MANAGING ARMED CONFLICTS
IN THE 21st CENTURY

THE CASS SERIES ON PEACEKEEPING

ISSN 1367-9880
General Editor: Michael Pugh

This series examines all aspects of peacekeeping, from the political, operational and legal dimensions to the developmental and humanitarian issues that must be dealt with by all those involved with peacekeeping in the world today.

1. *Beyond the Emergency: Development within UN Missions*
   edited by Jeremy Ginifer

2. *The UN, Peace and Force*
   edited by Michael Pugh

3. *Mediating in Cyprus: The Cypriot Communities and the United Nations*
   by Oliver P. Richmond

4. *Peacekeeping and the UN Specialized Agencies*
   edited by Jim Whitman

5. *Peacekeeping and Public Information: Caught in the Crossfire*
   by Ingrid A. Lehman

6. *US Peacekeeping Policy under Clinton: A Fairweather Friend?*
   by Michael G. MacKinnon

7. *Peacebuilding and Police Reform*
   edited by Tor Tanke Holm and Espen Barth Eide

8. *Peacekeeping and Conflict Resolution*
   edited by Tom Woodhouse and Oliver Ramsbotham

The editors are grateful for the help of
the International Peace Academy
in preparing this volume.

Managing
Armed Conflicts
in the
21st Century

Editors
ADEKEYE ADEBAJO
CHANDRA LEKHA SRIRAM
International Peace Academy, New York

FRANK CASS
LONDON • PORTLAND, OR

First published in 2001 in Great Britain by
FRANK CASS PUBLISHERS
Crown House, 47 Chase Side, London N14 5BP, England

and in the United States of America by
FRANK CASS PUBLISHERS
c/o ISBS, 5824 N.E. Hassalo Street
Portland, Oregon 97213-3644

Website http://www.frankcass.com

British Library Cataloguing in Publication Data

Managing armed conflicts in the 21st century. – (The Cass series
on peacekeeping ; 9)
1.Peace 2.Security, International
I.Adebajo, Adekeye II.Sriram, Chandra Lekha
327.1'72

ISBN 0 7146 5094 3 (cloth)
ISBN 0 7146 8136 9 (paper)
ISSN 1367 9880

Library of Congress Cataloging-in-Publication Data:

Managing armed conflicts in the 21st century / editors, Adekaye Adebajo,
Chandra Lekha Sriram
    p. cm. – (The Cass series on peacekeeping, ISSN 1367-98880; 9)
Includes bibliographical references and index.
ISBN 0-7146-5094-3 (hbk.) – ISBN 0-7146-8136-9 (pbk.)
1. Peace. 2. Conflict management. I. Adebajo, Adekaya, 1966-
II. Sriram, Chandra Lekha, 1971- .III. Series.
JZ5595 .M36 2001
341.5'84–dc21

                                                    2001028822

This group of studies first appeared in a special issue of
International Peacekeeping, [ISSN 1353-3312] Vol.7, No.4 (Winter, 2000)
published by Frank Cass and Co. Ltd.

Printed in Great Britain by
Antony Rowe Ltd, Chippenham, Wiltshire

Contents

Acronyms and Abbreviations

ACE	Allied Command Europe
ACRI	African Crisis Response Initiative
AFRC	Armed Forces Revolutionary Council
ANC	African National Congress
ARRC	Allied Rapid Reaction Corps
BSA	Bosnian Serb Army
CBM	Confidence building measure
CDR	Comité pour la Defense de la République
CIA	Central Intelligence Agency
CIVPOL	Civilian Police
COPAZ	Government Peace Commission in Guatemala
DGMO	Director-General of Military Operations
DMO	Director of Military Operations
DNS	Doctrine of National Security
DoD	United States Department of Defense
DPA	United Nations Department of Political Affairs
DPKO	United Nations Department of Peacekeeping Operations
DRC	Democratic Republic of the Congo
DSL	Defense Systems Limited
ECCAS	Economic Community of Central African States
ECOMOG	Economic Community of West African States Cease-fire Monitoring Group
ECOWAS	Economic Community of West African States
EPLF	Eritrean People's Liberation Front
EZLN	Ejercito Zapatistia de Liberacion Nacional
FAR	Forces Armées Rwandaises
FAR	Forces Action Rapide
FLN	Front Line States
FNLA	National Front for the Liberation of Angola
FRELIMO	Front for the Liberation of Mozambique
FRY	Federal Republic of Yugoslavia
GDP	Gross Domestic Product
IAF	Indian Air Force
ICC	International Criminal Court
IFI	International financial institution
IGAD	Intergovernmental Authority for Development
INTERFET	International Force for East Timor
IPTF	International Police Task Force

JMGs	Joint Monitoring Groups
KFOR	International Kosovo Force
KLA	Kosovo Liberation Army
LF	Lebanese Forces
LoC	Line of Control
LRA	Lord's Resistance Army
MNC	Multinational Corporation
MONUC	United Nations Mission in the Democratic Republic of the Congo
MOU	Memorandum of Understanding
MPLA	Popular Movement for the Liberation of Angola
NATO	North Atlantic Treaty Organization
NGO	Non-Governmental Organization
NPFL	National Patriotic Front of Liberia
OAS	Organization of American States
OAU	Organization of African Unity
OCHA	Office for the Coordination of Humanitarian Affairs
ODA	Overseas Development Assistance
ONUC	United Nations Operation in the Congo
ONUMOZ	United Nations Operation in Mozambique
ONUSAL	United Nations Observer Mission in El Salvador
OSCE	Organization for Security and Cooperation in Europe
PAF	Pakistan Air Force
PKO	Peacekeeping Operation
PLO	Palestinian Leadership Organization
PMC	Private military company
PSC	Private security company
PSO	Private security organization
PSO	British Peace Support Operation
QRF	Quick Reaction Force
RECAMP	Renforcement des capacités africaines de maintenir la paix
RENAMO	Resistencia Nacional Mocambicana
RMA	Revolution in Military Affairs
RPF	Rwandan Patriotic Front
RRF	Rapid Reaction Force
RUF	Revolutionary United Front
SADC	Southern African Development Community
SAS	Special Air Service
SDP	Serb Democratic Party
SLORC	State Law and Order Restoration Council
SNA	Somali National Alliance
SPLA	Sudanese People's Liberation Army

SRSG	Special Representative of the Secretary-General
TMD	Theatre missile defence
TNC	Transitional National Council
UAV	Unmanned Aerial Vehicle
UNAMIR	United Nations Assistance Mission in Rwanda
UNAVEM	United Nations Verification Mission in Angola
UNCIVPOL	United Nations Civilian Police
UNITA	National Union for the Total Independence of Angola
UNITAF	Unified Task Force in Somalia
UNMIBH	United Nations Mission in Bosnia and Herzegovina
UNMIK	United Nations Interim Administration Mission in Kosovo
UNOMIL	United Nations Observer Mission to Liberia
UNOSOM	United Nations Mission to Somalia
UNPROFOR	United Nations Protection Force
UNTAC	United Nations Transitional Authority in Cambodia
UNTAES	United Nations Transitional Administration for Eastern Slavonia, Baranja and Western Sirmium
UNTAET	United Nations Transitional Administration in East Timor
UNTAG	United Nations Transitional Assistance Group
UNTSO	United Nations Truce Supervision Organization
USAID	United States Agency for International Development
USC	United Somali Congress
ZANU	Zimbabwe African National Union
ZALU	Zimbabwe African Liberation Union

Foreword

After living through decades of the Cold War, the most dangerous conflict in all of history, with moments when the human species teetered on the brink of self-induced extinction, the world hoped that an interlude of peace might follow. But the experience of the past decade has been one of serious violence in many parts of the world – ethnic, religious, and hyper-nationalist aggression – that left millions of people maimed, killed or driven forcefully from their homes. Indeed, some of these fights have not only been ruthless and vicious, but crossed the line into genocide.

Yet, even as these atrocities have recurred, most peoples, governments and organizations in the affluent and powerful parts of the world have been reluctant to face the problems of deadly conflict, typically dismissing any responsibility to act with a variety of self-justifying rationalizations.

One important response to these critical problems has been the emergence of international non-governmental organizations oriented to conflict resolution and violence prevention. One of the most valuable of these is the International Peace Academy. Over three decades – with superb leadership from Indar Rikhye, Olara Otunnu, David Malone and Rita Hauser – it has carved out a unique niche. It is close to the UN and therefore has deep insight into that uniquely universal organization, its problems and potentials; yet it is also fully independent and therefore can provide well-informed, objective analysis on international questions influencing war and peace.

One of its valuable attributes is its deliberate efforts to foster the work of excellent young scholars on a truly worldwide basis. This provides opportunities for exceptional international, interdisciplinary collaborations. The present volume shows clearly the value of this approach. It has the particular merit of addressing a wide range of problems pertinent to the management of contemporary conflicts, and it explores novel ways of strengthening the search for peace with justice in exceedingly difficult situations. It illuminates opportunities for the UN, regional inter-governmental organizations and non-governmental organizations to contribute to this great mission. The knowledge, insight, ingenuity and dedication of these authors are apparent in their work. It is a matter of extraordinary satisfaction to me that four of them served with distinction as Hamburg Fellows at Stanford University: Adekeye Adebajo, Bruce Jones, Chris Landsberg and Marie-Joëlle Zahar.

Altogether, this work is at the frontier of conflict management and deserves careful study by anyone who seeks a less violent world.

DAVID A. HAMBURG
President Emeritus
Carnegie Corporation of New York

Introduction

ADEKEYE ADEBAJO and
CHANDRA LEKHA SRIRAM

This volume examines the important issues related to the management of conflicts in various regions of the world. Written largely by young scholars from Africa, Asia, Europe, the Middle East and North America, it focuses on the conflicts of the 1990s and projects into the future, suggesting new approaches and tools for conflict management. The diverse topics covered include the paradoxical similarities between war and peace, the role of natural resources in fuelling conflicts, the changing nature of UN peacekeeping, the use of force in peace operations, building peace through transitional authority mandates, truth commissions and the quest for justice, civil–militia relations and the protection of civilians in conflicts, the role and utility of private security firms or 'mercenaries', the rise and fall of UN peacekeeping in Africa, the need for greater burdensharing within the NATO alliance, and the travails of keeping peace in nuclear South Asia.

Four important clusters of issues emerge from these essays which contain some provocative findings. The first of these is the paradox of conflict as cooperation and the economic benefits of war, which are inextricably linked to the role of natural resources in conflict. A counterintuitive lesson is that the traditional distinction between 'war' and 'peace' may not hold, particularly in contemporary instances of intrastate conflict. The traditional understanding of such conflicts as occurring between two (or more) groups competing for power, divided by ideological, ethnic, religious, or other distinctions becomes complicated when these groups collaborate with one another in their pursuit of power and wealth while continuing to proclaim adherence to particular identities. In such cases, transitions to peace may not mark the end of conflict and predatory behaviour by these groups. Thus, the very core of transitions as events marking a shift from war to peace may have to be re-conceptualized. This lesson is particularly salient in regions where conflicts occur not, or not solely, over the role of a state, but over particular natural resources such as valuable minerals.

The second cluster of issues addresses the changing nature of the role played by the United Nations in peace operations in the post-Cold War era, particularly with regard to the use of force.[1] Actions by the UN in cases like

Bosnia and Somalia have moved well beyond traditional peacekeeping operations in which forces were inserted into conflict zones with the consent of the parties after the conclusion of negotiated peace accords. Such activities now include intrusive military enforcement actions in what may be viewed as domestic issues, as with the recent actions in Kosovo to bring yet another Balkan conflict to a halt. Forces have also been stationed in novel ways, as in the preventive deployment of UN peacekeepers in Macedonia.

In many post-Cold War missions, once these forces have arrived, they do more than interpose themselves between previously warring parties; they often take up the more complicated task of what is often referred to as 'nation building'. These new UN peacebuilding operations not only seek to keep the peace, they now often assume the role of police force and temporary judiciary where such institutions have ceased to exist or lost all efficacy or legitimacy. Even in instances where the UN does not directly assume such governance roles, it may play a central role in assisting transitional states to restructure their police and military forces, or rebuilding their judiciaries, civil services and other state institutions. This work is often carried out against the backdrop of instability and impunity in which contending goals of justice and stability must be balanced increasingly through truth commissions, war crimes tribunals and other mechanisms.

A third cluster of issues in this volume addresses the growing importance and changing status of non-traditional actors in conflicts and conflict management, ranging from predatory warlords and private security firms to mercenaries and militias. Armed conflict is being addressed not only by international and regional organizations whose roles are changing; non-traditional actors like private security firms are also playing an increasingly important and controversial role in internal armed conflicts. Such actors may seek different goals and respond to different incentives. They often have very different interactions with the civilian population than states, a finding which clearly has important implications for those seeking to mitigate or negotiate an end to conflicts. On the other end of the spectrum, some analysts have argued that private military services, often dismissed as 'mercenaries', can play an important role in supporting and maintaining internationally-brokered peace agreements. But they can only play this role if their utility and efficacy is recognized and criteria for their legitimacy established.

Finally, a fourth cluster of contributions examines salient problems of conflict management in three regions of the world: Africa, Europe and Asia. In light of the uneven performance of the UN in conflict management and the continued resistance of the United States, its most powerful member, to

American participation in most peacekeeping operations, several authors have argued for strengthening the capacity of regional actors to manage their own conflicts. Faced with the threat of wider regional instability from war and refugees, these actors often have more at stake in such conflicts and are therefore more likely to commit time and resources to resolving them. Wherever possible, such operations should be undertaken in cooperation with the UN, with the active participation and political and financial support of the US and key regional actors.

In Africa, a division of labour may be slowly emerging between the UN and fledgling regional organizations as the disinterest of the most powerful members of the UN Security Council in politically risky interventions in Africa is forcing a rethinking of how best to guarantee a *Pax Africana* on the world's most volatile continent. In Europe, a NATO that is still excessively dependent on the US in the new military missions of the post-Cold War era will require not only greater burdensharing on the part of states like Britain, France and Germany, but also smaller powers like Canada, Spain and the Netherlands. Conflict might also flare in regions in which conventional myths might suggest otherwise because parties possess nuclear weapons or because one party possesses conventional superiority. Such is the case with India and Pakistan in South Asia, where recent strife in Kargil suggests that the risks of conflict remain high and that a negotiated settlement needs to be reached, probably with the facilitation of external powers like the US which has been active in informal mediation efforts on the sub-continent.

The first three clusters examine broad problems which the international community faces in managing conflict in the new millennium. The essays are informed by comparative case analysis, by analyses of institutional processes and non-state actors, and by sophisticated theoretical claims about internal conflicts, peacekeeping and peacebuilding. The final cluster of contributions casts further light on these issues through deeply informed empirical analyses in three important regions of the world.

*   *   *

In the opening essay, 'War and Peace: What's the Difference?', David Keen notes that war and peace are normally considered to be opposites, but asks what they have in common. He argues that answering this question is particularly important to understanding transitions from war to peace and from peace to war. Rather than simply being concerned with 'winning', many of the actors helping to shape violence during a conflict have other aims, which often foster a limited but enduring violence. It is also important to note that peace can be quite violent. It may be difficult to account for mass violence or civil war without examining the violence embodied in peace.

Abiodun Alao and Funmi Olunisakin, in their essay, 'Economic Fragility and Political Fluidity: Explaining Natural Resources and Conflicts', examine the age-old link between natural resources and conflicts. The authors reject some of the arguments in the recent literature on natural resources and conflicts, which attribute the emergence of armed conflict and civil wars largely to a ploy by protagonists to exploit the natural resources in a particular area rather than to problems resulting from state collapse. The authors argue instead that the real explanation involves elements of both economic greed and state collapse. They conclude that transparent, accountable structures of governance and the promotion of a buoyant and educated civil society will best enhance the management of resource-based conflicts.

David Malone and Karin Wermester note in 'Boom and Bust? The Changing Nature of UN Peacekeeping' that with the end of the Cold War, the notion and practice of peacekeeping has undergone something of a revolution. The authors outline the two major shifts, spearheaded by the UN Security Council, that have occurred in peacekeeping in the past decade. First, the goals pursued by peacekeeping operations have changed from assisting in the maintenance of ceasefires to implementing the foundations of self-enforcing peace through, in particular, the increasingly detailed electoral, humanitarian, human rights and civilian police components in peacekeeping mandates. Second, the level of enforcement brought to bear by peacekeeping operations has increased dramatically. The increasing use of Chapter VII mandates to authorize the use of force under 'coalitions of the willing', the implementation of mandatory sanctions regimes, and the humanitarian intervention missions of the 1990s all represent new trends in UN peacekeeping.

In the fourth contribution, 'Lessons Not Learned: The Use of Force in "Peace" Operations in the 1990s', Mats Berdal notes that the armed forces of several western countries have embraced the view that 'peace enforcement' constitutes a type of military activity that, while coercive in nature, remains distinct from 'war'. This view rests on two basic assumptions: that military force can be used impartially to enforce compliance with a given mandate without designating an enemy, and that using force in this manner will not prejudice the political outcome of the conflict in question. Employing two case studies from Bosnia and Somalia, Berdal argues, however, that the experience of military operations in support of humanitarian objectives in the 1990s suggests that these assumptions are empirically unsustainable and optimistic in the extreme. Instead, he urges decision-makers to think in terms of a broad yet still basic distinction between consent-based operations and enforcement which must still allow for the logic of war and war-fighting.

In 'Building Peace through Transitional Authority: New Directions, Major Challenges', Michèle Griffin and Bruce Jones assess two new surprisingly far-reaching peace operations in East Timor and Kosovo that were authorized by the UN Security Council in 1999. The authors note that these operations are more challenging than previous similar peacebuilding missions in Namibia, Cambodia and Eastern Slavonia, because they involve the UN assuming vastly greater executive and legislative authority. The authors note that the UN is assuming such powers in unstable environments lacking functioning institutions and in the context of increasingly severe financial, political and logistical constraints on the UN's capacity to manage conflicts.

In 'Truth Commissions and the Quest for Justice: Stability and Accountability after Internal Strife', Chandra Lekha Sriram examines a key dilemma: whether and to what degree accountability ought to be pursued after the end of civil conflicts or military dictatorships. Drawing on nearly 30 cases, Sriram argues that three factors frequently make accountability more or less possible: the international political and historical context, the history of past abuses, and the nature of civil–military relations and/or the balance between the government and opposition. She argues that there may be instances in which limiting, though not jettisoning, accountability may enable transitional regimes (and by extension external donors) to pursue greater levels of reform of security forces. This can be done, in particular, by transitional regimes cutting military budgets and personnel and also instituting wide-ranging reforms in doctrine and education, actions which may help to ensure long-term stability.

Marie-Joëlle Zahar notes in 'Protégés, Clients, Cannon Fodder: Civilians in the Calculus of Militias' that the incentives of belligerents either to respect or to violate the rights of civilians are little understood and have been even less systematically studied. She develops a typology of civil–militia relations, ranking warring groups from most to least challenging in terms of their expected compliance with the letter and spirit of the provisions of the Hague conventions on the protection of non-combatants, the Geneva conventions, and other humanitarian laws. Zahar identifies two broad classes of factors that influence civil–militia relations: the impact of militia objectives and structure, and the nature of the ties between the combatants and the population.

In 'Messiahs or Mercenaries? The Future of International Private Military Services', Doug Brooks argues that private military companies (PMCs) or private security companies (PSCs) are very different from the 'freelance mercenaries' of the past, both in terms of motivation and adherence to legal norms. Brooks further argues that the bias against these companies stems from two major concerns: that they threaten the traditional authority of the state and that they are a key factor in the growth of multinational corporations. The author stresses, however, that what makes private military services viable is their ability to offer military services in a more efficient, timely, and inexpensive manner than state militaries or non-military companies. Brooks predicts a rapid growth in the activities and functions of these companies, including their increased use in peace operations, particularly due to the weakness of some recent UN operations.

In 'NATO's Underachieving Middle Powers: From Burdenshedding to Burdensharing', Brian Finlay and Michael O'Hanlon observe that the degree of US military supremacy in the post-Cold War era is unprecedented and ultimately harmful to the future of the NATO alliance. They note that while the world decries *Pax Americana*, the international community is often helpless to conduct many of the military operations necessary to deter conflicts and maintain and re-establish peace without US military support. Finlay and O'Hanlon call for a more equitable burdensharing mechanism within NATO, suggesting that the alliance's underachieving middle powers should restructure their armies to shoulder a heavier military burden in post-Cold War missions. Using Canada as a case study, the authors draw a road map by which the NATO allies can potentially reconfigure their militaries to become more self-sufficient and more rapidly reactive. The authors recommend that America's NATO allies develop their military high-technology and strategic transport and logistics capabilities, reducing their dependence on the US while simultaneously increasing their ability to operate in conjunction with American forces.

In sharp contrast, Adekeye Adebajo and Chris Landsberg argue, in 'Back to the Future: UN Peacekeeping in Africa', for a strengthening of regional organizations in Africa and call for the establishment of a new division of labour between the UN and these organizations to manage African conflicts. The essay focuses on seven important cases of UN peacekeeping in Africa, including the recent missions in Sierra Leone and the Democratic Republic of the Congo. From these cases, the authors identify factors that have often contributed to success in UN peacekeeping missions in Africa: first, the willingness of internal parties to disarm and accept electoral results; second, the lack of economic resources that often fuel conflicts; third, the existence of a political accord between the warring parties and the cooperation of regional players in peace processes; fourth, the support of extra-regional actors in stopping military assistance to local clients and in providing financial support for peace processes; and finally, the presence of skilful mediators.

Finally, in his contribution 'In the Shadow of Kargil: Keeping Peace in Nuclear South Asia', Waheguru Pal Singh Sidhu argues that the 1999 Kargil conflict, the latest in a series of 'nuclear crises' between India and Pakistan, challenged two myths: that stability is inherent between a pair of nuclear-armed states, and that states, particularly nuclear-armed states in a dyad setting, can alter a boundary – even a disputed boundary – by force. The Kargil episode proved that while stability cannot be taken for granted, boundaries – even disputed ones – can. In fact, any attempt to change such boundaries by force is not only likely to fail but may lead to dangerous escalation. Sidhu notes that although, in the wake of Kargil, both India and Pakistan have sought unilateral and antagonistic approaches to ensure their security, this approach is fraught with danger and could lead to inadvertent escalation. The author explains why it is in the interest of India and Pakistan to adopt a more cooperative and verifiable approach to keeping peace in South Asia and suggests ways for India and Pakistan to move in this direction with the facilitation of influential external actors like the United States.

* * *

It is the goal of this volume to serve as a resource for scholars and policymakers alike, drawing largely on the difficult experiences of managing conflicts in the post-Cold War era. The volume is also an attempt to derive lessons for managing conflicts in a new century even as the actors, approaches, tools and techniques, continue to evolve and expand. The diverse perspectives reflected here will hopefully bring to the study of conflict management a vital but often overlooked aspect of a sometimes excessively parochial approach to international relations. We have not only sought scholars of diverse backgrounds, but we have urged them to reflect views and voices that are not always heard above the Anglo-American din. Such perspectives should serve to enrich the important debates about tools and approaches to managing armed conflicts in the twenty-first century, and will hopefully contribute to making the *dialogue de sourds* between North and South a more fruitful exchange.

NOTE

1. The need for further change in UN doctrine and practice with regard to peace operations was addressed within the UN system by the *Report of the Panel on United Nations Peace Operations*, available at http://www.un.org/peace/reports/peace_operations/docs/ (August 2000) (*Brahimi report*).

War and Peace: What's the Difference?

DAVID KEEN

At one level, the question posed in the title of this contribution can be quickly dispensed with: war is violent and peace is, well, peaceful; in other words, peace is the antithesis of war. This is certainly the common-sense view, and it is one usually reinforced by the media. Journalists, after all, are interested in *change*: theirs is a world of news (what is *new*), of events, discontinuities and drama. What could be more dramatic than the change from one thing into its opposite? Historians, by contrast, are often interested in continuities, and it is this approach that informs this essay. What do war and peace have in common? Answering this question is particularly important if we hope to understand *transitions*: the transition from peace to war and the transition from war to peace. Perhaps we can also take a cue here from the natural sciences: how can one thing change into another – a bulb into a plant, a liquid into a gas – unless it has already begun to resemble it?

A conventional model of war portrays it as a conflict between two sides with opposing aims. These aims are typically presented as 'political': in the case of international wars, the aim is seen as furthering the political interests of a state; in the case of civil wars, the aim is seen as changing the policies and the nature of the state. It follows, for the conventional model of conflict, that the aim in a war is to win (and thereby gain a favourable political settlement). This is war as a continuation of politics by other means, as Clausewitz famously noted. How to make a peace in the face of such a war? The obvious way is to secure a compromise between the opposing political aims of the two sides. Another is simply for one or other side to secure an outright victory.[1]

The idea of a war between 'sides' (usually two, often 'ethnic') is easy to grasp; it helps to make complex events digestible and (apparently) comprehensible. James Fallows has argued that the US media covers American politics as if it were covering sport. Favoured questions include: Who is going to win? Who is ahead in the polls? And what are the tactics? Other questions – like 'What are the policy issues?' – are hard to answer and easy to neglect.[2] Much contemporary coverage of violent conflict also follows this 'sporting' model. Who is it between? Who is going to win? What are the tactics? And who (if we are delving really deeply into the matter) are the goodies and baddies? Again, we may be left with little idea of the complex issues behind the conflict. For those who do wish to know what is at stake in a conflict, the parade of warring initials is likely to leave them frustrated. For those who might wish to ask about the (diverse) reasons why (diverse groups of) people are orchestrating, funding and carrying out acts of violence, the perfunctory reference to a conflict's 'underlying causes' may be similarly unenlightening.

In practice, many wars deviate from the conventional model of a battle between two sides, and recent civil conflicts usually deviate considerably from this model. In order to think sensibly about peace, we need to think clearly about what war actually *is*. Rather than simply being concerned with 'winning', many of those helping to shape violence during a conflict have other aims, aims which often foster a limited but very enduring violence. Among the most important aims in contemporary conflicts are: limiting exposure to violence, accumulating resources and suppressing political opposition. If we assume we know what 'war' is, we are likely to miss the importance of these aims. We are also likely to miss important continuities with peacetime. Part of the function of war may be that it offers a more promising environment for the pursuit of aims that are also prominent in peacetime. In these circumstances, keeping a war going may assist in the achievement of these aims, and prolonging a war may be a higher priority than winning it. While conflict is an undeniable reality in many countries, the fault-lines of that conflict should not be taken at face value. What are the systems of collusion obscured by 'war'? And what are the hidden conflicts (for example, class conflict or conflict between armed and unarmed groups, conflict between the military and civil society) that are obscured when officials and journalists portray civil war as a more or less unproblematic contest between two or more 'sides'?

Limiting Violence

Opposing factions or armies have often been concerned with *limiting* violence. This does not necessarily result in violence that is small-scale; on the contrary, the violence may be massive. What is stressed here is that key actors in conflict have repeatedly given priority to minimizing *their own exposure* to violence. Ideally, violence will not happen to you, to your political constituency, or even to your armed forces. There are a variety of means for achieving this goal of limiting violence. One key step is to avoid directly confronting an armed enemy. Where such a confrontation is necessary, children (who can often be easily manipulated) have sometimes been used as 'front-line' troops (Sierra Leone and Liberia). In many conflicts (for example, Sudan, former Yugoslavia and Burma/Myanmar) there has been an attempt to exploit – and foment – divisions within civil society, for example by encouraging the formation of ethnic militias (see Zahar in this volume). This method can help avoid the necessity of raising a large, conscripted army – something that is likely to be expensive and politically unpopular both at home and abroad.

Within many recent civil conflicts, cooperation between armed groups has often been significant. Pitched battles have been the exception rather than the rule. And civilians have borne the brunt of the violence. In Angola, there were reports of trading and fraternizing between UNITA and government forces after the war resumed in 1992. In Liberia, faction leaders were reported drinking together in Monrovia while violence raged upcountry. Pitched battles between armed groups were relatively rare, with civilians consistently targeted for violence.[3] During the ongoing conflict in Algeria, elements of the national army have often appeared to be cooperating with Islamic extremists – perhaps because the 'Islamic threat' has tended to legitimize military control and undemocratic government.[4]

Although the superpowers of the Cold War era were sometimes drawn into direct participation in conflicts (the US in Vietnam, the Soviet Union in Afghanistan), they most often conducted their ideological struggle by means of proxies (for example, in Guatemala, Nicaragua, Angola, and Ethiopia). Noticeably absent were direct (and almost certainly suicidal) attacks on one another. This was in many ways a system for limiting conflict and for ensuring that it happened to *other people*. It is notable that, for all the obscenity (and profitability) of large nuclear arsenals, only two nuclear weapons have so far been detonated in combat, and these in Hiroshima and Nagasaki in 1945, against a nation lacking the ability to strike back. In recent years, the desire of the US to avoid casualties to its own troops has powerfully shaped American foreign policy, with the Somalia *débâcle* in 1993 (see Adebajo and Landsberg, and Berdal, in this volume) compounding persistent fears of 'another Vietnam'. This aversion to risk has helped to shape patterns of intervention (high-altitude bombing over Kosovo) and non-intervention (the reluctance to recognize, or counter, genocide in Bosnia and Rwanda). In these circumstances, much of contemporary peacekeeping has been delegated to *other people*, whether private military companies[5] (see Brooks in this volume) or regional peacekeeping organizations such as ECOMOG in West Africa.[6]

Accumulating Resources

Making money is an important – and increasingly prominent – aim in warfare.[7] With capitalism having 'won' the Cold War, socialist movements lost much of their remaining allure, and at the same time the pursuit of economic self-interest has arguably been elevated to a position of ideological hegemony – a fertile climate for the world's most genuinely aggressive entrepreneurs. Falling support for governments and rebels from the superpowers during the Cold War often fed into an increasing emphasis on funding fighting through *internal* predation.[8]

Contemporary conflicts have frequently taken on a paradoxical quality. A concern with economic accumulation has often prompted actions that are counter-productive from a purely military point of view. One such is selling arms to the other side.[9] Another is economically-motivated raiding that predictably radicalizes its victims and *encourages* support for a rebel group. In Sudan, for example, northern Sudanese militia raiding on a variety of groups *preceded* and *helped to create* their affiliation with the rebel Sudan People's Liberation Army.[10]

The case of conflict in Sierra Leone brings out the importance of accumulating resources (as well as the desire to limit conflict). Peacetime corruption in the diamond economy has mutated into (collaborative) conflict. In a pattern that some Sierra Leoneans dubbed 'sell-game', government soldiers in the early and mid-1990s were observed attacking civilians, engaging in illegal diamond mining, dressing up as rebels, selling arms to rebels, and coordinating movements with rebels so as to minimize clashes and maximize the exploitation of civilians.[11]

Significantly, the pattern of 'sell-game' during the civil war in Sierra Leone has been a variation on a peacetime phenomenon: prior to the outbreak of war in 1991, state officials repeatedly participated in the smuggling they were supposed to be suppressing. Anti-corruption drives proved again and again to be fertile ground for extending corruption. Meanwhile, the corruption of government officials helped to ensure, first, a lack of genuine development in Sierra Leone and, second, a lack of treasury revenue to suppress either smuggling or the growing discontent engendered by precisely this lack of development.

During periods of relative clam, conflict has tended to mutate back into more institutionalized forms of corruption. Sierra Leonean rebels and government soldiers have tended to share an interest in perpetuating insecurity and in exploiting civilians. During peace negotiations at the time of the handover of power to a democratic government in 1996, witnesses reported something distasteful in the warmth with which supposedly opposing commanders embraced each other during peace negotiations.[12] Government soldiers and rebels – who staged a joint coup in May 1997 – shared important interests not just in preserving systems of economic exploitation that had flourished under the cover of war but also in preventing recriminations or prosecutions under a democratic government.

Also in the early and mid-1990s, another kind of 'sell-game' was going on in Cambodia. After the Paris peace agreement of 1991, exporting timber and gems through Thailand helped the Khmer Rouge to resist UN pressures for disarmament. At the same time, Cambodian government officials and especially the armed forces had become heavily involved in the logging business, helping to denude Cambodia's forests. In 1994, the Cambodian Defence Ministry was awarded the sole right to licence timber exports and to receive all the revenue from those exports. This gave the armed forces, particularly senior officers, a powerful interest in *not eliminating the Khmer Rouge altogether*, and the army in fact winked at timber concessions in areas they knew would provide funding for the Khmer Rouge. Between 1994 and 1997, elements of the army came to arrangements with the Khmer Rouge over the control of economic resources in respective areas of influence, and cooperated in exporting, and in getting the best prices for, some commodities. Some soldiers were even reported to be selling armaments to the Khmer Rouge.[13]

While the focus of this contribution is on civil conflicts, it is worth noting that at the international level, the military-industrial complexes dating from the Cold War era can be argued to have a vested interest in the continuation of conflicts of some kind. Certainly, the waning of the Cold War should draw attention to the economic as opposed to political or ideological reasons for the still-large spending on armaments. Arms industries (particularly in the former eastern bloc) pursue markets in conflict zones, and weapons and personnel decommissioned by NATO and eastern bloc countries have found their way into a variety of conflict zones. The five permanent members of the UN Security Council (the US, Russia, China, France and Britain) although charged with the primary responsibility of preserving global peace and security, are still responsible for 85 per cent of global arms sales. When industrialized countries do opt for conflict, this is usually against much weaker countries or regions where there is a reasonable certainty of winning (Britain versus Argentina; the US versus the might of Panama, Grenada, Libya or Iraq; and Russia versus the – admittedly underestimated – Chechens). The closely-controlled media coverage of such conflicts preserves their status as 'wars' (rather than somewhat one-sided punitive operations) and can sometimes serve as good advertising for military hardware – points emphasized by Jean Baudrillard in relation to the Gulf War of 1991 following Iraq's invasion of Kuwait.[14]

Weakening or Eliminating Political Opposition

A third major goal in contemporary conflicts has been weakening or eliminating political opposition. Fomenting ethnic conflict has frequently proved a useful way of dividing the opposition, and indeed ethnic nationalists have often fed off one another's nationalism. Genocide and massacres have been used as a tool for political survival and for weakening the opposition in many contexts, including Sudan, Rwanda, the former Yugoslavia and Guatemala.

In its analysis of the war in Guatemala, the report of the Commission for Historical Clarification notes that guerrilla groups did not have the strength or numbers to pose a serious threat to the Guatemalan state. The widespread attacks on civilians served a much wider function than simply suppressing the guerrillas, namely the suppression of a wide band of political and cultural opposition.[15] In these circumstances, the problem goes beyond simply ending the war or reaching a compromise between government and rebels and extends to how to institutionalize widespread popular participation in politics – and how to do so without prompting an elite backlash of the kind that fired the war in the first place.

The Functions of 'Us and Them'

Deficiencies in the portrayal of civil conflicts are more than deficiencies in understanding; they frequently play directly into the hands of those manipulating or profiting from violence. The idea that a conflict is bi-polar – in other words, that conflict is 'really' about government troops fighting rebel troops or about Serbs fighting Muslims or about Hutus fighting Tutsis – has proven extremely useful to elites protecting their own privileges. There are three main reasons for this.

First, international confusion and pessimism in the face of 'intractable, ancient ethnic hatreds' or 'irrational rebels' allows time for planning and carrying out human rights abuses with minimal international repercussions. These abuses are often carried out by forces linked to the government; yet government responsibility is obscured when the focus is on 'ethnic' conflict or on a particularly reviled rebel group such as UNITA in Angola, the Revolutionary United Front (RUF) in Sierra Leone, or the Lord's Resistance Army (LRA) in Uganda.

Second, the image of bi-polar conflict helps in suppressing political dissent since dissenters can be readily labelled as supporters of 'the other side' (whether these are 'rebels' or some reviled and demonized ethnic group). It is precisely the distinction between 'us' and 'them' which those manipulating conflict wish to encourage. Once this distinction is established, it follows that if you are not with us, you are against us. Ethnic fault-lines harden. Those manipulating conflict in this way may include ethnic nationalists or warlords but also democratic leaders who find that war boosts their popularity. In Russia, Vladimir Putin rode to the Presidency on the back of war-fever over Chechen 'terrorists', and there are serious concerns over possible involvement by Russian oligarchs linked to Putin in the Moscow apartment bombings that did so much to ignite anti-Chechen feelings.[16] In Pakistan, military brass-hats have used the conflict with India (notably, the nuclear stand-off and the conflict over Kashmir) to justify their continued interference in politics and a large military budget (see Sidhu in this volume); at the same time, many within the military establishment have benefited from drugs-trading links with the Taliban in Afghanistan, a nexus threatened by pressure from the US and perhaps defended by the October 1999 military coup.[17]

A third function of presenting conflicts as bi-polar is that the image of an enemy may assist those benefiting from the political economy of conflict. These benefits may take a number of forms. They may include the profits arising from preparation for war and from weapons procurement during conflict – a major source of profits for a small ruling cabal in Angola, for example.[18] They may also include access to minerals (often in areas partially depopulated by conflict and famine), access to agricultural commodities (usually through forced labour), and access to the profits of illegal trading that may flourish under conditions of conflict and of minimal government control and taxation (most notably, the drugs trade).

The tactics of divide and rule often depend on 'ethnic' war being talked into existence. Local media have often played a key role in instilling fear of the ethnic 'other', apparently a necessary condition for genocide.[19] And as the Croatian writer Dubravka Ugresic notes, the passion for naming and labelling during ethnic conflicts can put pressure on a writer to abandon their sense of ambiguity and multiple truths. Suddenly there is an army of petty informers ready to point the finger at those who reject this new passion for labelling; petty jealousies can fuel this finger-pointing.[20]

In Turkey, the government has blamed the burning of villages by the army on the rebel PKK (Kurdistan Workers' Party), and the distortion has usually been uncritically reported by the Turkish press. Paradoxically, as the Kurdish dissident Yasar Kemal notes, resisting this conspiracy of silence and pursuing an objective truth can be seen as taking sides.[21] We have seen the same thing[22] in Cambodia and Sierra Leone. Enoch Opondo in his analysis of conflict in Kenya[23] – and Phillip Knightley in his more general analysis of truth as the first casualty of war[24] – have both suggested that in wartime, those who try to be 'objective' may quickly be accused of complicity with the enemy and/or undermining the morale of friendly forces.

International journalists often play their part in solidifying ethnic divisions by taking these divisions as an immutable given, rather than questioning how ethnicity has come to be important, how this process has been manipulated, and how conflict generates ethnicity.[25] Similarly, immeasurable damage is done when international journalists take divisions between government forces and rebels as a given, rather than investigating the violent, exploitative and exclusionary processes which this discourse may facilitate. Insofar as the simplistic model of conflict as sport or ethnic hatred proves cheaper to produce and easier to digest than a more nuanced understanding, we can see here the local political economy of war interacting damagingly with the international political economy of news. Foreign journalists face fewer obstacles than local journalists in scrutinizing and resisting the politics of 'us and them'. But often such opportunities are wasted.

Part of the construction of ethnicity and ethnic hatred in the media is done through denigrating or demonizing entire nations rather than simply groups within nations. Jonathan Mermin shows how the US often pumps up the fear of the foreign 'other' – even (perhaps especially) in relation to small states like Panama and Grenada.[26] In many ways, the Anglo-Saxon axis of Britain and the US constitute a major ethnic group on the world stage, and one that is sometimes prepared to act outside of UN channels (as over Kosovo and Iraq).

For those seeking to divide the world into 'us' and 'them', any neutrals or 'undecideds' may constitute a powerful *cognitive* threat, a threat to the world view and moral universe of the chief combatants, as Antonius Robben has argued in relation to Argentina's 'dirty war' in the 1970s.[27] This argument can be extended onto the world stage to help explain the strong hostility to analysts like Noam Chomsky and Edward Said.

Violence in Peace

If war can involve elements of cooperation and collusion, of limiting violence, and of the consolidation of various kinds of order, then it is also important to note that peace can be quite violent. Indeed, it may be difficult to account for mass violence or civil war without examining the violence embodied in peace.

Violence in many ways lies at the heart of democracy and of capitalism. Democracies have tended to emerge from a process of violent struggle. And capitalism, too, has its roots in violence, notably the looting of commodities, the forcible appropriation of land (creating a pool of industrial workers), and the appropriation of labour in the form of slavery.[28] Much of the violence surrounding the origins of capitalism and democracies has simply been forgotten, though some ethnic groups are more interested in remembering it than others. Moving into the present, capitalist democracies may also involve large elements of militarism, which begs the following question: to what extent can a society be said to be at peace when it is planning for war?

Closely related to the assumption that peace is not violent are two common assumptions, first, that 'the rule of law' is at the opposite end of the spectrum from lawless violence and, second, that development is at once non-violent and an insurance against violence.

Yet the apparent lawlessness of civil war is often supported by the state in some way: it is *sanctioned illegality*, as when the state supports the creation of violent ethnic militias. As for peace, Jenny Edkins – in her critique of Amartya Sen and his limited consideration of the role of violence in creating famine – has rightly emphasized the violence embodied in the law.[29] Johan Galtung distinguishes 'structural violence' from 'direct violence', using the former to include processes of exploitation and marginalization, indeed anything that limits human well-being to levels below what is possible.[30] Peter Uvin has written about the 'humiliations' of the development process in Rwanda and its contribution to violence and genocide.[31]

In Sudan, much of the development process has been violent, including the forcible ejection of people from land, and this violent process helps to explain the more overt and visible violence of civil war.[32] Here and elsewhere, vulnerable groups have fallen partially below the protection of the law in peacetime, and after this process has propelled significant numbers into rebellion, these marginalized groups have been further marginalized and stigmatized in conditions of war, and have fallen still further below the law's protection. Those falling below the law have not just been in the south of Sudan but also the west and, increasingly, the east.

Much of the violence in peacetime consists of crime. Peace may be riddled with violent crime; it may not feel particularly peaceful. Much of this crime may be organized crime, and since war can also take the form of organized crime, the distinction between peace and war is further eroded. The murder rate in El Salvador is about 15 times as high as in the United States. War in El Salvador (between 1980 and 1992) destroyed families, often leaving children living with distant relatives who have been unable to afford schooling. This, together with widespread unemployment and perhaps also a culture of violence encouraged by the war, seems to have created a susceptibility to joining criminal gangs. On top of this, the US has been deporting large numbers of illegal and legal Salvadoran immigrants who are convicted of crimes in America, and these have often played a key role in gang warfare inside El Salvador.[33]

In Guatemala, crime has also been very high since the advent of 'peace'. Where ordinary people feel their physical security remains under threat and where police forces have not been developed and supported to provide security, one temptation has been to vote for 'hard-line', rightist candidates who promise law and order. This has created opportunities for those associated with the old counter-insurgency, adding to the problem of impunity and to the difficulties of ending the war.

Nor is Europe immune to large-scale organized crime, whether in peacetime or wartime. In southern Italy, an estimated 10,000 people were killed by organized crime during the 1980s.[34] In contemporary Russia, the inability of the state to provide a secure environment for property-ownership has combined with a surplus of ex-soldiers and security personnel to encourage a growth of mafia activity. These conditions bear a significant resemblance to those that fostered the emergence of the Sicilian mafia in the late-nineteenth century, as Federico Varese has shown.[35] In a development that has some parallels with patterns of cooperation between 'enemies' in war-time (and the phenomenon of soldiers turning into rebels in Sierra Leone), Russian policemen have been leaving their posts in large numbers and joining the ranks of the criminals. Others (again echoing Sierra Leone) have cooperated with criminals while still in their posts. More broadly, the sale of Russian state assets to a small clique of oligarchs at 'knock-down' prices can be seen as a form of organized pillage,[36] albeit a pillage that has for the most part been organized under conditions of 'peace'. Organized crime has been a marked feature of the various conflicts in the former Yugoslavia.[37]

War economies tend to be linked to *regional* trading systems, with surrounding countries – though perhaps formally 'at peace' – getting drawn into illegal trading (often drugs and arms) that can bring growing insecurity. As with the states presiding directly over a war economy, surrounding countries may lack the resources or the will to control smuggling that further saps their revenue.[38]

The Transition from War to Peace

How are we to understand the transition from war to peace? This tends to be presented as a move from madness to sanity, or from evil to good, but if we are mindful of the violence in peace and the cooperation in warfare, the transition from war to peace takes on a different complexion.

A 'transition from war to peace' is unlikely to see a clean break from violence to consent, from theft to production, from repression to democracy, or from impunity to accountability. Peace is likely to institutionalize violence in some form; indeed, peace may not be possible without institutionalizing violence in some way. One way of looking at the problem of contemporary conflicts is to consider those who mobilize violence from above and to consider those who embrace it – willingly or unwillingly –

from below.[39] External interventions will need to try to make peace appear a more attractive option than war for both of these groups. This may be a messy, compromising business. Peace could also be called 'order', a word that carries a different set of associations and assumptions.

Relationships of cooperation during wartime may create important opportunities for peace, though it would be wise to ask: peace on what basis? It may, for example, be a peace that is deeply infused with violence and exploitation.

Ethnic nationalists, having benefited from one another's extremism in wartime, may agree to cooperate in creating (more or less) ethnically pure states. This can be called peace. Others might call it the institutionalization of 'ethnic cleansing', a charge that has been levelled at the Dayton agreement of 1995 in the former Yugoslavia.

Some things seem almost self-evidently useful in the business of conflict resolution and conflict prevention. These things include justice (to put an end to the climate of impunity); reconstruction and development (to give people hope and put what is often seen as the 'madness' of violence behind them); democracy (to empower the oppressed and restrain the rulers); and a ceasefire (to strengthen negotiations and build up trust). According to the so-called 'Washington consensus', economic liberalization is another policy that will promote peace, as growth reduces resentments and trade becomes too lucrative to disrupt through warfare. It is tempting, moreover, to imagine that 'all good things go together', and that the solution to conflict lies in a package of justice, reconstruction, development, democracy, ceasefires and liberalization.

However, one also needs to ask why people should accept these apparently benign phenomena? Do the key actors (whether elites, fighters or 'ordinary people') have an interest in justice, reconstruction, development, democracy, ceasefires and/or liberalization? And if they do not, how might these phenomena – and the goal of democracy stands out as particularly problematic here – be rendered acceptable to them? One has to remember the profits and limited exposure to risk that frequently characterize contemporary conflict. Ensuring that armed groups agree to some kind of peace is likely to involve a range of compromises. Unless armed groups are given some kind of stake in peace, including perhaps a material reward, why then would they choose to accept it?

Justice

A common idea is that peace and justice are indivisible. Amnesty International has often leaned towards this position, emphasizing a legalistic solution to the problem of violence based on the need to ensure and enforce human rights by holding abusers accountable.

Certainly, there is a link between impunity and violence, and correspondingly it is dangerous to leave human rights abuses unpunished. A particularly troubling example is the history of accommodation to Cambodia's Khmer Rouge, including the support of the Khmer Rouge in exile in the 1980s by the West, Thailand and China, in opposition to the Vietnam-installed government in Phnom Penh. In Cambodia itself, the August 1996 deal between the government and elements of the Khmer Rouge under Ieng Sary (a former Foreign Minister under Pol Pot), while critical in weakening the Khmer Rouge, can also be seen as sending out potentially damaging signals on the acceptability of violence and corruption. Amnesty International observed that the deal contributed further to a climate of impunity in Cambodia.[40] China has been particularly keen to avoid a war crimes tribunal for Khmer Rouge leaders that might highlight Beijing's own role in supporting the Khmer Rouge.

At the same time as there are dangers in accommodating violence, there are dangers in a rigid policy of punishing abuses. As Charles King notes:

> The prospect of war crimes tribunals, the arrest of belligerent leaders and assigning blame for atrocities committed during the war all create great disincentives for leaders to enter negotiations and generate equally strong incentives for them to renege on commitments during the implementation of peace agreements.[41]

The art of facilitating a transition from war to peace may lie, to a considerable extent, in ensuring that some of those benefiting from war are in a position to benefit to a greater extent from peace. In practice, these benefits may (at least initially) be secured under some kind of 'armed peace' in which a number of players remain in a position to use the threat of force to underwrite control of economic activity. Charles Tilly has traced this process in relation to the establishment of European states.[42] Groups that have been able to use violence to secure control of production, trade and emergency aid in wartime may be able to carve out for themselves a degree of control over production, trade and development or reconstruction aid after a peace settlement. (Indeed, part of the point of wartime violence may be precisely to secure a commanding and lucrative position within the peacetime economy.)

In Somalia, mafia-type operations have benefited from a degree of order as conflict abated somewhat. Ken Menkaus and John Prendergast argue that this had the effect of assisting trade and minimizing turf battles while holding out the prospect of attracting foreign donors.[43] Alex de Waal points to the shared interest of many Somali landlord-elders in a particular kind of peace, one that excludes politically-marginalized agriculturalists from land they used to cultivate before it was taken away by quasi-legal means or simply by force. He notes that clan analysis has often obscured class analysis.

In Cambodia, some progress towards peace was achieved through a combination of offering rewards for impunity and tightening economic sanctions. The holding of elections without Khmer Rouge participation – what Stephen Stedman calls the 'departing train' strategy – had already weakened the Khmer Rouge.[44] Then the threat by the US Congress to impose sanctions on countries aiding the Khmer Rouge seems to have prompted Thailand to tighten control of trading with the rebel group in late 1996. This created incentives for Thai officials, military officers, and gem and log traders on the ground to deal directly with elements of the Cambodian government, in turn encouraging defections from those elements of the Khmer Rouge – including Ieng Sary, who had benefited most from doing business with Thai officials. Ieng Sary and his supporters were offered a pardon and access to lucrative gem and timber concessions within the Cambodian government system.[45] The links that Sary had built up with traders, army commanders and the Cambodian government contrasted with the more isolated and ideologically 'pure' world inhabited by Pol Pot himself, and these links seem to have prepared the way for Sary's defection from the Khmer Rouge.[46]

The ambiguities of peace and war have also been notable in Burma. Here, many rebellious ethnic groups signed ceasefire agreements with the SLORC (State Law and Order Restoration Council) military government, apparently in return for government tolerance of their drug-trafficking within their respective areas. The Burmese opium warlord Khun Sa, who apparently 'surrendered' to the government in January 1996, was reported to be living unpunished in Rangoon, investing in casinos and, most bizarrely, funding a portion of the Burmese army.[47]

It is doubtful whether South Africa's security services would have accepted the end of apartheid without the prospect of some kind of amnesty for abuses that could be shown to be politically motivated. Many Ugandans still reject the idea of bringing Lord's Resistance Army (LRA) rebels to justice, seeing this as a recipe for continued LRA violence.[48] In international wars, a concern with bringing criminals to justice can also be argued to be risky. For example, the indictment of Serbian President Slobodan Milosevic as a war criminal during the conflict over Kosovo was seen by some as impeding a negotiated solution.[49]

An alternative policy to punishing those who have perpetrated violence is to reward them for giving up violence. In practice, peace often has a quality of pragmatism. Charles King mentions awarding control of significant portions of Bosnia to the Serb Republic, or granting diamond concessions to companies set up by UNITA in Angola, as examples of such pragmatism. Mozambique's RENAMO was bought off with funds to transform itself into a political party. The award to the Revolutionary United Front (RUF) leader, Foday Sankoh, of the chairmanship of a Commission for Strategic Resources to manage Sierra Leone's diamonds failed to achieve the peaceful outcome desired by its American architects. Indeed, the RUF appears to have built up its military muscle with the help of officially-sanctioned control of mining revenue. The distinction between rewarding someone for giving up violence and rewarding them for the violence they gave up may not always be clear. In Sierra Leone, elements of the old government army used hostage-taking to draw attention to their dissatisfaction at being largely excluded from the peace agreement between the Ahmed Tejjan Kabbah government and the rebel RUF. Violence in Sierra Leone has been a response to exclusion, underlining the dangers in peace agreements that include some but exclude large numbers of others. What looks to some people like realism and pragmatism may look to others like appeasement and a prolongation of impunity. Similarly in Liberia, the appeasement of Charles Taylor, who was elected President in 1997, has led to the exclusion of some groups from the political process and security institutions and a potential recourse to armed violence.

Reconstruction/Development

We hear a lot about rehabilitation, reconstruction, resettlement and all the various 're's of post-conflict work. But if you could recreate and reconstruct the exact social and economic conditions prevailing at the outset of a civil war, would it simply break out all over again – for the same reasons as before?

The role of structural violence and of peacetime violence in creating conditions for war implies a need, in the aftermath of a war, to *re-form* a state, to *re-form* an economy, and to *reorient* development. Zygmunt Bauman argued in relation to the Holocaust that violence is likely to be generated by society and its norms, rather than simply representing the breakdown of these norms.[50] Rather than simply representing a breakdown in development, violence is often generated by particular patterns of development. This should call into question the advisability of resuming these patterns of development in the aftermath of a conflict.

The end of Sudan's first civil war (in 1972) did not produce a political system that remedied the underdevelopment of the south or the marginalization of significant groups in the north. In the absence of lasting political protection for the south, the economic rehabilitation of the area merely served to regenerate resources (notably cattle) that could be raided by northern pastoralists who themselves continued to be marginalized within the north, notably by the growth of mechanized farming. In circumstances where rebel leaders have been bribed into peace (as happened to a significant extent in Mozambique and later in Sierra Leone and Liberia), then a failure to tackle underlying grievances may be particularly likely and particularly damaging in the long run.

In our haste to separate the evil perpetrators of violence from the innocent victims of violence – and this tendency applies particularly to the media – we often forget that soldiers are recruited from civilians and that civilians' disillusionment with peace may provide one of the critical clues to why violence is taking place. Rather than simply reconstructing an economy, one might want to think about how to put into reverse the process by which diverse groups took up arms or persuaded others to do so.

The fact that fighters – whether in Sierra Leone or in criminal gangs in the industrialized countries – often have shared goals and shared needs (for money, status, security, a sense of belonging) suggests a need to think of conflict resolution not only as a compromise between two divergent positions but as *the simultaneous provision of what both sides need*. This resonates with John Burton's 'human needs' approach to conflict resolution, which sees conflict as an attempt to meet basic human needs not being met in peacetime.[51] If we take seriously the diverse reasons why ordinary people participate in violence, rather than simply concentrating on states or leaders (as has been common in international relations), then this alerts us to the importance of shared goals. This way of thinking tends to put education, employment and ensuring the rule of law at the heart of conflict prevention and resolution. In other words, it highlights the need for development – but probably not the kind of development that preceded the conflict.

Patterns of development and reconstruction that meet the needs of ordinary people – whether these are needs for resources, for education or for security – will tend to weaken the position of warlords, extremist politicians and faction leaders who offer to meet these needs through more violent means. Menkaus and Prendergast argue that UN intervention in Somalia actually did the opposite by giving resources and legitimacy to the major warlords, and encouraging conflict over central authority in a context where resources were concentrated in Mogadishu. Moreover:

> The failure of the UN mission in Somalia is to a large degree the extension of a bankrupt donor policy which for decades supported overly centralised, unsustainable government structures in Mogadishu whose legitimacy came primarily from the barrel of a gun.[52]

As in Somalia, Liberian civilian organizations have often opposed recognition of armed faction leaders in peace negotiations, arguing that this boosts their prestige and their ability to attract a following.[53]

When it comes to the demobilization of armed groups, there is a danger that demobilization, like emergency aid, will be tackled as a discrete programme, isolated from a wider understanding of political and economic processes. For example, Save the Children Fund staff accused the Structural Adjustment Programmes in Mozambique of undermining economic opportunities just at the point when demobilized soldiers needed to be absorbed. Commenting on peace agreements signed in January 1992 in El Salvador, one Oxfam report noted:

> Generally it was recognised that whilst the Agreements dealt in detail with issues related to the demobilisation and demilitarisation processes, limited attention was given to fundamental economic and legal issues which constituted the root causes of the internal conflict.[54]

Land reform, in particular, was not given a high priority. Indeed, the failure to fulfil expectations of demobilized combatants jeopardized security and contributed to the high crime rates mentioned earlier.

One of the obstacles to constructing the kind of political economy that will not generate a resumption of war is a lack of adequate funding. There is often a contrast, noted for example by Menkaus in relation to Somalia,[55] between very large sums spent on emergency relief and then very small sums spent on rehabilitation once the cameras, and perhaps the international peacekeepers, have gone away. In Kosovo, there have been major shortfalls in funding for rehabilitation. No recent rehabilitation programme has seen anything remotely comparable to the estimated $88 billion (at present-day prices) that was pumped into the rebuilding of Germany under the Marshall Plan after the Second World War. Analysing the roots of the latest conflict in Chechnya, Anatol Lieven, author of *Chechnya: Tombstone of Russian Power*, has written:

> Since being defeated in that war [that is, the war of 1994–96], Moscow...failed to give President Aslan Maskhadov any serious aid to reconstruct Chechnya's shattered economy. By doing so, the Kremlin fatally undermined the only Chechen leader who has combined a desire for pragmatic relations with Russia with real prestige at home. The ruin of the Chechen economy obviously contributed enormously to the dangerous anarchy of the region, as thousands of unemployed, heavily armed ex-fighters turned either to kidnapping or raiding or to Islamist and nationalist extremism.[56]

Democracy

Democracy has sometimes been presented as a panacea for peace. But securing *consent* for democracy may not be easy. Securing consent even from ordinary people may sometimes be a problem. Why, for example, should the Tutsis accept democracy in Rwanda, where the Hutus constitute a large majority? Moreover, a rapid push towards democracy has sometimes been destabilizing, as in neighbouring Burundi. In the former Yugoslavia, Milosevic and his cabal have defended themselves against democracy with a series of conflicts that reinforce a Serb 'siege mentality', deepen politically – and economically – profitable sanctions, legitimize undemocratic rule, stigmatize political opposition as 'Western collaborators', and allow various kinds of asset transfer from ordinary people to this cabal (not least from ordinary Serbs through a variety of pyramid schemes, taxation and monopolistic pricing).[57] In Rwanda, encouraged by international prevarication and French support, extremist Hutu factions defended their privileged position against democracy with a ruthlessness that embraced carefully planned genocide. In East Timor, the Indonesian army reacted to the threat of secession by encouraging militias to attack and intimidate civilians. More broadly, the army seems to have been stirring up conflict in Indonesia to underline its continuing political importance and to guard against the sidelining of the military and its economic interests in a process of democratization.

In Sierra Leone, the advent of democracy in 1996 (something the UN and its member states failed to back with peacekeeping) proved unacceptable to rebels and soldiers alike, who saw in it an end to their impunity, an end to the lucrative war economy, and a return to corrupt pre-war politics – hence, in large part, the May 1997 coup. In Liberia, democracy in 1997 meant the appeasement of Charles Taylor and an electoral victory based on the veiled threat of a return to war if he did not win.

Ceasefires

Ceasefires have often been a step on the road to peace. But there are circumstances in which a call for an immediate peace, or a ceasefire, may represent an accommodation – and even an invitation – to massive violence. War and genocide frequently run alongside each other. Part of the rationale for the Allied war effort in the Second World War was putting an end to the Nazi genocide. Few would question the legitimacy of this. Yet some 25 years later, most of the world condemned the Vietnamese invasion of Cambodia in 1978 – even though it was this event that brought an end to genocide by the Khmer Rouge. In April–June 1994, a ceasefire in the war between the Rwandese Patriotic Front (RPF) and the Rwandan government – called for by the UN Security Council – would actually have halted the RPF's advance in circumstances where this advance was the most realistic hope of ending the genocide, something the RPF was eventually able to achieve.[58]

Liberalization

The liberalization of an economy may sit uneasily with a process of democratization. In Rwanda, as African Rights has argued, the international drive towards democratization in Rwanda appears to have run aground, in part, on the resource shortages fostered by internationally-generated austerity packages.[59] In Sierra Leone, privatization proved to be a means of transferring state assets to a small monopolistic oligarchy, reinforcing the vested interests opposed to the end of one-party rule.[60] And in Russia, the partial criminalization of business has been linked to the transition from a command economy to a market economy operating with institutions (banks, accounting systems, means of enforcing contracts) that organize and regulate markets. The process has been accelerated by the collapse of state agencies, which became unable or unwilling to control this criminalization.[61] And democratization has been compromised by deals between former President Boris Yeltsin and the newly-enriched oligarchs controlling much of the Russian economy and much of the media on which politicians rely for generating electoral support.

Conclusion

The existence of peace begs a number of questions: Whose peace are we talking about? Peace on what terms? Peace in whose interests? And peace negotiated by which individuals or groups? In one sense, everybody wants peace; it is just that they want their own version of peace. This line of analysis prompts Eftihia Voutira and Shaun Brown to be particularly sceptical in relation to NGOs involved in conflict-resolution: 'What kind of a peace are you working towards,' they ask.[62] It is a good question.

Who are you excluding in a peace settlement? To what extent is it an agreement between armed factions to the exclusion of most elements of civil society? If an agreement between government and rebels can exclude civil society, in extreme cases, the rebels themselves are excluded from peace agreements. The Sudan Peace Agreement of 1997 was in many ways an agreement between military allies – the Sudan government and southern factions with which it was already linked. The rebel SPLA was excluded. The agreement coincided with a marked escalation of the war. In Liberia and Sierra Leone, civil society groups were eventually marginalized in the peace agreements reached in 1995 and 1999, respectively.

What forms of corruption are you institutionalizing in the peace process? And what exactly is the difference between peace and war in circumstances where peace institutionalizes violence and where war involves forms of covert cooperation and tacit non-aggression between ostensibly warring parties?

In a sense, for a peace agreement to succeed, two factors are essential: first, one needs an agreement between leaders; second, these leaders must be legitimate individuals who can maintain a following that encompasses all important sectors of the population and who, moreover, do not sacrifice a significant part of this following by the very act of making a peace agreement. One immediately thinks of the nascent Palestinian state, and the split between Yassir Arafat and those who would wish to see a more far-reaching solution to the Palestine/Israel problem. Members of the Palestinian Leadership Organisation (PLO) leadership have certainly profited from international aid and business monopolies while militant groups like Hamas and Hizbollah have attracted more support because of economic crisis in the small area controlled by the Palestinian elite.[63]

The diverse aims of those involved in warfare (and in crimes during war) should be taken into account by those who are seeking to intervene in some way, whether such intervention takes the form of long-term aid, of emergency aid, of attempts to broker or militarily enforce a peace, or of rehabilitation efforts. Rather than simply concentrating on negotiations between the 'two sides' in a war, it may be helpful to try to map the benefits and costs of violence for a variety of parties and to seek to influence the calculations they make. This will include attempts to reduce the economic benefits of violence (for example, through sanctions such as the freezing of bank accounts), to increase the economic benefits of peaceable activities (for example, through the provision of employment and more geographically-even forms of development), and to reduce the legal (and moral) impunity that may be enjoyed by a variety of groups (for example, by publicizing abuses, initiating international judicial proceedings, and making aid explicitly conditional on human rights observance). We need to investigate what international interventions (aid, diplomacy, publicity, investment, trade) are doing to accelerate or retard the processes by which people fall below the protection of the law.

'Interventions' are not simply something that 'the West' or 'the international community' does to remedy humanitarian disasters once they occur; more often than not, interventions occur prior to the disaster, perhaps helping to precipitate it – witness, for example, the international support for abusive and unrepresentative governments like those of Siad

Barre in Somalia, Samuel Doe in Liberia and Juvenal Habyarimana in Rwanda. In order to develop effective strategies for ending conflict, one must first understand its complex dynamics and the various interests involved in perpetuating conflicts. One of the best ways to minimize the suffering resulting from 'war' is to combat the strategies and misinformation of those who seek to use 'war' as cover for their anti-democratic and/or criminal agendas.

NOTES

1. Charles King has argued that when one side wins, the peace is often more long-lasting, in *Ending Civil Wars*, Adelphi Paper 308, Oxford University Press/International Institute for Strategic Studies, 1997.
2. James Fallows, *Breaking the News: How the Media Undermine American Democracy*, New York: Pantheon, 1996.
3. Stephen Ellis, 'Liberia 1989–1994: A Study in Ethnic and Spiritual Violence', *African Affairs*, Vol.94, No.375, Apr. 1995.
4. David Hirst, 'Escalation of Blood', *The Guardian*, 25 Sept. 1997, p.17; and John Sweeney, 'We Accuse, 80,000 Times', *The Observer*, 16 Nov. 1997.
5. David Shearer, *Private Armies and Military Intervention*, Adelphi Paper 316, Oxford University Press/International Institute for Strategic Studies, 1998.
6. Adekeye Adebajo, 'Nigeria: Africa's New Gendarme?', *Security Dialogue*, June 2000, Vol.31, No.2, pp.185–99.
7. David Keen, *The Economic Functions of Violence in Civil Wars*, Adelphi Paper 320, International Institute for Strategic Studies/Oxford University Press, 1998; and Mats Berdal and David Malone (eds.), *Greed and Grievance: Economic Agendas in Civil Wars*, Boulder, CO and London: Lynne Rienner, 2000.
8. Jean Francois and Jean-Christophe Rufin (eds.), *Economie des Guerres Civiles*, Paris: Hachette, 1996.
9. See, for example, Carlotta Gall and Thomas de Waal, *Chechnya: A Small Victorious War*, London: Pan Original, 1997, on the Russian army in Chechnya.
10. David Keen, *The Benefits of Famine: A Political Economy of Famine and Relief in Southwestern Sudan, 1983–89*, Princeton and Chichester, UK: Princeton University Press, 1994
11. David Keen, 'When War Itself Is Privatized: The Twisted Logic That Makes Violence Worthwhile in Sierra Leone', *Times Literary Supplement*, 29 Dec. 1995, pp.13–14.
12. Focus on Sierra Leone, London, Feb. 1996.
13. Mats Berdal and David Keen, 'Violence and Economic Agendas in Civil Wars: Considerations for Policymakers', *Millennium*, Vol.26, No.3, 1997.
14. For an interesting discussion, see Nicholas Zurbrugg (ed.), *Jean Baudrillard: Art and Artefact*, London: Sage, 1997.
15. Commission for Historical Clarification, *Guatemala: Memory of Silence, Conclusions and Recommendations*, n.d.
16. See, for example, George Soros, 'Who Lost Russia?', *The New York Review of Books*, 13 Apr. 2000, Vol.XLVII, No.6, pp.10–16; and Jonathan Steele, 'The Ryazan Incident', *The Guardian*, 24 Mar. 2000, 22.
17. Malik Mohan, 'Front Line, Fault Line', *The World Today*, Feb. 2000, Vol.56, No.2, pp.14–16.
18. Anna Richardson, 'Police Aid Angola Oil Demo', *Independent on Sunday*, 12 Mar. 2000, p.20.
19. See, for example, Mark Thompson, *Forging War: The Media in Serbia, Croatia, Bosnia and Hercegovina*, Luton: University of Luton Press, 1999; and 'Rwanda: Death, Despair and Defiance', *African Rights*, London, 1994.

20. Dubravka Ugresic, 'Goodnight Croatian writers', in W.L. Webb and Rose Bell (eds.), *An Embarrassment of Tyrannies*, London: Victor Gollancz, 1997, pp.204–10.
21. Yasar Kemal, 'The Dark Cloud over Turkey', in Webb and Bell (eds.), pp.251–6.
22. William Shawcross, 'Tragedy in Cambodia', *New York Review of Books*, 1 Nov. 1996, pp.41–6 and Dec. 19 pp.73–4; and author's research in Sierra Leone.
23. Enoch O. Opondo, 'Representation of Ethnic Conflict in the Kenyan Media', in T. Allen, K. Hudson and J. Seaton (eds.), *War, Ethnicity and the Media*, London: South Bank University, 1996.
24. Phillip Knightley, *The First Casualty: From the Crimea to Vietnam: The War Correspondent as Hero, Propagandist and Myth Maker*, London: Pan, 1989.
25. David Turton, *War and Ethnicity: Global Connections and Local Violence*, New York: University of Rochester Press, 1997, Introduction.
26. Jonathan Mermin has analysed media coverage of US intervention in Grenada in 1983 and Panama in 1989, as well as the build-up to the Gulf War. He shows that the range of debate in the American media was closely tied to the degree of criticism coming from the Democrats in any given crisis. Where there was little criticism, there was little debate. He also argues that polls showing public support for an aggressive military line had a circular quality, since limited media coverage had powerfully shaped the public opinion that was then polled. Where memory of abuses by one ethnic group is suppressed (and abuses by the other side are played up), this feeds into the 'us' and 'them' mentality. If the US and the English-speaking allies in the UK are considered as an ethnic group, one can add that the US and UK media often suppress abuses by this ethnic group and play up threats against it. See Jonathan Mermin, *Debating War and Peace: Media Coverage of US Intervention in the Post-Vietnam Era*, Princeton: Princeton University Press, 1999.
27. Antonius Robben, 'The Fear of Indifference: Combatants' Anxieties about the Political Identity of Civilians during Argentina's Dirty War', in K. Koonings and D. Kruijt (eds.), *Societies of Fear: The Legacy of Civil War, Violence and Terror in Latin America*, London: Zed, 1999.
28. Karl Marx, *Capital: A Critical Analysis of Capitalist Production*, London: Oxford University Press, 1999 edition.
29. Jenny Edkins, 'Legality with a Vengeance: Humanitarian Relief in Complex Emergencies', *Millennium Journal of International Studies*, 1996, Vol.25, No.3, pp.547–75; and Amartya Sen, *Poverty and Famines: An Essay on Entitlement and Deprivation*, Oxford: Clarendon Press 1981 (reprinted 1984).
30. Johan Galtung, *Peace by Peaceful Means: Peace and Conflict, Developments and Civilization*, London: Sage, 1996.
31. Peter Uvin, *Aiding Violence: The Development Enterprise in Rwanda*, West Hartford, CT: Kumarian Press, 1998.
32. David Keen, 1994 (n.10 above)
33. Lucy Jones, 'LA's deportees send murder rate soaring in El Salvador', *The Guardian*, 29 Feb. 2000, p.16.
34. Alexander Stille, *Excellent Cadavers: The Mafia and the Death of the First Italian Republic*, Vintage Books, 1996.
35. Federico Varese, 'Is Sicily the Future of Russia? Private Protection and the Rise of the Russian Mafia', *Archives é de Sociologie*, 1994, Vol.35, No.2, p.249.
36. Manuel Castells, *End of Millennium*, Malden, Mass: Blackwell, 1998.
37. Mary Kaldor, *New and Old Wars: Organised Violence in a Global Era*, Cambridge: Polity Press, 1999.
38. On Afghanistan see, for example, Ahmed Rashid, *Taliban: Islam, Oil and the New Great Game in Central Asia*, London, 2000: I.B. Tauris; and Kaldor (n.37 above).
39. See David Keen, 1998 (n.7 above).
40. William Shawcross (n.22 above).
41. Charles King (n.1 above).
42. Charles Tilly, 'War Making and State Making as Organised Crime', in Peter Evans, Dietrich Rueschemeyer and Theda Skocpol (eds.), *Bringing the State Back In*, New York: Cambridge University Press, 1985.

43. African Rights, 'Land Tenure, the Creation of Famine and Prospects for Peace in Somalia', *Discussion Paper No.1*, London, Oct. 1993.
44. Stephen John Stedman, 'Spoiler Problems in Peace Processes', *International Security*, Fall 1997, Vol.22, No.2.
45. William Shawcross (n.22 above).
46. Pierre P. Lizée, 'Cambodia in 1996: Of Tigers, Crocodiles and Doves', *Asian Survey*, 1997, Vol.37, No.1; and Mats Berdal and David Keen (n.13 above).
47. *The Guardian*, 27 Nov. 1996.
48. Personal communication, Andrew Mawson.
49. See, for example, Ian Black and Stephen Bates, 'War crimes move dims peace hopes', *The Guardian*, 28 May 1999, p.1.
50. Zygmunt Bauman, *Modernity and the Holocaust*, Cambridge: Polity, 1989.
51. John W. Burton (ed.), *Conflict: Human Needs Theory*, Basingstoke: Macmillan, 1990.
52. Ken Menkaus and John Prendergast, 'Political Economy of Post-Intervention Somalia. Somalia Task Force', Issue Paper No.3, Apr. 1995, pp.1–18.
53. Samuel Kofi Woods II, 'Civic Initiatives in the Peace Process', in Jeremy Armon and Andy Carl (eds.), *ACCORD: The Liberian Peace Process, 1990–1991*, London: Conciliation Resources, 1996, pp.27–32.
54. Oxfam/Community Aid Abroad, 'United Nations Interventions in Conflict Situations', A submission to Ambassador Richard Butler, Chair of the UN Preparatory Committee for the Fiftieth Anniversary, Oxford, 1994, p.A3.
55. Ken Menkaus, 'US Foreign Assistance to Somalia: Phoenix from the Ashes?', *Middle East Policy*, Vol.5, No.1, Jan., 1997.
56. Anatol Lieven, 'The Only Hope for Ending the Chechen Nightmare', *Independent*, 5 Nov. 1999, p.5.
57. Author's research in Belgrade, 1999.
58. *African Rights*, 1994 (n.19 above).
59. Ibid.
60. William Reno, *Corruption and State Politics in Sierra Leone*, Cambridge University Press, 1995; and author's research in Sierra Leone.
61. Castells (n.36 above); Soros (n.16 above).
62. Eftihia Voutira and Shaun Brown, *Conflict Resolution: A Review of Some Non-governmental Practices – 'A Cautionary Tale'*, Uppsala: Nordiska Afrikainstitutet/Swedish International Development Cooperation Agency, 1995.
63. David Hirst, 'Shameless in Gaza', *The Guardian*, 21 Apr. 1997, pp.8–10; and Edward Said, *Peace and Its Discontents: Gaza-Jericho 1993–1995*, London: Vintage, Parker, 1995.

Economic Fragility and Political Fluidity: Explaining Natural Resources and Conflicts

ABIODUN ALAO and 'FUNMI OLONISAKIN

One subject that has enjoyed much interest and attention, particularly in the post-Cold War era, is natural resource-based conflicts. There are three primary reasons for this interest. First, the drastic increase in the number of such conflicts is caused, in part, by the downward spiral in the economic fortune of many states, particularly in Africa, and in part, by the structural problems of governance that exist in many of these countries. Second, many of these conflicts are related to other major security problems, especially the proliferation of small arms, the activities of warlords and the re-emergence of mercenaries. Attempts to address these problems have forced many analysts to examine more profoundly the issue of resources and conflict. Finally, resource-based conflicts are often marred in the complexities surrounding the collapse, or near collapse, of many states. From Liberia and Sierra Leone to Cambodia and the Democratic Republic of Congo, the politics of resource control have played an important part in the weakening of institutional and administrative structures.

This essay presents an overview of post-Cold War resource conflicts, focusing largely on how such conflicts have affected structures of governance. The essay is divided into six sections. The first examines the complexities of the link between natural resources and conflict; the second focuses on the characteristics and manifestations of post-Cold War natural-resource conflicts; the third section briefly assesses three contemporary resource-based conflicts in Liberia, Zimbabwe, and the Democratic Republic of Congo; the fourth investigates the external dimensions of natural resource conflicts in Africa; the fifth considers how natural-resource conflicts have affected governance in Africa; and the final section briefly summarizes the main conclusions.

Natural Resources and Conflicts: Explaining the Complexities of a Connection

Human history is replete with examples in which natural resources have featured prominently in fuelling conflicts. The connection between natural resources and conflicts is easily established. Conflicts fought over natural resources are exploited to prosecute war, and the resource endowment of enemies is destroyed to weaken their military capabilities during conflicts. However, conceptualizing and explaining the politics of natural resources has not always been an easy task. One reason that has been advanced for this is that 'because the world is environmentally diverse, problems are rarely universal [and] societies will differ in details of their understanding'.[1] This diversity of views on how best to address the future of the environment emerged clearly during the 1992 Rio conference on the environment, where developing countries disagreed fundamentally with the advanced industrial nations on how to exploit the environment for development.[2]

In modern academic writing, the resource issue that first attracted attention was scarcity. This concern, which was popularized by Thomas Malthus' apocalyptic warning in 1798 on the possible implications of population explosion on resource availability,[3] was to attract more disciples among subsequent generations. By the beginning of the twentieth century, concerns about resource scarcity were widespread. The search for natural resources was among the major factors in European imperialism in Africa and Asia by the end of the twentieth century.

Public and academic interest in the politics of natural resources underwent a *renaissance* during the second half of the twentieth century. There are three possible explanations for this. First, there was an increase in the number of academic disciplines interested in the issue of natural resources and conflict. While historically the subject was studied by geographers and their affiliate disciplines like geology and demography, the de-compartmentalization of academic disciplines which occurred in the 1950s brought other disciplines, including social sciences, law and even the natural sciences, into the study of conflict. The multiplicity of interpretations that emerged from these subjects increased interest in the study of the politics of natural resources.[4] The second possible explanation for the increased interest in this subject involved the heightened media focus on topics related to the future of a world that was seen to be adopting a *laissez-faire* approach of benign neglect to the environment and its support systems. Issues like the depletion of the ozone layer and the 'green-house effect' that were to attract attention in later years, had begun to attract the attention of a critical public. Finally, the increase in the number of resource-based conflicts around the world helped fuel interest in the politics of natural resources. From oil in the Middle East to land in Africa to solid minerals in Asia to control of sea resources in Latin America, conflicts centred on natural resources dominated attention and ignited public awareness of resource issues.

Despite the universal acknowledgement of the importance of resource-based conflicts, there were no concrete attempts to develop a special focus on the link between natural resources and conflict. Even today, most of the studies on the subject are still brought under the wider discussion of 'Environment and Security'. While this may not be altogether inappropriate, it has the potential danger of subsuming important natural-resource conflicts under the less important controversies that may sometimes surround environmental issues.[5]

Broadly speaking, the link between natural resources and conflict can be brought under two main headings: cases in which natural resources have *caused* conflicts, and cases in which natural resources have *fuelled* conflicts. As will be demonstrated below, the distinction between these two cases is sometimes blurred. It is ironic that only in a few cases is it obvious that natural resources are a direct cause of conflict. More often, natural resources form a core factor in conflicts but are subsumed under explanations like ethnicity, religion or border disputes. As a prolongation of conflict, the role of natural resources has been mainly to provide financial resources to warlords and fighters in order to finance their wars. As will be discussed below, the characteristics of this aspect of warfare have changed somewhat in the post-Cold War era.

It has recently become apparent that a balanced and in-depth analysis of the role of natural resources in conflicts is yet to emerge. On the one hand, some analyses see recent conflicts characterized by chaos and exploitation of mineral resources as the result of a collapse of structures of state and governance and, as such, attempts to resolve these conflicts must focus on putting the state back together.[6] On the other hand, some of the emerging literature on natural resources and conflict tends to pay much less attention to the 'state collapse' argument, and sometimes even dismisses it altogether as a major factor in generating civil wars.[7] Instead, some of this literature highlights the greed of the protagonists as the most prominent factor in generating war, and argues that the resulting chaos and plundering are a result of carefully orchestrated efforts aimed at reaping the benefits of natural resources.[8] Furthermore, the Clausewitzian concept of 'war as a continuation of policy by other means' is seen to have little or no place in the new post-Cold War conflicts, where the main aim of the parties is not necessarily victory, but a continuation of war.[9]

Paul Collier, for example, tends to over-simplify and over-generalize the greed factor as a motivation for armed conflict when he states that 'the true cause of much civil war is not the loud discourse of grievance but the silent force of greed'.[10] The real explanations appear to lie somewhere in between this explanation and the 'breakdown' or 'collapse' argument. The breakdown factor can be found at the root of both levels of explanation – causes and prolongation. While it is true that ethnicity, religion and other factors are usually advanced by the protagonists as their reasons for resorting to often brutal armed conflicts, failure over time to address group demands and to distribute available natural resources equitably between groups cannot be excluded as one of the major factors generating armed conflicts. In many cases, the exclusion of the majority from access to the centre of political power (where tight control of natural resources is often maintained) serves to exacerbate these conflicts.[11] Thus, over time, in many parts of the developing world that have experienced an outbreak of violent conflict or suffer from continuing conflict in the post-Cold War era, the marginalization of certain groups has served to weaken structures of governance. The absence of a reliable structure through which these conflicts could have been mediated is often a factor in the eventual slide to violence. Peacemakers in such environments must examine ways of not necessarily returning these countries to their pre-war state, but of creating strong and accountable institutions of governance that will manage group demands in a just and equitable manner.

At the level of prolongation, once a conflict (particularly one over natural resources) remains unresolved and is allowed to turn violent, the conflict often assumes a life of its own. Unscrupulous characters often take advantage of the resulting chaos and leadership vacuum. However, political goals do not always cease to exist as a result of the complexities associated with armed conflict. Other factors like the need to sustain the war effort simply make the road to achieving desired political ends more difficult. Fighters have to be rewarded and alliances and supply lines maintained. The exploitation of natural resources is therefore often a primary objective for warring parties in post-Cold War environments, particularly in the developing world, where material support from affluent allies in the North is no longer as readily available and can only be accessed under new conditions. While the warlords still have political goals, the same may not necessarily be the case for their followers, and faction leaders may not be able to maintain tight control over all their fighters.

How, for example, could arguments that see the prolongation of war as an end in itself adequately explain Charles Taylor's unflinching goal of becoming Liberia's President (even when he controlled natural resources) or Foday Sankoh's belief that the presidency of Sierra Leone is his manifest destiny? Such explanations must be sought through a deeper analysis of the weak, over-centralized state systems that excluded the periphery from the centre and the fusion of economic and political power in one source – the state. Such systems created the motives and opportunities for war and produced a mix of both scrupulous and unscrupulous citizens searching for different ways to redress the perceived wrongs committed against them. While it is tempting to see the overarching political objective of rebel leaders who seek political power as the desire to use the state machinery to consolidate their control over acquired material wealth, other factors cannot be neglected. These factors could include, for example, other expressions of grievances, like the desire to avenge wrongs committed by previous regimes, the need to gain political power for reasons of prestige and, in some cases, to seek protection of the state from possible prosecution for past atrocities, whether committed before or during wars. Therefore, analyses such as Collier's tend to apply a broad-brush explanation that fails to take into account the complex socio-political issues at the root of many contemporary civil wars. Because recent civil wars, particularly in Africa, are not waged in ways that resemble the familiar patterns of pre-Cold War Europe or indeed other wars fought in the Cold War period in many parts of the developing world, there is sometimes a tendency to ignore the political motivations at the root of these conflicts and to pay greater attention to the elements of greed such as the exploitation of natural resources. The nature of greed is such that it can be found at the root of almost every human interaction and it is therefore easy to offer explanations of greed without seeing other complex ramifications.

Bringing peace to societies torn apart by war as a result of resource-based conflicts must therefore entail a process that carefully blends two things – wresting control of mineral resource areas from warring parties, and recreating structures of governance that will successfully manage future conflicts and prevent a recourse to war or violence. Thus, while there is a consensus that natural resources can serve as both a cause and a prolongation of armed conflict, there is a need for more systematic study of the political and economic motivations behind armed conflicts with particular emphasis on the socio-political realities of the war-affected communities. This would contribute to the creation of effective strategies for bringing stability and peace to these environments. The rest of this essay provides a broad overview of the manifestations of natural resource-based conflicts in the post-Cold War period.

Post-Cold War Natural Resource Conflicts: Characteristics and Manifestations

The post-Cold War era has witnessed an increase in resource-based conflicts, both in prominence and in number. The increase in prominence has been due to the string of security issues that now seem to be associated with these conflicts. These issues have further drawn global attention to the fragility of the political and economic structures in many states, particularly in Africa. Indeed, the ultimate collapse of some of these states was to provoke concerns about how best the international community could respond to the challenges created by fragile societies.[12] Perhaps the best evidence of international concern was the plethora of phrases that entered into the security lexicon, including 'complex-emergency',[13] 'peace enforcement',[14] 'peace-creation'[15] and a host of others.

Under the post-Cold War dispensation, the causes of resource-based conflicts have not changed. They remain rooted in the differences between groups concerning the ownership and control of these resources and how best to manage their proceeds. However, while the root causes remain the same, their manifestations have changed. These changes are due to two main factors. The first is the agitation for democratic change that came with the end of the Cold War in countries like Benin, Togo, Niger, Zambia and Zaire. The impact of this development on natural resource conflicts has been profound. First, in many countries, active civil society groups emerged, determined to 'ask questions' about the management of natural resources. Second, a vocal opposition emerged, many of whose members were willing to use force in order to redress what they saw as the political injustices in their societies. Third, the role of ethnicity in politics increased, with both incumbent governments and the opposition whipping up ethnic sentiments to pursue their respective claims. It is, indeed, not surprising that most of these resource-centred conflicts were manifested along ethnic lines.

The second factor in the changing circumstances of resource-based conflicts, particularly in Africa, is the depression that characterized the economy of many developing countries in the last decade, which increased the debt burden and the quality of life of ordinary people in these societies. This development has two main implications for resource-based conflicts in Africa. First, it puts further strain on the environment, forcing many people to eke out a living on limited resources. This inevitably increases the propensity for violent inter-group relations. Second, it has created a disaffected army of people, especially among the youth, many of whom became determined to employ violence in their demand for equitable economic justice from their governments. Some of the best examples of this tendency can be seen in Sierra Leone and Liberia, where disaffected youths were transformed into armed fighters during the civil wars in both countries.

A Tale of Three Conflicts

This section examines three major resource-based conflicts in post-Cold War Africa. The cases selected are Liberia, Zimbabwe and the Democratic Republic of Congo. These countries have been selected for four reasons. First, these conflicts have mostly occurred after the Cold War. Second, taken together, they reflect some of the complexities that have been associated with resource-based conflicts in post-Cold War Africa. Third, they satisfy the geographical spread of sub-Saharan Africa, with cases selected from west, central and southern Africa; finally, these cases reflect different typologies of states in conflict. Liberia represents a state that completely collapsed; Congo represents a state that was severely damaged but still maintained some structures of governance; and Zimbabwe represents a state whose structure of central governance has not been threatened despite the security problems emanating from its resource-based conflict.

Liberia

On the surface, the conflict in Liberia did not appear to be over natural resources. It seemed to be purely an attempt to fight what was seen as the tyranny of the late Samuel Doe's regime.[16] A closer look however reveals that even the outbreak of the conflict had major natural resource components. Over decades, political groups in Liberia had exploited its resource endowment to finance a standard of living that was not indicative of the general economic situation of the country. Thus, Liberia's civil war of 1989 to 1997 was, in a sense, the reaction of the neglected majority to an unjust social order. Although Charles Taylor, who led the rebellion, was a member of the tiny Americo-Liberian elite class,[17] the crop of his followers were mostly Gios and Manos who had not benefited from the country's natural resource endowment. However, if the role of natural resources as a primary cause of the Liberian conflict is not immediately evident, the same cannot be said about the role resources played in the course of the conflict.

The main natural resources that featured in the Liberian civil war include timber, diamond and iron ore. These were the main natural resources on which pre-war Liberia earned most of its foreign revenue, and it was unsurprising that the warring factions exploited these resources to fund their war efforts. It is estimated that Charles Taylor earned over US$400 million per year from trade in natural resources during the war between 1992 and 1996.

It is difficult to arrive at the exact number of actors that took an active part in the struggle to control natural resources in Liberia during the country's civil war, but two distinct groups can be identified. These were (1) the main warring factions, which at one stage grew to seven,[18] and (2) the peacekeeping missions, both the regional team, the Economic Community of West African States Ceasefire Monitoring Group (ECOMOG) and the UN Observer Mission in Liberia (UNOMIL). There were three ways in which these actors benefited from the exploitation of natural resources during the war. First was through the direct exploitation of these resources and their sale in international markets. This was reportedly done through neighbouring countries, and the main rebel movement, Charles Taylor's National Patriotic Front of Liberia (NPFL) exploited this opportunity most, especially because the faction controlled the largest and most resource-endowed sections of the country. The second way through which Liberia's warlords benefited from natural resources was through the protection fees often obtained from foreign, mostly European, multinational corporations operating in Liberia during the war. Finally, Liberia's factions benefited through taxes imposed on goods entering or leaving the country.[19]

Zimbabwe

The key natural resource that has historically been at the root of conflict in Zimbabwe is land. What, however, makes land more controversial in Zimbabwe is the racial ramifications of the land controversy in the country. This is a subject on which there is an extensive literature, and we will thus limit discussion here to the key themes that have affected governance in Zimbabwe in recent years.[20] Zimbabwe's war of liberation was fought as much for independence as it was for land. The white population which accounted for less than 20 per cent of the total population controlled about half of the land. However, the compromise that secured independence for Zimbabwe at the Lancaster House talks in 1979 made the land issue one on which there would be gradual rather than radical restructuring.

From 1992, three major issues emerged to complicate land politics in Zimbabwe, and to serve as the antecedent to the major land conflict that brought the country to the focus of international attention in the early months of 2000. First was the dwindling popularity of President Robert Mugabe and his Zimbabwean African National Union (ZANU) party which increased the level of political opposition to the government. Contrary to the previous opposition, which took the pattern of the old ZANU/ZAPU (Zimbabwean African People's Union) political divide, Zimbabwe's opposition after 1992 was more ideologically focused. The second issue that complicated Zimbabwe's land politics was the growing depression of the country's economy. Although the downward plunge in the country's economic fortune had started since the second half of the 1980s, the problem became more acute after 1992. This depressed economy increased the domestic demand for land while, at the same time, further increasing the pressure on the government. The third factor was the alleged corruption that characterized the redistribution of acquired land. It was alleged, with some justification it would appear, that much of the land acquired under the 1992 'Land Acquisition Act' was later re-distributed to top ZANU party members and to President Mugabe's cronies. White farmers and opposition politicians thus argued that the whole purpose of re-claiming land from white owners would ultimately be defeated if they were not given to poor and landless Zimbabweans.

All these issues came to a head in February 2000 when a referendum took place on a revised constitution for Zimbabwe. Although technically the issue at stake was a referendum over a new constitution, land issues emerged as a major source of concern. The ruling party argued that the President needed more power to be able to acquire land from white farmers for redistribution to landless blacks. The opposition, however, argued that what was needed was not a new constitution, but for the government to respect the existing one. White farmers also supported the opposition politicians in the referendum, which the government lost. This defeat has led to the latest land crisis in Zimbabawe. Having lost the referendum over a new constitution, the government encouraged war veterans to take over white farms. The crisis reached a disturbing stage in April 2000 when the war veterans started killing opposition party supporters and white farmers. This has not resolved the problem, and many white Zimbabweans have fled the country.

Democratic Republic of the Congo

Of all the post-Cold War civil conflicts in Africa, none reflects the complexities of the connection between natural resources and conflict like the civil war in the Democratic Republic of Congo. The war that began as an effort to remove the tyranny of the Mobutu regime had, by the end of 1999, resulted in multi-dimensional conflicts involving more than five Congolese factions and up to seven countries within the region (see Adebajo and Landsberg in this volume).

The natural resources at stake in the Congo crisis are mainly solid minerals, especially diamond, gold, cobalt and tantalum. Perhaps because of the enormous interest in recent developments in the conflict, many observers are apt to forget that the management of natural resources was itself a major cause of the imbroglio. The years of Mobutu Sese Seko's dictatorship (1965–97) saw the massive plundering of revenues from natural resources to the great dissatisfaction of the majority of the population.[21] It was an alliance of this disaffected population that eventually deposed the Mobutu regime.

Since 1998, when the local and regional alliance that removed Mobutu disappeared and a multi-dimensional civil conflict ensued, natural resources have come to play a more prominent role. Most of the attention has focused on the role that these resources have played in determining external involvement in the war. Since all the countries involved in the conflict (Rwanda, Uganda, Burundi, Zimbabwe, Angola and Namibia) are known to have weak economies, it is believed that the main motivation for their involvement is the mineral resources they can extract from the country. This is especially the case with a country like Zimbabwe whose security can not be said to be directly threatened by the situation in the Congo. There are also allegations that the war has been exploited by senior military officers and politicians in some of these countries to make quick business deals and financial gains from the Congo. The extent of the regional involvement in the Congo's mineral resources can be seen in the Kisangani debacles between August 1999 and June 2000 in which Uganda and Rwanda, two countries with long historical and military relationships, engaged in conflict. Although a number of political explanations have been employed in a bid to explain these clashes, many close observers believe that the problem had more to do with disagreements over the management of the town's abundant mineral deposits.

As in Zimbabwe, the controversy in the Congo still continues, and its enormous mineral deposits will remain an important determinant in the conflict's future directions, particularly as it relates to the nature and extent of foreign involvement in the country.

Foreign Involvement in Post-Cold War Africa's Resource-based Conflicts

One area in which there seems to be a consensus among security scholars is that the pattern of foreign involvement in African conflicts has changed. The blatant interventions of the Cold War era have disappeared, leaving behind the more subtle activities of non-state actors, especially private security firms, multinational corporations and Non-Governmental Organizations (NGOs). Before going into a discussion of foreign involvement in resource-based conflicts in Africa, it is necessary to point out that 'foreign' in this context is taken to mean countries and agencies outside the continent. This distinction is necessary because of the increasing involvement by other African countries in civil conflicts taking place in neighbouring states. While this is technically 'foreign', what we consider here are interventions from outside the continent.

In general terms, foreign involvement in Africa's resource-based conflicts has come from three main quarters. First, and perhaps most controversially, are the foreign mercenary firms, euphemistically described as Private Security Organizations (PSOs) (see Brooks in this volume). Although mercenaries first mounted the African stage during the Cold War era, their re-entry onto the stage in the early 1990s has evoked concerns, especially since they are actively involved in conflicts that centre mainly around natural resources. Among the mercenary companies that have featured in recent African conflicts are the Gurkhas, Sandlines and Executive Outcomes. A second source of external involvement in African conflicts is foreign multinational corporations, many of which have exploited situations of conflict to maximize their own profits. There have also been cases where these corporations have taken an active part in the politics governing civil conflicts. A good example of this is the activities of Shell in Nigeria.[22]

The third source of external involvement in African conflicts is the governments of the United States and some European countries. As a result of the lack of a recognizable security structure within Africa to deal effectively with resource-based and other conflicts, subtle external intervention has been encouraged. For example, several external peacekeeping capacity-building initiatives have been put forward by the United States and France. The former initiated the African Crisis Response Initiative (ACRI), while France backed *Renforcement des Capacités Africaines de Maintienir de la Paix* (RECAMP), both focusing on training, rather than providing much needed equipment and logistics. In comparison, however, France has provided more substantial logistical support under RECAMP, than the US support under the ACRI arrangement, which is limited to provision of non-lethal equipment.[23] These schemes have, however, not always been well received by many African countries, most of which see them as a divisive attempt to frustrate regional alliances that could address these resource-based conflicts. Apart from inadequate logistical support, some of the training programmes pay greater attention to doctrines that are likely to be irrelevant to many conflict environments in Africa. Perhaps the most difficult challenge that these training initiatives face is the perception among many Africans that they are intended to keep the West out of politically-risky African conflicts.

Natural Resource Conflicts and Governance

One of the main features of the post-Cold War order is the frequent calls for 'good governance' particularly among external donors. Although what this exactly means may be open to debate, it is generally assumed to encompass ensuring that citizens are empowered to participate actively and democratically in decisions related to how they are governed. Contained in this definition is the active participation of citizens in the management of the natural resource endowment of their countries. While historically the national interest has been seen in terms of the state controlling rent over its resources, local communities are now interested in controlling rent outside of the tentacles of the state.

Armed challenges against the state over control of natural resources have come mainly from two quarters: the local communities, as in the case of the Niger Delta communities in Nigeria, and local warlords, as evidenced in Liberia and Sierra Leone during their civil conflicts. The principal desire of local communities is to ensure greater participation and accountability for the resources extracted from their land, while the objectives of warlords have often been centred on political and economic gains.

The strategies adopted by governments to counter armed challenges against their control over natural resources have depended largely on the strength of the state and on the importance of the natural resource to state survival and elite interests. Where the central government is weak, its response to the challenge has often been uncoordinated, and in some cases, external assistance has been sought or welcomed. Recent examples of this can be seen in Sierra Leone where the government of Captain Valentine Strasser turned for help to the South African mercenary group, Executive Outcomes, in 1992, and in the Democratic Republic of Congo, where Laurent Kabila welcomed the assistance provided by a host of friendly neighbours in 1998. The importance of the resource in dispute to state survival in countries where there are strong central governments has been a strong determinant of state responses to challenges against its authority. In almost all cases, the reaction has been swift and brutal, as can be seen, for example, in the reaction of General Sani Abacha's regime to the problems in the Niger Delta, which involved the hanging of Ken Saro-Wiwa and eight other activists in 1995.

Since many of the resource conflicts in the continent have been communal, managing them sometimes involves intricate politics. It is ironic that governments in Africa often encourage such conflicts in order to advance their short-term political goals or else ignore them long enough to try to maximize political advantage. It is believed in many quarters, for example, that the on-going land conflict in Zimbabwe may be calculated by the Mugabe administration to reap political gains, especially as it reached its peak at the time when the country was preparing for a general election.

Conclusion

Natural resources serve as both a cause and a prolongation of armed conflict. Certainly the experience of the post-Cold War era has shown how the availability of natural resources introduces other complexities, particularly when a conflict has assumed a violent dimension. Experience has shown that the potential for armed conflict in societies that are endowed with natural resources is great when group demands are not managed effectively and access to these resources is denied through a process of fair and just distribution. Thus, when armed conflict erupts under these circumstances, the ready availability of some natural, particularly mineral, resources serves other purposes – fuelling and creating opportunities for the involvement of a cross-section of external actors. This has served to complicate efforts to create peace and stability in many conflict areas. More systematic research is therefore required to enhance the understanding of peacemakers about the different roles that natural resources can play in conflicts.

From the panoramic survey presented in this essay, it is clear that the complications surrounding resource politics are likely to remain key issues in the new millennium, especially as countries in Africa attempt to use their limited resources to meet apparently limitless needs. It is also clear that, as conflicts of this nature increase, their impact on governance will become more profound. It is early as yet to know what the outcome of all this will be, but the best option for African countries collectively and individually is to develop strong civil societies and accountable institutional structures to meet the challenges of resource-based conflicts. It is only by achieving this that durable peace can be established in many conflict areas on the continent.

ACKNOWLEDGEMENT

The authors would like to thank the Ford Foundation for the grant given to undertake study on Resource Conflicts in Sub-Saharan Africa.

NOTES

1. Quoted from Judith Rees, *Natural Resources: Allocation, Economics and Policy*, London: Routledge, 1990.
2. For a detailed discussion of this, see, Abiodun Alao, 'The Environment and Security in Africa', in Adebayo Oyemade and Abiodun Alao, *Africa After the Cold War: The Changing Perspective on Security*, Trenton: African World Press, 1996.
3. Thomas Malthus, *First Essay on Population, 1798 Essays on the Principle of Population*, London: Macmillan; St. Martins Press, 1966.
4. See, for example, recent studies like Paul Richards, *Fighting for the Rainforest: War, Youth and Resources in Sierra Leone*, London: James Currey, 1996; and Robert Kaplan, 'The Coming Anarchy', *Atlantic Monthly*, Feb. 1994.
5. For a fuller discussion, see Abiodun Alao, *The Tragedy of Endowment: Natural Resources and Conflict in Sub-Saharan Africa* (forthcoming).
6. See, for example, William Zartman, *Collapsed States*, Boulder and London: Lynne Rienner, 1995.
7. See Mats Berdal and David Malone (eds.), *Greed and Grievance: Economic Agendas in Civil Wars*, Boulder and London: Lynne Rienner, 2000. See in particular Paul Collier, 'Doing Well out of War: An Economic Perspective' (ch.5) and David Keen, 'Incentives and Disincentives for Violence' (ch.2).
8. Paul Collier, for example, places greater emphasis on greed as a motivating factor for armed conflict, rather than grievance.
9. See Keen (n.7 above).
10. Collier (n.7 above), p.101.
11. While Collier accords more prominence to greed as a motivating factor for war, Keen, in his analysis of the economic agenda in wars, finds that certain experiences highlight the importance of grievance rather than greed. See Keen (n.7 above), p.31.
12. See, for example, I. William Zartman (ed.), *Collapsed States: the Disintegration and Restoration of Legitimate Authority*; and *State Rebuilding after State Collapse: Security and*

Democracy and Development in Post-war Liberia. London: Centre for Democracy and Development, 1998.

13. See, for example, John Mackinlay and Abiodun Alao, 'Liberia 1994: ECOMOG/UNOMIL Response to Complex Emergency', *United Nations University Occasional Paper Series* 1, 1996.

14. See, for example, Dennis J. Quinn, 'Peace Support Operations: Definitions and Implications', in Dennis J. Quinn (ed.), *Peace Support Operations and the US Military*, Washington DC: National Defense Press, 1994.

15. See, Funmi Olonisakin, *Reinventing Peacekeeping in Africa: Conceptual and Legal issues in ECOMOG Operations*, The Hague: Kluwer Law International, 2000.

16. See for example, Gus Liebenow, *Liberia: The Quest for Democracy*, Bloomington: Indiana University Press, 1987; and Amos Sawyer, *The Emergency of Autocracy in Liberia*, San Francisco: Institute for Contemporary Studies, 1992.

17. He was an Americo-Liberian, the group that had held power in the country for more than a century. He was also a prominent official in the Doe administration.

18. These include the National Patriotic Front of Liberia (NPFL), the Independent National Patriotic Front of Liberia (INPFL), two wings of the United Liberation Movement of Liberia for Democracy (ULIMO K and ULIMO J), the Liberia Peace Council (LPC), Bomi County Council, (BCC) and Lofa County Council (LCC).

19. Philippa Artkinson, *The War Economy in Liberia: A Political Analysis*, London: Overseas Development Institute, 1997.

20. See, Sam Moyo, *The Land Question in Zimbabwe*, Harare: SAPES Books, 1995.

21. Crawford Young, 'Zaire: The Shattered Illusion of the Integral State', *Journal of Modern African Studies*, Vol.32, No.2 (June 1994), pp.247–64.

22. For two opposing views on Shell's activities see Jedzej George Frynas, 'Political Instability and Business: Focus on Shell in Nigeria', and Allan Detheridge and Noble Pepple, 'A Response to Frynas', both in *Third World Quarterly*, Vol.19, No.3 (1998).

23. See, for example, Eric G. Berman and Katie E. Sams, *Peacekeeping in Africa: Capabilities and Culpabilities*, Geneva and Pretoria: United Nations Institute for Disarmament Research (UNIDIR) and Institute for Security Studies (ISS), 2000, p.385.

Boom and Bust?
The Changing Nature of UN Peacekeeping

DAVID M. MALONE and KARIN WERMESTER

The emergence of peacekeeping as one of the most important instruments of the United Nations Security Council was a product of necessity rather than design. Although Article 42 of the UN Charter left open the possibility of taking 'action by air, sea, or land forces as may be necessary to maintain or restore international peace and security', the Founding Members' notion of creating a permanent standing UN army to serve as the tool of collective security never materialized. Instead, peacekeeping emerged as an instrument for the UN to manage inter-state conflict.

With the end of the Cold War, peacekeeping has undergone something of a revolution. In the decade of the 1990s, the Council rose to the challenge of intra-state conflict, often in a strikingly intrusive manner and with mixed success. The changing nature of peacekeeping derived from a permissive political context in which, crucially, the five permanent members of the UN Security Council (P-5) more often than not cooperated in the maintenance of international peace and security. P-5 cooperation in the Security Council unfolded in three phases: the first, at the beginning of the decade, was marked by enthusiasm for far-reaching peacekeeping operations (PKOs); the second, mid-decade, saw a retrenchment in peacekeeping after the failure of UN missions in Rwanda, Somalia and Bosnia, even though working relations among the P-5 remained good; the third, at the end of the decade, saw the deployment (and in the case of Sierra Leone, expansion) of four significant PKOs in Kosovo, East Timor, Sierra Leone and the Democratic Republic of Congo *despite* serious disunity between members of the Council, and especially the P-5, on key issues.[1] With the Security Council now adrift on how to approach several major threats to peace and security across the globe, the ambitious peacekeeping mandates of 1999 appear to be improvisations of last resort.[2]

This contribution seeks to outline the two major shifts, spearheaded by the Security Council, that have occurred in peacekeeping in the past decade: first, in the goals pursued by PKOs, and second, in the level of enforcement they have brought to bear. After a brief survey of peacekeeping during the Cold War, this inquiry aims to address the new structure, components and tasks of PKOs. And the final section will examine the increasing resort to peace enforcement over the past ten years.

The Evolution of Peacekeeping

The first ever peacekeeping operation was christened the United Nations Truce Supervision Organization (UNTSO) and was deployed to Jerusalem in 1948, just three years after the signing of the UN Charter. Although more of a monitoring mission, it became the model on which subsequent peacekeeping operations were created.

Until the end of the 1980s, PKOs were developed and deployed in order to bolster peace processes, observe the peace, and keep the peace – with the exception of the UN intervention in the former Belgian Congo between 1960 and 1964, which involved peace enforcement[3] (see Adebajo and Landsberg in this volume). The 'blue helmets' were defenders of the status quo, and operated with light arms under the strict instruction to use force only in self-defence. Such operations were baptized 'Chapter VI and a half' PKOs and required, in principle, an invitation or consent on the part of the recipient state. They operated under UN command, and were primarily mandated with the implementation of activities agreed upon by belligerents, such as the cantonment and separation of warring parties, the monitoring of borders, the withdrawal of foreign troops, and the verification of the cessation of aid to irregular or insurrectionist movements. These missions have come to be known as 'classic' or 'traditional' PKOs.

Although the P-5 were often instrumental in the provision of superior logistical support, they rarely provided troops for UN peacekeeping missions. Instead, middle and small powers such as the Scandinavian countries, Poland, Canada, Bangladesh, Fiji, Ghana and Nepal became regular 'troop contributing nations', and served to uphold the impartiality of the operations. The initial PKOs largely served as deterrents to the renewal of conflict.[4] Between 1948 and 1987, the Security Council launched 13 peacekeeping and military observer operations of this nature. The majority of these operations (seven of the 13) were deployed in the Middle East, a region of clear geostrategic importance to key permanent members of the Security Council.

The UN Transition Assistance Group (UNTAG) operation in Namibia, 1989–90, marked a transition from 'traditional' to 'complex' PKOs.[5] UNTAG was formally established in 1978 with the mandate of assisting the Special Representative of the Secretary-General to ensure the independence of Namibia through free and fair elections under the supervision and control of the UN.[6] However, UNTAG remained effectively dormant until 1989 when, in the improved post-Cold War international climate, implementation of the peace plan began.[7] Between 1978 and 1988, 'Chapter VI and a half' operations had been 'on hold': no new operations were launched during this period despite a rash of regional conflicts around the globe. This *de facto* suspension of PKOs was largely due to a lack of political will within the Security Council to address threats to international peace and security. The reticence of Member States resulted from several factors including continuing tension between East and West, a global economic downturn and perceptions in Washington that the UN had become the bastion of Third World agitation, as demonstrated by demands for a New International Economic Order (NIEO) and the 1975 General Assembly resolution equating Zionism with racism.[8]

In spite of various violations of the agreements underpinning the UN's presence in Namibia, elections there were ultimately successful and Namibia joined the UN on 23 April 1990. This achievement proved to be a watershed. It helped anchor confidence within the Council that its decisions, even ambitious ones involving significant nation-building components within states, could be implemented. Although Namibia in some ways constituted a late case of decolonization (which the UN had also asserted elsewhere in modest ways), it also encouraged the Council to experiment further with concepts such as the resolution of intra-state conflicts through elections and the promotion of democracy.

With the thaw in the Cold War, the Security Council, between 1989 and 1993, was able to draw on an unprecedented level of political will on the part of most of its 15 members, most significantly the P-5, to address a broad range of internal conflicts erupting throughout the world. Many of these conflicts were legacies of Cold War rivalries often conducted through local proxies. Five UN PKOs were launched in 1988 and 1989. By 1993, an additional 12 PKOs had been launched. Most of these addressed situations of *internal* conflict and generally represented a serious departure from past peacekeeping models.

Multifunctional Peacekeeping Mandates in the 1990s

The transformation of PKOs in the past decade reflects more than mere hybridization. The goals of PKOS have in fact changed significantly: from assisting in the maintenance of ceasefires during the Cold War, peacekeeping operations, during the 1990s, increasingly became peacebuilding missions, launched with the goal of implementing the foundations of a truly self-enforcing peace – no small undertaking.[9] Indicative of the change in strategy was an April 1999 report by the UN Department of Peacekeeping Operations (DPKO) titled *Multidisciplinary Peacekeeping: Lessons from Recent Experience.* The report stated that 'mandates should be conceptualized flexibly and could include elements of peace-building and emergency reconstruction of war-torn economies.'[10] The changing goals of peacekeeping have seen concomitant changes in the structure of PKOs, the creation of new components, and the assignment of additional tasks. These changes will be addressed in the following sections.

Emerging Structure of PKOS

PKOs, traditionally, were mostly military operations with limited political goals and tasks. Consequently, they were generally placed under the supervision of a Force Commander, with any political functions directed from UN Headquarters. However, given the nature of the 'new generation' of multidisciplinary PKOs and the need for rapid decision-making in the field in areas of considerable political sensitivity, these new missions were normally placed under the overall supervision of a Special Representative of the Secretary-General (SRSG) to whom both military and civilian components reported. A number of these diplomats achieved widely recognized distinction in difficult circumstances. Particularly notable were Alvaro de Soto (ONUCA, Central America, September 1989–February 1992); Iqbal Riza (ONUSAL, El Salvador, July 1991–March 1993); Aldo Ajello (ONUMOZ, Mozambique, October 1992–December 1994); and Lakhdar Brahimi (several missions but perhaps most notably UNMIH, Haiti September 1994–March 1996).[11] The increasing use of SRSGs endowed PKOs with a greater political mediation capacity in the field. In addition, SRSGs were able to communicate country-specific requirements to UN headquarters, allowing for context-specific adaptation of mandates. In this way, Special Representatives were able to spearhead, in many instances, the consolidation of peace at the local level. Indeed, the function of the SRSG is now understood to be critical, and is examined incisively in *Command from the Saddle: Managing United Nations Peace-building Missions*,[12] a report arising from discussions with and among a large group of mostly successful SRSGs in 1998.

Adapting Components and Tasks

The past decade has also witnessed the proliferation within PKOs of civilian components, corresponding to the fundamentally altered objectives of these missions. These include civilian police functions (CIVPOL), electoral monitoring and democratization, humanitarian relief, economic reconstruction and longer-term development work, civil engineering, human rights monitoring and, increasingly, protection, de-mining, and occasionally other tasks. The following section will address four components of multifunctional peacekeeping mandates that have either emerged or undergone significant transformation in the past decade: elections, humanitarian assistance, human rights and civilian police.

Electoral Components

In the early 1990s, in missions like UNTAG in Namibia, the UN Transitional Authority in Cambodia (UNTAC), the UN Operation in El Salvador (ONUSAL) and the UN Operation in Mozambique (ONUMOZ), the Security Council relied primarily on elections as a means of fostering stability and creating legitimacy for new governments. The success of this approach has been mixed. In Cambodia, 1993 saw the promulgation of a new Constitution for the Kingdom of Cambodia, elections on 23–28 May 1993, and the creation of a new government. However, UNTAC's success at establishing self-enforcing peace was undermined by the palace coup of Cambodian Second Prime Minister Hun Sen against his co-Prime Minister Norodom Ranariddh in July 1997. Hun Sen subsequently won a majority in parliament in highly questionable elections in 1998. Similarly, although the UN was not directly involved in the implementation of elections in Bosnia, the experience of the international community did little to usher in a genuine democracy or self-sustaining economic growth in any part of the country. There, the international community focused heavily on promoting 'multi-ethnicity,' almost as if the mere co-existence of different groups would create a modern, liberal democracy.[13] But experience was to demonstrate that the elections in Bosnia were held too early after the Dayton Peace Agreement of December 1995. Elections were to prove only one feature of democratization, a lesson the UN seemed to learn only in the latter part of the decade, and an experience pregnant with implications for future PKOs. It is a lesson that seems to have been borne in mind in the design of more recent PKOs in Kosovo and East Timor, where elections will be held only after conditions are seen as favourable and, in the case of Kosovo, with a multi-tiered approach, starting with local elections.

In an effort to improve upon this mixed track record, the electoral mandate of PKOs was broadened in the 1990s, adopting a more multifaceted approach to elections and democratization. For instance, the UNMIK mandate in Kosovo included a subsection of the 'institution-building component' described as 'democratization and institution-building', as well as one on 'elections'.[14] Similarly in East Timor, the mission includes a 'governance and public administration' component, in addition to an 'electoral operations' component.[15] In both cases, UN staff have been tasked under this rubric with multiple short and medium-term electoral duties – from voter registration and creating electoral law to supporting capacity building for self-government – in an effort to build institutions that can serve as local conflict management mechanisms.

Humanitarian Assistance Components

At the start of the decade, the Security Council responded to humanitarian crises by expressing concern and by prodding states and UN agencies to take more robust action. For instance, Security Council Resolution 688 on Iraq in 1991 made clear the Council members' concern over humanitarian conditions in the northern regions of Kurdistan and mandated some humanitarian activities there.[16]

The international community's initial involvement in Somalia intensified the Security Council's focus on humanitarian affairs, hitherto a domain perceived as resting mainly within the purview of UN agencies like the UN High Commissioner for Refugees (UNHCR). Early in the decade, UN peacekeeping missions like the Somalia operation (UNOSOM I)[17] and the UN Mission in Rwanda (UNOMUR)[18] were given a coordinating role and in certain instances were tasked with escorting humanitarian convoys. However, successful efforts to coordinate the operational tasks of humanitarian agencies require serious attention to the political and security dimensions of crises on the ground.[19] The Council, recognizing that its efforts were being consistently thwarted in Somalia and, as a result, its credibility undermined, sought a new approach. Basking in the afterglow of Operation *Desert Storm* against Iraq in early 1991, the Council authorized the use of force in order to ensure the delivery of humanitarian assistance. Resolution 794 of 3 December 1992 called for the 'use of all necessary means', under a Chapter VII mandate, to establish a US-led Unified Task Force to create a safe and secure environment for the delivery of humanitarian assistance. Earlier that year, the Council had expanded the UN Protection Force's (UNPROFOR) mandate in Bosnia, calling on states to 'take nationally or through regional agencies or arrangements all measures necessary' to facilitate, in coordination with the UN, the delivery of humanitarian assistance in Bosnia and Herzegovina.[20]

By the end of the decade, it became clear that the use of force to protect the delivery of humanitarian assistance was of limited effectiveness, and at worst detrimental, unless it was combined with, or preceded by, serious strategic coordination and planning.[21] Inattention to strategic coordination led to continued overlaps and significant gaps in the mandates of UN agencies, even when combined with the mandates of the multiplicity of NGO humanitarian actors in the field, and posed the single greatest challenge to the successful delivery of humanitarian assistance in conflict-torn societies. Moreover, the provision of humanitarian relief did little to promote medium and long-term stability and development. Bridging the gap between relief and development was no small task. On the ground, humanitarian assistance lent itself to manipulation by spoilers. In Somalia, for instance, peacekeepers were accused of upsetting, even destroying, the local economy.[22] In other contexts of prolonged armed conflict perpetuated by complex and highly organized 'shadow' economies, humanitarian assistance was denounced for contributing to the continuation of war, as in the Great Lakes region for instance.[23]

With renewed authorization of large-scale peacekeeping late in the 1990s, the Council took serious steps to tackle obstacles to the successful delivery of humanitarian assistance by incorporating, for the first time, humanitarian tasks under the rubric of a 'humanitarian component' in the PKO mandates for Kosovo and East Timor. Instead of coordinating the actions of others and providing protection, humanitarian tasks were, for the first time, delegated to peacekeepers themselves. These tasks included the delivery of humanitarian assistance, protection of returning displaced persons and provision of adequate needs upon their return, rehabilitation of key infrastructure, and the promotion of social well-being and restoration of civil society: all markedly new developments[24] (see Griffin and Jones in this volume). In the Democratic Republic of Congo, when MONUC was expanded in early 2000, its mandate included enhanced responsibilities in the field of humanitarian assistance (although it remained woefully understaffed to fulfil the tasks).[25] The development of humanitarian assistance components within UN PKOs and the far-reaching tasks entrusted to them constituted significant developments in peacekeeping practice.

Human Rights Components

A by-product of the effort to bring peace to countries wracked by internal strife was a growing understanding among member states that the transition from self-enforcing ceasefires to self-enforcing peace is next to impossible in the face of continued gross violations of human rights. The increasingly widespread, although selective, media coverage of humanitarian devastation and massive human rights breaches (the so-called CNN effect) resulting *inter alia* from intense pressure exerted by NGOs, served to highlight, in the deliberations of the Security Council, the challenges faced by civilians in countries engaged in civil war and in post-conflict societies. As a result, in the past decade, the Security Council started to link the security and human rights agendas of peacekeeping operations. On the ground, the UN often integrated human rights components into PKOs and, where this was not the case, as in Haiti and Rwanda, provided encouragement for the General Assembly to authorize separate human rights missions operating alongside PKOs.

At the beginning of the decade, the promotion and monitoring of human rights became an important component of the peacekeeping strategy in countries like El Salvador, Guatemala, Cambodia, Haiti and Rwanda. In these cases, peacekeepers or related UN personnel provided observation and reporting on human rights issues. The success of the first of these, with ONUSAL in El Salvador, which was tasked with the verification of the implementation of the Human Rights Agreement, was critical to the subsequent wider success of the peace agreement in spite of many other obstacles along the way.

At the peak of the Security Council's human rights fervour, involving widespread human rights abuses and, in Rwanda, genocide, it established two International Criminal Tribunals under Chapter VII of the UN Charter with mandates to prosecute individuals responsible for the perpetration of gross human rights abuses in the former Yugoslavia (1993)[26] and in Rwanda (1994).[27] The creation of these tribunals, in turn, intensified pressure for an International Criminal Court (ICC) with universal jurisdiction. Within a few years, the Statute of an ICC was agreed in Rome in 1998. Sufficient ratifications for the Court to become operational should be registered within the next five to seven years.

By the mid 1990s, significant failures and manifest inaction – not least in Africa's Great Lakes region and the Balkans – called into question bold peacekeeping endeavours to protect human rights. Moreover, many states, in particular members of the G-77, were reluctant to accept the emergence of a universal human rights norm. As a result, there emerged, in some instances, a tacit and only implicit agreement on incorporating human rights objectives as a baseline for new PKO mandates. For instance, while the UN Transitional Authority in East Timor (UNTAET) and the UN mission in Sierra Leone (UNAMSIL) do not in themselves have a 'human rights component,' many if not all tasks mandated speak to the protection and promotion of human rights, and not least, in Sierra Leone, to the protection of civilians.[28]

Indeed, the protection of civilians in war became the major theme at the end of the decade through which the Council addressed the issue of human rights. In September 1999, the Council passed Resolution 1265 which called for a broad range of measures to protect civilians in armed conflict, including a measure for PKOs to provide special protection and assistance for women and children in war.[29] In a significant development in early 2000, UNAMSIL in Sierra Leone was authorized, under Chapter VII of the Charter, to use force to protect civilians where resources and circumstances allowed.[30] This represented not only a major shift in focus from states to individuals within states on the part of the Council, but an increasing willingness to use force to protect the human rights of individuals.

Civilian Police Components

The role of local civilian police has become understood as both one of the most important peacebuilding mechanisms in war-torn societies and one of the most significant challenges facing the Security Council today.[31] In the past decade, the role of UNCIVPOL has expanded dramatically in countries where local police have been unable – or unwilling – to fulfil their proper functions. Although police units were deployed in previous missions such as ONUC in the Congo and the UN Temporary Authority (UNTEA) in West New Guinea (now Irian Jaya), the units were attached *ad hoc*, with insufficient attention paid to the provision of resources and strategic planning. The first formal UN civilian police component was deployed in 1964 as part of the UN peacekeeping force in Cyprus (UNFICYP). Under the broad mandate of restoring peace and security to the island, its specific tasks included liaising with the local Cypriot police, accompanying local police patrols and monitoring checkpoints.

Despite their uncertain beginnings, these fledgling civilian police components served as a model for UNCIVPOL during the 1990s. In March 1990, the Council sent a contingent of 1,500 police officers from 25 countries to Namibia with the mandate of monitoring local police forces and assisting in the creation of the necessary conditions for the holding of elections. Subsequent missions encompassing large civilian police components were deployed as part of UNTAC in Cambodia, UNPROFOR and successor missions in Bosnia, the UN Mission in Haiti (UNMIH) and its successor missions, and the UN Mission in Kosovo (UNMIK) and UNTAET in East Timor.

During the Cold War, CIVPOL contingents fulfilled two main functions: monitoring and supervising local law enforcement units; and training and mentoring local police forces.[32] In the 1990s, a third role, with far reaching goals and significant implications for peacekeeping emerged: the performance of law enforcement functions.

The problems encountered by CIVPOL, particularly in the domain of law enforcement, have been significant. The 'blue berets', as they became known, faced the same dilemma as the 'blue helmets': unarmed, they were unable to enforce the law, and armed, they potentially became part of the problem rather than the solution, and constituted targets for spoilers. In practice, the perception of increased security created by their presence was often unmatched by capacity and the illusion of their effectiveness in some instances rapidly collapsed. In addition, although there is a clear underlying logic in separating the military component (authorized to provide macro-level security over the short term in the immediate aftermath of the cessation of hostilities) from the policing component (entrusted with ensuring micro-level public security and begin to reconstitute trust and confidence over the long-term), problems have abounded. At best, the trade-off on the ground has been the division of legitimacy, and thus accountability, of public security writ large. At worst, this has led to not insignificant security 'gaps'. The lack of a pre-existing judicial structure with legal, institutional and logistical capacity to sustain policing functions encountered in 'failed states' has only exacerbated these difficulties.[33]

Significant differences in policing 'culture' among countries providing personnel to the UN have also plagued CIVPOL in the field. For example in Haiti, the values and methods of the French contingent of *gendarmes* clashed with the 'community based' policing culture of the Royal Canadian Mounted Police (RCMP) contingent, leading to raw hostility between the two groups at times.[34] In addition, some UN police officers, notably in ONUSAL (El Salvador), proved corrupt and brutal. In Kosovo, bitter criticism of the CIVPOL contingents by ethnic Albanians sparked finger-pointing by UN police against the military command of the local NATO-led security force (KFOR) in northern Kosovo.[35] Such divisions among international personnel in Kosovo contributed little to the image of a united effort that has often been depicted in the media and by UNMIK's leader, Bernard Kouchner, as failing on several fronts.

At the end of the 1990s, the Security Council bowed to realities on the ground. For the first time, as part of the UNMIK and UNTAET mandates, UN police officers were authorized to be on 'active patrol', and in Kosovo, they were armed and given 'executive law enforcement authority'.[36] In these transitional authorities, CIVPOL in fact acts *in lieu* of local police forces, an unprecedented occupation of political and administrative space at the local level.[37] However, the roster of such dangerous law-enforcement assignments adds up to many more police officers than the organization can assemble, and will need to be addressed urgently if the Council is to avoid another – potentially calamitous – failure.

The changing goals of peacekeeping in the past decade have seen peacekeepers become, in a sense, peacebuilders. With mixed success, PKOs have become involved in the creation of an operational and political space in which international actors – from grass-roots NGOs to the UN and its family of agencies – have come to take on a host of peacebuilding activities that seek at once to consolidate peace in the short term and increase the likelihood that future conflicts can be managed withouta resort to violence.[38]

Enforcement Action

The Security Council's willingness to involve itself in a broad range of *internal conflicts* – encompassing inter-communal strife, crises of democracy, fighting marked by a fierce struggle for control of national resources and wealth, and several other precipitating causes or incentives for continuation of war – forced it to confront hostilities of a much more complex nature than the inter-state disputes with which it had greater experience.[39] In so doing, it brought to bear an unprecedented level of enforcement under Chapter VII of the UN Charter. Despite this, the Council's ambitious objectives proved significantly more difficult to attain in many circumstances than it seemed to have anticipated. Even Security Council-mandated military activities encountered significant resistance by frequently shadowy belligerents, leading to incidents involving heavy loss of life among peacekeepers and civilians (in Rwanda, Somalia and the former Yugoslavia). The Council's inability to induce compliance with its decisions fuelled two apparently contradictory but all too frequently complementary responses: on the one hand, the Council moved to enforce decisions which had failed to generate consent in the field, notably in the former Yugoslavia,[40] Somalia[41] and Haiti;[42] on the other, in the face of significant casualties, the Council cut and ran, as in Somalia and at the outset of genocide in Rwanda.[43]

The Use of Force

Resort to the provisions of Chapter VII of the UN Charter and to the enforcement of Security Council decisions was not new: Council decisions were enforced in Korea in the 1950s and to a much lesser extent in the Congo in the 1960s. Nevertheless, the extent to which the Council adopted decisions under Chapter VII during the 1990s was totally unprecedented. At first, it was hoped that the UN would prove capable of launching and managing enforcement operations. In the face of disappointing, occasionally catastrophic results in the former Yugoslavia and Somalia, it became clear to Member States – as many within the UN Secretariat, notably Under-Secretary General for Political Affairs, Marrack Goulding, had argued all along – that the transition from peacekeeping to peace enforcement represented more than 'mission creep' (see Berdal in this volume). The two types of operations were, in fact, fundamentally different – one requiring consent and impartiality, the other requiring international personnel to confront one or several belligerent groups, even if in defence of a Council mandate conceived as neutral relative to the parties to the conflict. Decision-making for enforcement operations also proved more difficult than for most 'classic' UN PKOs, given the attendant risks for UN personnel.[44] Powerful Security Council members like the US and UN Secretary-General Boutros Boutros-Ghali, concluded by 1994 that the UN should not itself seek to conduct large-scale enforcement activities. Consequently, for enforcement of its decisions the Security Council increasingly resorted to 'coalitions of the willing', such as Operation *Uphold Democracy* (in Haiti, 1994–95); the NATO-led implementation force (IFOR) and subsequent stabilization force (SFOR) in Bosnia since 1995; the Inter-African Mission to Monitor the Implementation of the Bangui Agreements (MISAB) in the Central African Republic, 1997; and the International force in East Timor (INTERFET) in 1999.[45] The Council also alternately both worried about and supported in qualified terms enforcement activities by regional bodies, notably ECOMOG, the Ceasefire Monitoring Group of the Economic Community of West African States (ECOWAS), in Liberia and Sierra Leone.[46] One enforcement technique, employed only once previously by the Council, against Rhodesia, was the resort to naval blockades to control access of prohibited goods to regions of conflict. Such blockades were mandated with varying success during the 1990s: against Iraq in the Persian Gulf and the Gulf of Aqaba, against various parties in the former Yugoslavia on the Danube and the Adriatic Sea, and against Haiti.[47]

One problem relating to both the use of force and persuasion by international actors is the now widely understood notion that third parties cannot, in most circumstances, impose peace if there is no political will among the protagonists to solve the problem.[48] The withdrawal of much of the UN Angola Verification Mission (UNAVEM I) from Angola in 1993 in the wake of failure of the rebel group, the National Union for the Total Liberation of Angola (UNITA) to respect the outcome of UN-monitored elections, is a case in point. In establishing UNAVEM II in early 1995, the Council requested that the Secretary-General condition UN deployment on the behaviour of parties on the ground.[49] Even this failed, over time, as signalled by the withdrawal of the UN Mission of Observers in Angola (MONUA, the successor observer mission to UNAVEM III) in February 1999, in the face of considerable hostility by both protagonists.[50]

An exceptional and controversial case was NATO's bombing of Serbia, Montenegro and Kosovo in the spring of 1999 in a bid to halt 'ethnic cleansing' by Serb forces in Kosovo. NATO's action followed the failure of negotiations at Rambouillet, which involved Belgrade and a 'contact group' of countries (including the USA, France, the UK and the Russian Federation) seeking the implementation of earlier Security Council resolutions on Kosovo.[51] NATO countries proceeded to attack Serb targets from the air, as of 24 March 1999, without Security Council authorization, pointing to threatened vetoes by Moscow (and possibly Beijing) in justifying their decision to forego such authorization.[52] Russian efforts to rally Security Council condemnation of, and an end to, NATO's action failed, on 26 March 1999, with 12 countries opposed to Moscow's text and only three in favour.[53] A settlement of sorts was negotiated within the veto-free Group of Eight (G8) forum in May 1999 and estimated in Security Council Resolution 1244 of 10 June 1999. NATO countries retained the lead role in the military force (KFOR, a coalition operation rather than a UN PKO, authorized under Chapter VII of the UN Charter), providing security in Kosovo, alongside a UN police force, which as of 1 March 2000 remained woefully under-staffed and inadequate to the task. But the UN was placed in charge of the civil administration of the province, working with the European Union and the Organization for Security and Cooperation in Europe (OSCE).[54] Strong differences remain over the legality of NATO's action (although perhaps less so its legitimacy). NATO, undergoing something of an existential and, to a lesser degree, operational crisis in the wake of its successful Kosovo operation – a campaign marked by a great deal of luck – did not seem particularly keen to engage in any further such interventions.[55] Nevertheless,

NATO will continue to play an important role alongside the UN in promoting stability in the Balkans (and possibly elsewhere in Europe). This insight is hardly new: as early as 1993, Kofi Annan, at the time UN Under-Secretary-General of Peacekeeping, suggested that NATO could play a key role in 'peacekeeping with teeth'.[56]

Humanitarian Intervention

At the end of the 1990s, a wide-ranging and unusually sharp debate arose over humanitarian intervention as a result, in part, of NATO's air campaign against Serb forces in the Balkans, which had not been explicitly authorized by the UN Security Council. This debate coincided with greater resort by the Council to the provisions of Chapter VII of the Charter and an increasing focus by its members on the plight of civilians in war. However, many states were reluctant to accept that an 'international norm in favour of intervention' had developed, as claimed by Kofi Annan in a landmark speech to the General Assembly on 20 September 1999.[57] In response to Annan's speech, Algerian President Abdelaziz Bouteflika stated that at least three questions would need to be resolved before the debate on intervention, or indeed 'interference' as he called it, could be closed: 'First, where does aid stop and interference begin? Second, where are the lines to be drawn between the humanitarian, the political, and the economic? Third, is interference valid only in weak or weakened states or for all states without distinction?'[58] Annan was widely seen as being on strong moral and political ground in advocating humanitarian intervention without Security Council authorization in extreme cases, but, by the end of 1999, there seemed little hope of developing a legal framework of principles to govern such intervention.[59] Thus, humanitarian intervention was likely to continue to be practised only in exceptional circumstances and authorized only on a case-by-case basis by the Security Council. Harsh Russian military tactics employed against civilians in Chechnya in late 1999 and early 2000 demonstrated that humanitarian action would remain subject to double standards, as has been the record of the UN and of the Security Council since 1945. Nonetheless, Annan was widely admired for championing a meaningful debate over humanitarian action and for promoting human rights at every opportunity. By the turn of the millennium he had contributed to a significant development of norms favouring the citizen over the state, and civilians over militaries.

Sanctions

More common than military enforcement decisions by the Council was the resort to mandatory economic (and, increasingly, diplomatic) sanctions under Chapter VII of the UN Charter.[60] While arms embargoes remained in vogue, the imposition of comprehensive trade and other economic sanctions, once seen as more benign than the resort to force, faded noticeably once the humanitarian costs of sanctions regimes against Haiti and Iraq became widely known by the end of the 1990s. The capacity of government elites in countries struck by sanctions to enrich themselves greatly by controlling black markets in prohibited products also took some time to sink in. Indeed, the criminalization of the economies of Iraq, the former Yugoslavia and Haiti while under sanctions was striking. By the mid-1990s, more targeted sanctions such as the ban on air flights to and from Libya aimed at inducing Tripoli's cooperation with Council efforts to address several terrorist aircraft bombings, gained favour. Diplomatic sanctions, such as the reduction in the level of diplomatic representation mandated by the Council against Sudan following an assassination attempt in Addis Ababa against Egyptian President Hosni Mubarak, also gained favour.[61] Targeted sanctions (addressing financial transactions and air links) also went into effect on 14 November 1999 against the Taleban in Afghanistan in response to the protection the regime has provided to the alleged terrorist Osama Bin Laden.[62]

Several research projects have recently illuminated the difficulty of designing and implementing effective sanctions, including the 'Interlaken process' (dealing with financial sanctions) sponsored by the Swiss, and a German-sponsored project on arms embargoes and other forms of targeted sanctions.[63] The Canadian government has also recently brought to the attention of the Security Council the need for more effective, less counter-productive sanctions regimes in general,[64] and has emphasized the need for more rigorous application of the Council's sanctions mandate in Angola to suffocate UNITA's ability to fund its war effort through the sale of diamonds.[65] This has resulted, *inter alia*, in the decision of the De Beers corporation to close down its operations in Angola.[66] The Security Council has recently undertaken to curb the sale of 'conflict' diamonds in Angola and Sierra Leone.[67]

The distinction between 'classic' peacekeeping operations of interposition adopted under Chapter VI of the UN Charter and those involving an element of enforcement adopted under Chapter VII had, by the end of the 1990s, become fairly moot. Indeed, the new operations launched in 1999 by the Security Council in Kosovo, East Timor, Sierra Leone and the Democratic Republic of the Congo, were all Chapter VII operations. The only non-Chapter VII operation on the planning boards in early 2000 was a hypothetical deployment between Eritrea and Ethiopia.

Conclusion

The UN Security Council's willingness to tackle complex civil wars during the 1990s owed much to a favourable conjunction of events involving a new-found political will, particularly among the P-5, that led to the Council expending considerable resources and running some real risks to promote global peace. However, in spite of the significant efforts by the UN system and many of its member states, results have been mixed at best. Complex PKOs involving a multiplicity of civilian components, such as ONUMOZ in Mozambique, UNMIH in Haiti, ONUSAL in El Salvador, MIGUA in Guatemala, UNTAC in Cambodia and UNTAG in Namibia, proved successful to varying degrees. Several others, such as UNOSOM I and II in Somalia, UNPROFOR in Bosnia, UNAMIR in Rwanda and the successive incarnations of UNAVEM in Angola failed, sometimes spectacularly. 'Coalitions of the willing', sometimes able to command greater resources and enjoying much greater administrative and decision-making flexibility, were generally more adaptable. A great number of case studies have generated useful 'lessons learned' material. However, the Council's woolly decision in early 2000 to authorize conditionally a woefully understaffed and unclearly-tasked peacekeeping operation for the Democratic Republic of Congo and the appalling shortcomings of UNAMSIL in Sierra Leone as of early 2000 suggest that while individuals may absorb lessons and benefit from experience, collective bodies like the Security Council have limited memories and are prepared to seize upon any benefit of doubt to indulge political expediency.[69]

Depressing as these conclusions may be, there is little doubt that the Council's decisions in the 1990s, often of a strikingly intrusive nature, fundamentally altered conceptions of state sovereignty and promoted further international intervention (with or without the consent of belligerent parties, across borders and within states).[70] Whether the trends of the 1990s will survive the newly heightened tensions among the Permanent Five following NATO's war in Kosovo remains to be seen. Nevertheless, as pointed out elsewhere in this volume (see Griffin and Jones), the expansion of peacekeeping in the post-Cold War era to embrace ambitious programmes of civil administration often underpinned by the threat or actual use of force appeared only to intensify in 1999 with sizeable operations in both Kosovo and East Timor. The next two years should instruct us as to whether these missions represent a 'bridge too far' for the UN, although here again results may well be mixed and clear lessons with universal application hard to extract.

ACKNOWLEDGEMENTS

We are grateful to friends and colleagues for their extremely helpful comments and suggestions, in particular Bruce D. Jones, Leila Kazemi and Katia Papagianni.

NOTES

1. On 24 Feb. 2000, paradoxically under heavy US pressure, in Security Council Resolution 1291, the Security Council agreed conditionally to expand its monitoring operation, the UN

Mission in the Democratic Republic of the Congo (MONUC) into a medium-scale, although no doubt ill-fated (5,537 strong) PKO in a bid to build momentum towards a cessation of hostilities.

2. See the 'Report of the Panel on United Nations Peace Operations – A far-reaching report by an independent panel', 23 Aug. 2000, which notably argues that 'the United Nations has repeatedly failed to meet the challenge, and it can do no better today'. The report is available on the UN's website at: www.un.org/peace/reports/peace_operations/.

3. Thomas G. Weiss, David P. Forsythe and Roger A. Coate, *The United Nations and Changing World Politics*, 2nd Ed., Boulder, CO: Westview Press, 1997, p.53.

4. See Chantal de Jonge Oudraat, 'The United Nations and Internal Conflict', in Michael E. Brown (ed.), *The International Dimensions of Internal Conflict*, Cambridge Mass: Center for Science and International Affairs, John F. Kennedy School of Government, Harvard University, 1996.

5. Note that this does not imply that there is a linear evolution from traditional to other forms of peacekeeping operations, as the possibility of new PKOs of interposition remains. The point is simply that the 1990s have witnessed a proliferation of substantively new peacekeeping activities.

6. UN Security Council resolution 435, 29 Sept. 1978.

7. UN Security Council resolution 632, 16 Feb. 1989.

8. UN General Assembly resolution 3379, 10 Nov. 1975.

9. In 1992, Boutros Boutros-Ghali defined post-conflict peacebuilding as 'the creation of a new environment to forestall the recurrence of conflict' in *An Agenda for Peace*, A/47/277-S/24111, 17 June 1992. For an excellent articulation of the evolution and current state of the art of peacebuilding, see Elizabeth M. Cousens' Introduction, in Elizabeth M. Cousens and Chetan Kumar (eds.) with Karin Wermester, *Peacebuilding as Politics: Cultivating Peace in Fragile Societies*, Boulder, CO: Lynne Rienner, forthcoming 2000.

10. 'Multidisciplinary Peacekeeping: Lessons from Recent Experience', United Nations DPKO, Apr. 1999.

11. Kofi Annan also briefly served as SRSG in Bosnia (UNPROFOR, 1 Nov.–20 Dec. 1995); see *The Blue Helmets: A Review of UN Peacekeeping*, New York, NY: UN Department of Public Information, 1996.

12. Rick Hooper and Mark Taylor, 'Recommendations Report of the Forum on the Special-Representative of the Secretary-General: Shaping the UN's role in Peace Implementation', Fafo report No.26, Oslo, Norway: *Peace Implementation Network, Programme for International Cooperation and Conflict Resolution*, 1999.

13. Alexander T. Knapp, 'Vision and Craft – Elections in Kosovo', presentation to UNA-USA, 30 Nov. 1999, New York.

14. UN Security Council resolution 779, 12 July 1999.

15. UN Security Council resolution 1024, 4 Oct. 1999.

16. UN Security Council resolution 688, 5 Apr. 1991.

17. UN Security Council resolution 751, 24 Apr. 1992.

18. UN Security Council resolution 872, 5 Oct. 1992.

19. See Sue Lautze, Bruce D. Jones and Mark Duffield, 'Strategic Humanitarian Coordination in the Great Lakes Region, 1996–1997: An Independent Study for the Inter-Agency Standing Committee', New York: Office for the Coordination of Humanitarian Affairs (OCHA), UN (Mar. 1998).

20. UN Security Council resolution 770, 13 Aug. 1992.

21. Ibid. According to Lautze, Jones and Duffield, strategic coordination refers to two sets of tasks in particular: (1) 'negotiating access to affected populations, advocating respect for humanitarian principles and law, and liaising with international political and military actors' and (2) 'setting the overall direction and goals of the UN humanitarian programme, allocating tasks and responsibilities within that programme, ensuring correspondence between resource mobilization and established priorities, and monitoring and evaluating system-wide implementation of the programme' (see n. 19 above), p.2.

22. See in particular, Ameen Jan, 'Somalia: Building Sovereignty or Restoring Peace?', in Cousens and Kumar (eds.) with Wermester, *Peacebuilding as Politics*.

23. See Alex de Waal, 'En toute impunité humanitaire,' *Le Monde Diplomatique*, Apr. 1998, p.32.
24. See, on Kosovo, S/1999/779, 12 July 1999, and on East Timor, S/1999/1024, 4 Oct. 1999.
25. See UN Security Council Resolution 1291, 24 Feb. 2000, and S/2000/30, 17 Jan. 2000.
26. UN Security Council resolution 808, 22 Feb. 1993.
27. UN Security Council resolution 955, 8 Nov. 1994.
28. UN Security Council resolution 1024, 4 Oct. 1999.
29. UN Security Council resolution 1265, 17 Sept. 1999. Olara Otunnu, President of the International Peace Academy, 1990–98, had undertaken a vigorous campaign as UN Under-Secretary-General to highlight the plight of children in war. The Security Council's decision underscores his remarkable success in this endeavour.
30. UN Security Council resolution 1270, 22 Feb. 2000.
31. See Tor Tanke Holm and Espen Barth Eide (eds.), *Peacebuilding and Police Reform*, London and Portland, OR: Frank Cass,1999.
32. Robert B. Oakley, Michael J. Dziedzic and Eliot M. Goldberg, *Policing the New World Disorder: Peace Operations and Public Security*, Washington DC: National Defense University, 1998, p.23.
33. See Gareth Evans, *Cooperation for Peace: The Global Agenda for the 1990s and Beyond*, Sydney: Allen & Unwin, 1993.
34. See David M. Malone, *Decision-Making in the UN Security Council: The Case of Haiti*, 1990–1997, Oxford: Clarendon Press, 1998.
35. R. Jeffrey Smith, 'French Troops in Kosovo Accused of Retreat; UN Police Cite lack of Support in Mitrovica Uprising, Inadequate Aid to Civilians', *The Washington Post*, 9 Feb. 2000, p.A14.
36. See Barbara Crossette, 'The UN's Unhappy Lot: Perilous Police Duties Multiplying', *The New York Times*, 22 Feb. 2000, and for quote see UN Security Council resolution 779, 12 July 1999.
37. See Michèle Griffin and Bruce D. Jones in this volume for an elaboration of this point.
38. See Cousens (n.9 above).
39. For a discussion of the importance of economic factors in many civil wars of the 1990s, see Mats Berdal and David M. Malone (eds.), *Greed and Grievance: Economic Agendas in Civil Wars*, Boulder, CO: Lynne Rienner, 2000.
40. There is a plethora of literature regarding the former Yugoslavia and constraints and obstacles encountered in the field, including: Adam Roberts, 'Communal Conflict as a Challenge to International Organization: The Case of Former Yugoslavia,' *Review of International Studies*, Vol.21 (1995), pp.389–410; International Crisis Group, 'Kosovo: Let's Learn from Bosnia – Models and Methods of International Administration,' Sarajevo, Bosnia, 17 May 1999.
41. See John L. Hirsch and Robert Oakley, *Somalia and Operation Restore Hope: Reflections on Peacemaking and Peacekeeping*, Washington DC: United States Institute for Peace Press, 1995 and more recently Mark Bowden, *Black Hawk Down: A Story of Modern War*, Atlantic Monthly Press, 1999.
42. Malone (n. 35 above); also James F. Dobbins, 'Haiti: A Case Study in Post-Cold War Peacekeeping', *ISD Reports* II.I, Washington DC: Institute for the Study of Diplomacy, Georgetown University, Oct. 1995; and on Haiti and Somalia see David Bentley and Robert Oakley, 'Peace Operations: A Comparison of Somalia and Haiti,' *Strategic Forum* 30, Washington DC: Institute for National Strategic Studies, National Defense University, May 1995.
43. See in particular Gérard Prunier, *The Rwanda Crisis : History of a Genocide,* New York: Columbia University Press, 1995; Michael Barnett, 'The UN Security Council, Indifference and Genocide in Rwanda,' *Cultural Anthropology*, Vol.12, No.4 (1997), p.551; and J. Matthew Vaccaro, 'The Politics of Genocide: Peacekeeping and Disaster Relief in Rwanda,' in William J. Durch (ed.), *The UN, Peacekeeping, American Policy and the Uncivil Wars of the 1990s*, New York: St. Martin's Press, 1996. See also Adebajo and Landsberg in this volume.
44. The UN Secretary-General's report on UNPROFOR's catastrophic failure to deter attack at Srebrenica in 1995 details a case in point. See A/54/549 of 15 Nov. 1999.

45. For an excellent reference work covering UN peacekeeping operations from 1947 to the present, see Oliver Ramsbotham and Tom Woodhouse, *Encyclopedia of International Peacekeeping Operations*, Santa Barbara, CA: ABC-CLIO, 1999.
46. For an excellent analysis of regional peacekeeping, see Hilaire McCoubrey and Justin Morris, *Regional Peacekeeping in the Post-Cold War Era*, The Hague, The Netherlands: Kluwer Law International, 2000.
47. UN Department of Political Affairs, 'A Brief Overview of Security Council Applied Sanctions', *Interlaken 2*, 1998.
48. For a statement on this by the Secretary-General Boutros Boutros-Ghali, see SG/SM/5589, 21 Mar. 1995.
49. UN Security Council resolution 976, 8 Feb. 1995.
50. UN Security Council resolution 1229, 26 Feb. 1999.
51. UN Security Council resolution 1199, 23 Sept. 1998 and UN Security Council resolution 1203, 24 Oct. 1998.
52. See S/PV.3988, 24 Mar. 1999 and S/PV.3989, 26 Mar. 1999, and, for a justification of the NATO air strike, see the Press Statement by NATO Secretary-General Javier Solana No.041, 24 Mar. 1999.
53. UN Security Council draft resolution 328, 1998, failed to be adopted on 26 Mar. 1999.
54. See Crossette, 'The UN's Unhappy Lot: Perilous Police Duties Multiplying,' and Smith, 'French Troops in Kosovo Accused of Retreat; UN Police Cite Lack of Support in Mitrovica Uprising, Inadequate Aid to Civilians'.
55. Lieven, 'Kosovo: Implications for the International System', Ditchley Conference Report 00/01 reporting on a conference at Ditchley Park, 14–16 Jan. 2000.
56. Kofi A. Annan, 'UN Peacekeeping Operations and Cooperation with NATO,' *NATO Review* 41, no.5 (Oct. 1993).
57. UN document A/54/PV.4, 20 Sept. 1999, p.4.
58. UN document A/54/PV.4, 20 Sept. 1999, p.14.
59. For a sophisticated discussion of these issues, see Anatol Lieven (n.59 above).
60. For an in-depth discussion of the Council's experience with sanctions regimes since 1990, see David Cortright and George Lopez, *The Sanctions Decade: Assessing UN Strategy in the 1990s*, Boulder, CO: Lynne Rienner, 2000.
61. For another recent discussion of sanctions and the increasing use of targeted sanctions, see Daniel W. Drezner, *The Sanctions Paradox: Economic Statecraft and International Relations*, Cambridge: Cambridge University Press, 1999.
62. See Security Council resolution 1267 of 15 Oct. 1999.
63. See the German Permanent Mission to the UN website for details on this: http://www.undp.org/missions/germany/state.htm
64. See Canada on the UN Security Council 1999-2000: http://www.un.int/canada/english.html
65. For a recent articulation of the Canadian initiative on Angola, see Ambassador Robert R. Fowler, 'Notes for an Intervention by H.E. Robert R. Fowler, Ambassador and Permanent Representative of Canada, to the United Nations Security Council on the Humanitarian Situation in Angola,' Canada on the UN Security Council 1999–2000, 23 Aug. 1999.
66. 'Le négociant De Beers arrête tout achat de diamants d'Angola', *AFP*, 6 Oct. 1999.
67. The Sanctions Committee on Angola was established by UN Security Council resolution 864 in 1993. For a report regarding recent developments in the committee, see UN document S/1999/147.
68. The Report of the Panel (Brahmin Report) of August 2001 highlighted one growing problem: the unwillingness of industrialized countries to expose their troops to physical risks in far-off countries where they have no national interests at stake. On this practically and ethically reprehensible head, see Ramesh Thakur and David Malone, 'Rich and Afraid of Peacekeeping', *International Herald Tribune*, 25 October 2000.
69. MONUC, UN Security Council resolution 1291, 24 Feb. 2000.
70. See David M. Malone, 'The UN Security Council in the 1990s: Boom and Bust?,' Proceedings of the 28th Annual Conference of the Canadian Council on International Law, Keynote Address, in *From Territorial Sovereignty to Human Security*, Cambridge, MA: Kluwer Law International, forthcoming 2000.

Lessons Not Learned:
The Use of Force in 'Peace Operations' in the 1990s

MATS BERDAL

Before he assumed command of United Nations (UN) forces in Bosnia and Herzegovina in January 1995, General Rupert Smith, on different occasions and before various audiences, presented his views on the 'object and utility of the use of force in intervention operations' after the Cold War. The central question he raised was why the threat of and the actual use of force had often ended 'with disappointing or unlooked for consequences'.[1] A basic reason, he suggested, was that 'we had been unclear as to what it is we expect the use of force or forces to *achieve* as opposed to *do*'.[2] This contribution questions whether governments and international organizations have properly grasped this fundamental distinction and the consequences that flow from it.

As a category 'peace operations' has become a catchall phrase, where the term 'peace' or 'peace support' has less to do with the operational environment and the specific challenge it poses to an intervening force than with the wider objective which, it is hoped, military action will help to promote.[3] These operations are, ultimately, about righting wrongs and advancing wider humanitarian purposes. As such, they are supposed to transcend the pursuit of narrowly defined interests and national ambitions. Thus, the second UN Mission to Somalia (UNOSOM II) was deployed in May 1993 to assist 'the Somali people in rebuilding their shattered economy and social and political life'.[4] North Atlantic Treaty Organization (NATO) and UN military action in Bosnia in late August and early September 1995 were designed to prevent further 'ethnic cleansing'.[5] Both these cases involved what, according to many, ought properly to be considered a distinctive sub-category of peace operations, namely 'peace enforcement'. It is this category and its supposed utility, both as an analytical construct and as a key to understanding how force has in fact been used in the 1990s, that provide the main focus of this essay.

The view that 'peace enforcement' constitutes a type of military activity that, while 'coercive in nature', remains distinct from 'war', has been embraced by the armed forces of several countries, all of them understandably anxious to provide appropriate doctrine or guiding principles for their armed forces engaged in a growing number of international operations.[6] While different names have sometimes been used – French doctrine staff, for example, speak of 'peace restoration' operations (*restauration de la paix*) – the basic idea of 'peace enforcement' rests on two key assumptions.[7] The first of these is that military force, even though it involves coercion, can be used *impartially* to ensure compliance with a given mandate without designating an enemy. According to extant United Kingdom doctrine, Peace Support Operations (PSOs) 'are neither in support of, nor against, a particular party, but are designed to restore peace and ensure compliance with the mandate in an even-handed manner'.[8] John Ruggie has expressed the same basic idea, arguing that force can be 'used impartially, meaning without *a priori* prejudice or bias in response to violations of agreements, Security Council mandates, or norms stipulated in some other fashion'.[9] The second assumption flows directly from the first: using force in this manner, precisely because it is 'impartial and even-handed', will not prejudice the political outcome of the conflict in question.

There is something superficially appealing about this approach, and much of the doctrine literature in which it is elaborated is sophisticated and undoubtedly valuable as a means of instilling a 'peace operations' mindset among soldiers, especially among those whose traditional focus has been on high-intensity warfare. Yet, the necessarily abstract and generalized character of this literature has certain obvious limitations when it comes to understanding how military force has in fact been employed in support of humanitarian objectives over the past decade. Humanitarian or moral imperatives have clearly assumed a more prominent role in the minds of policy-makers, but decisions regarding the use of force and, above all, the manner in which force has actually been employed, have *also* been shaped by a range of other motivations and constraints. These have included considerations of prestige and credibility, competing perceptions of national interest, historical memories and fears, bureaucratic politics, and, not least, the particular outlook and personalities of key decision-makers. These sorts of influences, while often difficult to quantify, have always been present when governments make decisions about the use of military force. Other factors, notably the aversion to casualties and the unique pressures of modern media, are arguably more specific to the post Cold-War era. These have also influenced both the character and pattern of interventions in important ways.[10] The experience of 'peace operations' cannot be dissected for 'lessons' without an awareness of these wider considerations. And while doctrine and doctrinal revision have a role to play, the more urgent need is for political decision-makers to rethink, on the basis of what is now a significant body of experience, the requirements for the *effective* use of force, that is, to think of military force in terms of what it can *achieve* as opposed to what it can *do*.

To this end, this essay concentrates specifically on developments and decisions regarding the use of force taken during the critical period of two operations: UNOSOM II in Somalia and UNPROFOR in Bosnia. The former case involved American troops, nominally as part of a larger UN operation, in the impoverished and war-stricken country of Somalia in the summer and autumn of 1993. During a five-month period, American forces were used in a 'peace enforcement' capacity against forces loyal to Mohammed Farah Aideed, a faction leader or 'warlord' whose physical capture, UN Secretary-General Boutros Boutros-Ghali had persuaded the American administration, was critical to the success of the largest UN operation to date. The second case examined covers the military action and, significantly, the background to it by NATO and the UN in late August and early September 1995 against Bosnian Serb forces throughout Bosnia – an action which helped pave the way for a permanent ceasefire among the warring factions after four years of bloody and brutal fighting.

The Use of Force in Somalia and Bosnia: Argument in Brief

One reason for re-visiting these cases is that the 'international community' is still very much living with the consequences of the actions that were taken in each case. American policy towards peace operations generally, and the UN and Africa in particular, remain profoundly shaped by the events in Somalia. In Bosnia, military action in August and September 1995 helped create the conditions for a peace settlement to be negotiated in Dayton, a settlement which remains in place even though the country has increasingly assumed the character of a trusteeship with limited signs of genuine integration among its constituent parts. The background to Operation *Deliberate Force* in 1995 is also of interest for another reason. The decision by NATO leaders to launch an air campaign against Yugoslavia in March 1999, and the associated belief that a 'short, sharp shock' against the regime of President Slobodan Milošević would do the trick, were based on a particular and, as will be argued more fully, incomplete and simplistic reading of unfolding events in 1995.

There are two further reasons, however, why these cases deserve to be examined together. First, in each case, the use of force was tied to the promotion of a broader humanitarian objective. As such, they both reflect a trend whereby the use of military force internationally has increasingly come to be justified on humanitarian grounds. As indicated above, this is not to suggest that in either Somalia or Bosnia other motives did not influence the calculations of decision-makers and helped spur them into action.[11] Nor is it to suggest that there was complete convergence of views among states about the need for enforcement action to be taken. Yet, while it is true that Chapter

VII of the UN Charter, concerned with the maintenance and restoration of *international* peace and security, was invoked as a legal basis for military action in each case, these were not Chapter VII actions along the lines of the Gulf War. In 1990–91, a broad and unlikely coalition of states rallied behind the Security Council's decision to reverse, if necessary by the use of force, the entirely unambiguous case of Iraq's annexation of Kuwait. By contrast, in Somalia, Bosnia, and later in Kosovo, an intolerable situation, involving suffering and human rights violations on a scale offending the 'moral conscience of mankind', was deemed to have arisen *within* a country, and Chapter VII was sought, in part, as a procedural device enabling 'tougher action' to be taken.

The final reason for investigating these two cases together is that the level of force employed in both cases was designed to *create* military realities on the ground that would, in theory at any rate, facilitate the search for more lasting political solutions to the conflict at hand. The decision to take coercive action arose out of a conviction that relying on the consent and good will of the parties would only prolong an unacceptable situation. Indeed, disillusionment with consent-based peacekeeping, where the use of force had been restricted to self-defence (albeit with some variations in the interpretation of what constituted self-defence), provided an important backdrop to the decision to use force.

It is necessary to stress what this essay does not address. It does not cover the contentious issue of the *legitimacy* of military action in each case. It does recognize, however, that while the record of humanitarian action in the conflicts of the 1990s is uneven, and that the principle of humanitarian intervention itself has been applied with conspicuous inconsistency, a significant change in the normative climate has taken place.[12] Specifically, the view that what happens *within* a country should not be a matter of international concern has lost some of its force, or rather, has been tempered by countervailing pressures at least to consider intervention in circumstances involving violations of human rights on a 'massive' scale. The chief concern here, however, is about the actual use of force in support of humanitarian objectives. In brief, the argument put forward is not that enforcement should be ruled out as an option for decision-makers, but rather that the military and political consequences that inevitably flow from such action need to be carefully considered and not simply wished away. In its political and military consequences, enforcement cannot be impartial. As with the decision to commit military forces historically, enforcement action in support of humanitarian objectives requires tough and difficult choices – choices that some of the doctrinal literature on 'peace operations' in the West, if only inadvertently, has tended to underplay.

The Lessons from Somalia, 1993

In January 1991, after more than 20 years in power, President Siad Barre was forced to flee Somalia after a protracted and highly destructive period of civil war. Barre, an autocratic and ruthless ruler who had come to power in a military coup in 1969, left behind a depressing legacy of disintegrating institutions and economic mismanagement on a grand scale. His desperate attempt to hold on to power in the late 1980s resulted in a brutal civil war against an alliance of clan-based factions whose one common purpose was the ousting of the hated dictator. Partly for this reason, Barre's removal only hastened the collapse of the Somali state, as factions previously allied against him were unable to agree on the basis for a new political order. The result was a profound 'crisis of legitimate authority'.[13] In the summer of 1992, fierce rivalry and intense fighting between the two main factions of the United Somali Congress (USC) led by Mohammed Farah Aideed and Ali Mahdi Mohammed respectively, thwarted the efforts of a small-scale UN mission (UNOSOM I) to supervise the delivery of relief supplies to the country.[14] It was against the background of these developments – a collapsed state, continued fighting, and a large-scale famine – that Boutros Boutros-Ghali asked the United States, in late 1992, to lead a military task force (UNITAF) to Somalia that would secure humanitarian relief operations and, at the same time, prepare the ground for a second and much larger UN mission (UNOSOM II). The continuing precariousness of the situation in the country in early 1993 was deemed to require a more forceful mandate for any follow-on force. Consequently, the second United Nations Operation in Somalia (UNOSOM II) was 'endowed with enforcement powers under Chapter VII of the Charter' and became, in the words of Boutros-Ghali, the 'first operation of its kind to be authorised by the international community'.[15]

Presenting his plans to the Security Council in March 1993, the UN Secretary-General envisaged a role for UNOSOM II that involved far more than simply the continuation of UNITAF's efforts to establish 'a secure environment for humanitarian assistance'.[16] Indeed, Boutros-Ghali called for a mandate that:

> would also empower UNOSOM II to provide assistance to the Somali people in rebuilding their shattered economy and social and political life, re-establishing the country's constitutional structure; achieving national reconciliation, [and] recreating a Somali state based on democratic governance and rehabilitating the country's economy and infrastructure.[17]

Legitimate questions have been raised about the appropriateness of adopting such an ambitious mandate given the nature of the crisis in Somalia at the time. In particular, the emphasis on recreating a Somali state has been viewed by prominent scholars, as well as by some experienced NGOs, as running counter to 'powerful economic and social forces in contemporary Somalia militating against any central or centralising political arrangement'.[18] Mark Bradbury of OXFAM, writing in 1994, pointed out that 'centralised government is the very thing that many Somalis have been fighting against'.[19] A related criticism centred on the failure by outsiders to take proper account of the 'cultural specifics of the Somali context'.[20] Yet, as Ken Menkhaus also perceptively notes, while the various critiques of the UN's approach to reconciliation in Somalia 'grew louder and more caustic' as the situation deteriorated in 1993, 'collectively...they often contradicted rather than reinforced each other'.[21] What is surely beyond dispute is that the general nature of the objectives spelled out by the UN in March 1993 could only be achieved with the support and involvement of the Somalis themselves. This meant, as far as the central focus of this essay is concerned, that military operations would have to be subordinated to and closely coordinated with political efforts to control violence and set the country on the path of reconciliation. In the event, American-led military actions from early June 1993 onwards, actively encouraged by Boutros-Ghali himself, were to have the very opposite effect. Still, even as the situation on the ground deteriorated in the summer of 1993, UN and US officials continued to maintain that they were not in Somalia to fight a 'war', and that actions were not directed against any one party *as such*. It was a 'peace enforcement' operation with Chapter VII powers and the mission was not to fight an 'enemy' but to ensure that Security Council orders were implemented. That, at any rate, was the theory.

Shortly after the killing of 24 Pakistani UN peacekeepers on 5 June 1993, the Security Council passed a resolution condemning what it described as 'premeditated armed attacks launched by forces *apparently* belonging to the United Somali Congress (USC/SNA)'.[22] A Commission of Inquiry, set up by the UN to investigate the circumstances that had led to the deaths of its personnel, concluded much later that 'in the absence of a more convincing explanation from the USC/SNA', it believed that the SNA had indeed 'orchestrated the attacks' on 5 June.[23] It could find no 'conclusive evidence', however, to support the view that the attacks had been 'pre-planned and pre-meditated'.[24] Encouraged by Boutros-Ghali, Security Council Resolution 837 was nevertheless interpreted by the US leadership in Mogadishu as requiring a significant escalation in the use of force, including the targeting of the senior hierarchy of the SNA.[25] While professedly still not taking sides in the wider Somali conflict, a new phase of operations began on 12 June 1993 with a series of night and day-time attacks by American forces of the Quick Reaction Force (QRF) aimed at destroying weapons sites and Radio Mogadishu controlled by forces loyal to Aideed. Within weeks, Jonathan Howe, Boutros-Ghali's Special Representative in Somalia, had also announced a $25,000 bounty for the capture of Aideed who was increasingly described as an obstructionist warlord.

The key issue here is not whether Aideed could or should have been more unambiguously linked to the attack on UN forces; indeed he already had more than enough blood on his hands. The real question was whether the strategy adopted in response to that attack was the wisest policy under the circumstances. The Commission of Inquiry, whose final report Boutros-Ghali initially sought to suppress, noted laconically that it was 'arguable' whether Resolution 837 really envisaged the destruction of houses, garages and meetings.[26] In particular, the Commission singled out, as have most accounts of UNOSOM II's unhappy history, the decision to attack the house of Abdi Hassan Awale on 12 July 1993. Senior UN officials in Mogadishu at the time described the 'Abdi House' as a 'major SNA/Aideed militia command and control centre'. On the day of the attack, however, it was merely serving as a meeting place for elders, clansmen, intellectuals and militia leaders. Since the aim of the attack was to 'eliminate the SNA command centre and its occupants',[27] US commanders were determined to preserve the element of surprise. For this reason, the policy of prior notification before an attack, which up to that point had been adhered to in order to minimize 'collateral damage' in and around Mogadishu, was set aside. The results were predictable. In a carefully researched and graphic account of US military operations in Somalia in 1993, Mark Bowden has described how on that day 16 armour-piercing missiles slammed into a meeting of unsuspecting clan elders and religious leaders.[28] The attack was roughly estimated by the International Red Cross to have killed more than 50 Somalis and injured a further 170.[29] The Abdi House attack, for which President Bill Clinton's specific approval appears to have been sought,[30] did 'more than any single act to stir up local support for Aideed and the Habr Gidr, and turned many moderate Somalis who had supported the intervention against the international mission'.[31] The Commission of Inquiry rightly concluded that after the 5 June incident, and more unambiguously so after 12 July, the UN had become involved in what amounted to a war against Aideed's SNA in Mogadishu. Its report perceptively added that once the 'war' had started it 'followed its own dynamics'. The climax was reached on 3–4 October 1993, when 18 American soldiers were killed and 78 wounded in a firefight which resulted in the death of possibly as many as 1000 Somali civilians. The *Washington Post* aptly described the departure of US troops from Somalia as a 'guns-cocked withdrawal'.[32]

What, then, are the wider lessons from UNOSOM II's involvement in Somalia between May and October 1993? The first and most obvious lesson is that one cannot wage peace and make war in one location at the same time. As noted above, legitimate questions have been raised about the manner of the

UN's involvement in Somalia in the early 1990s, especially its lack of sensitivity to and understanding of the political realities of Somalia. This is not to suggest, however, that once UNOSOM II deployed in the country in May 1993, the course of events was doomed to follow the disastrous path described above. Gerard Prunier has shown how French troops, although deployed in a 'less tense' area of the country, were able to achieve a significant measure of stability and progress in their sector by adopting a 'very minimal, close-to-the-ground, down-to-earth approach', in sharp contrast to American forces in and around Mogadishu.[33] Likewise, Robert Patman in a comparative study of US and Australian policy in Somalia, argues persuasively that Australian soldiers were able to achieve an impressive amount in a short period of time (17 weeks) by adopting a radically different approach to that of US troops. Operating in the area around Baidoa – known as the 'city of death' until Australian troops arrived – they 'managed to create a stable situation…where relief agencies could freely operate and fulfil their work'.[34] The key to the comparative success of the Australian contingent, according to Patman, was similar to that of the French: a community-oriented style of operations, low-tech and participatory. These experiences suggest that there were certainly alternatives to the US mode of army operations. Yet it cannot be concluded from this that what happened in Somalia was simply a case of 'peace enforcement' that went awry.

'Peace enforcement' doctrine emphasizes that force can be applied impartially if the focus of military action is firmly geared towards ensuring compliance with a given mandate. The difficulty with this is that all Security Council resolutions, without exception, reflect a measure of political compromise which in turn lends the mandate to differing interpretations. In some cases, the nature of that compromise has involved the commitment to an 'end state' so vague as to provide little or no basis for translation into realizable military objectives. The case of Somalia illustrates how the adoption, interpretation and evolution of a mandate, including the question of the use of force, depend critically on the interplay of personalities, competing motivations and constraints of the kind alluded to above. Resolution 837 was rushed through the Council and left a number of questions about implementation unanswered. Boutros-Ghali's personal commitment to the Somalia operation and his direct involvement in decision-making turned out to be critical to the course of events. His subsequent claim that he was 'obliged' by the Security Council to take the actions that he did is anything but convincing. In his memoirs, Boutros-Ghali recalls how the aforementioned and critical Abdi House attack had in fact given rise to a 'debate' about the way forward.[35] Along with Madeleine Albright, he was convinced of the need to capture Aideed and dismissed, then as he does in his memoirs, those who claimed to have 'understood' the Somali people. These included the Italians (he regrets having brought them along in the first place); Mohamed Sahnoun (the highly capable Algerian UN Special Representative who he had first asked to undertake a fact-finding mission to the country in March 1992); and senior officials within the UN Secretariat. In fact, Boutros-Ghali's own approach to the UN mission and specifically to the Aideed coalition was fatally compromised by his previous involvement in the region as a senior Egyptian minister. Indeed, as Compagnon makes clear, in his capacity as Minister of Foreign Affairs, Boutros-Ghali was closely involved in support of Barre 'until the very end'. This was always likely to colour his judgement about the 'impartial application of force'. It almost certainly influenced the attitudes and perceptions of the Somalis.

The call in such cases is, of course, for the Security Council itself to ensure greater clarity of mandates, and much ink has been spilt by commissions of 'eminent persons' stressing the need for 'better mandates'. While this objective is laudable, the adoption of Resolution 837 provides grounds only for cautious optimism. A senior British diplomat involved in the informal Council deliberations preceding the adoption of this critical resolution, recalls how the British expressed 'some concern' about how it had been 'rushed' without an adequate assessment of its implications on the ground.[36] He noted, however, that London's central preoccupation and interest at the time were with events in Bosnia, where it had just played a key role in the drawn-out and politically difficult process leading up to the adoption of Resolution 836, extending UNPROFOR's role in relation to the so-called 'safe areas' in Bosnia. Given this hierarchy of priorities and the fact that the US and Pakistan (which was then on the Security Council) were pushing hard for a quick response to events in Somalia, the British view, understandably, was that taking the lead in Somalia (or even just raising awkward questions about 'the way forward' after Resolution 837) was not in their 'interest'.[37] It belongs to the story that the American Permanent Representative to the UN at the time, Madeleine Albright, was pushing hard for an immediate and 'tough' response in support of Pakistan, and that both of these countries had spent much of the previous three months expressing frustration about what they considered to be French and British pusillanimity over Bosnia. Indeed, only two days earlier, Pakistan had abstained in voting on Resolution 836 extending the 'safe areas' concept in Bosnia.[38] The adoption of 837 on Somalia is not untypical of the kind of dynamics that often drive the process of mandate formulation in the UN Security Council.

Operation *Deliberate Force* and the End of UNPROFOR's Mission

UNPROFOR's involvement in Bosnia came to an end with the signing of a comprehensive peace agreement for Bosnia and Herzegovina at Dayton, Ohio in late 1995.[39] To many observers and policy-makers, it was the air campaign initiated by NATO against Bosnian Serb targets throughout the country in late August and early September 1995 (Operation *Deliberate Force*) and it alone, which 'produced the results' that allowed agreement to be reached. This reading of the end-game in Bosnia has since been presented, and in many quarters accepted, as the central lesson for policy-makers regarding the use of force from that conflict. Indeed, it clearly informed the thinking of Western leaders and military planners in the run-up to Operation *Allied Force*, NATO's air campaign in Kosovo against the regime of Milošević in March 1999. In assuming, as was widely done, that the 'short, sharp shock' of a bombing campaign would quickly lead Milošević to abandon his repressive policies in the province of Kosovo, Western leaders were looking to and citing as evidence in support of their chosen policy, the supposed effect of NATO's aerial bombardment in Bosnia.[40] This is a crude and incomplete reading of what eventually brought the Serbs to the negotiating table and the war to an end. Drawing lessons regarding the use of force in 'peace operations' from the Bosnia experience requires examining the combined effect of four major developments which, by mid-August 1995, had created the conditions for the effective use of force to be initiated. These developments did not reflect a carefully coordinated strategic plan based on political consensus in NATO capitals about the 'way forward'. Instead, they came about as a result of events on the ground, by the willingness and ability of certain key actors to respond to those events, and ultimately by the American-led preparedness to support Croatia and take advantage of its military successes against Serb forces in both Croatia and Bosnia in 1995.

The first major development was the weakening of the military position of the Bosnian Serbs. This, however, had been substantially achieved well before the air campaign was launched. The dramatic success of Croatia's military offensives, first in Western Slavonia (Sector West) in May 1995 and later in the Krajina in August, had profoundly altered the strategic predicament of the Bosnian Serb Army (BSA). The Croat offensives, actively supported and strongly encouraged by the US (and to a lesser but significant degree by Germany) and eventually resulting in the single largest instance of forced population displacement in the brutal season of 'ethnic cleansing' between 1991 and 1995, was one of the preconditions for the effective use of force in September. The full background to the Croat military successes involved the American decision to assist in the creation of a professional and combat-capable force that could take on the Serbs (a process which started in the latter half of 1994).[41] American involvement also entailed assistance in the planning of operations, encouraging the Croat leadership at critical moments to pursue the 'military option',[42] and a readiness to accept, as distinct from condone, the more than likely violations of human rights and reprisals that would inevitably follow as interior forces moved in and reasserted control over areas 'liberated' by Croatia's 'crack' combat brigades.[43] The strategic significance of Croat victories on the battlefield, however, was clear: it decisively weakened the position of the Bosnian Serbs, both in terms of morale and strategic depth. The extent to which their position had been undermined became evident during the NATO air campaign a few weeks later when Bosnian government and Croat forces (in theory, supposedly operating together) provided an effective land component to NATO's air campaign.

The second development that facilitated the use of force in Bosnia was the withdrawal of UNPROFOR troops from isolated and exposed positions in Serb-controlled territory. Since the hostage crisis in May and June of 1995, General Rupert Smith, commander of UN forces in Bosnia, had been working towards this goal in order to reduce the vulnerability of UN troops to further hostage taking.[44] Specifically, this involved the abandonment of the Weapon Collection Points around Sarajevo and Gorazde, the only remaining 'safe area' in eastern Bosnia after the fall, at terrible cost, of both Srebrenica and Zepa to Bosnian Serb forces in July 1995. By late August, the process of concentrating forces away from exposed positions was nearly complete, with the significant exception of the remaining British troops in Gorazde. When a mortar round landed on the Markala market in Sarajevo on 28 August, General Smith, while seeking confirmation that the mortar attack originated from a Bosnian Serb position, stalled for time to allow British troops to be extracted from the enclave, to prepare for artillery bombardment of Serb positions around Sarajevo, and to allow enough time for Admiral Leighton-Smith, at NATO's southern command headquarters in Naples, to prepare for a sustained air campaign. Once confirmation had been obtained and the other elements were in place, both commanders turned their 'key'.[45]

The third development facilitating the use of force, in addition to removing points of military vulnerability throughout Serb-controlled territory, was the creation by Britain, France and the Netherlands of a Rapid Reaction Force (RRF) providing, for the first time, effective and accurate mortar and artillery support on Mount Igman near Sarajevo. This gave UN forces a capability that had hitherto been lacking to suppress Serb artillery positions around Sarajevo. When it was first announced that such a force would be deployed, it was unclear whether these reinforcements would be sent to assist a withdrawal or to help create the conditions for effective military action on the ground. At a meeting of senior UN officials, including the UN Special Representative, Yasushi Akashi, General Bernard Janvier and General Rupert Smith, held in Split on 9 June 1995 to assess the situation after the hostage crisis, Smith wished to know whether 'we [are] going to use them [RRF] to fight? – If not, I am not sure I want them – they will just be more mouths to feed, and create expectations that I cannot meet'.[46] By August, however, the

RRF artillery was in place around Sarajevo and was to play a key role in the unfolding campaign. When Operation *Deliberate Force* got underway, British and French artillery proved, especially in the initial stages of the campaign, to be more decisive in sustaining pressure on the Bosnian Serbs than NATO air power. The effectiveness of air power was hampered – not for the first, nor for the last time in the Balkans – by adverse weather conditions.[47] The precise and sustained use, and the continuing threat of use, of artillery in support of the air campaign allowed UNPROFOR to keep the roads around Sarajevo open – this, in spite of 'concerns' expressed by senior UN officials in New York, even at this late stage, about 'offensive actions' undertaken by the 'peacekeepers' of UNPROFOR.[48]

The final development which prepared the ground for effective use of force was the change in command and control arrangements for the use of NATO air power in support of UN forces that was made following the Srebrenica debacle. General Smith left the conference that had been convened, in London in July 1995, to assess the 'way forward' after the fall of Srebrenica and Zepa, disillusioned about the lack of progress and the obvious divisions that persisted among the major powers. However, steps were taken in early August to ensure more 'timely and effective use of air power'. These steps were enshrined in a memorandum of understanding between NATO and the UN, agreed between Admiral Leighton-Smith (CINCSOUTH) and General Janvier (FC UNPF). The document included a more detailed description of operational considerations, including targeting and the conditions for initiation of operations. These conditions were now considered to include more than just direct attacks, and the decision to initiate operations was left to the 'common judgement' of the senior NATO and UN commanders in theatre.[49]

Taken together, all of these developments meant that the ground was prepared for a deliberate transition to military *enforcement* action, which thus far in the conflict had been consistently rejected by the Security Council and troop-contributing countries. In the end, military force played a key role in bringing about a permanent ceasefire. This had involved, although resisted by some within the UN hierarchy, a taking of sides and a willingness to engage in war fighting to bring about a decisive result on the ground. In an article accompanying the British Peace Support doctrine of 1997, the events of mid-1995 and Rupert Smith's role in them are described as a 'switching to peace enforcement'.[50] Clearly, this was not 'peace enforcement' of the kind which the doctrine itself set out to elaborate.

A Doctrine for 'Peace Enforcement'?

Where does all of this leave the idea of peace enforcement as a form of 'active impartiality' that somehow falls short of war? To raise the question is, of course, not to dispute the fact that the armed forces of many countries have been called upon (and will continue to be called upon) to act in situations that are 'messy', volatile and dangerous by the standards of most traditional peacekeeping operations. The issue explored here is about the role and utility of military force in responding to such situations, and specifically whether the actual experience of 'peace operations' in the 1990s lends much support to the notion that 'peace enforcement' can meaningfully be treated as a distinct category of 'peace support' operations. Three basic difficulties stand out.[51]

In the first place, the fact that 'conflict environments are grey and messy' does not automatically suggest that the solution is to locate 'peace support operations on a spectrum of force'.[52] Indeed, by doing so, one is likely to 'encourage the notion that there can be military fixes of deep-rooted political problems, a notion that may be exacerbated by the pressure for quick exit strategies'.[53] There is, in other words, a danger that faith in doctrinal innovation – not unlike faith in technological 'fixes' and breakthroughs – may obscure the importance of maintaining a firm link between the employment of military force and the long-term political objective which the use of force is intended to achieve. This very basic point goes to the heart of the distinction which Rupert Smith was drawing in 1994 between what the use of force and forces can *achieve* as opposed to can *do*.

The second difficulty flows from the first: the idea that a 'peace enforcement' or 'peace restoring' operation can clinically apply force to manipulate the behaviour of various parties on the ground *without* designating an enemy while simultaneously assuming that such action will not influence the political dynamics of the conflict, is seriously to underestimate the impact of outside military action on the local balance of military, political and economic interests in the kind of complex intra-state conflicts we have seen in the 1990s (see Adebajo and Landsberg in this volume). It presupposes, in effect, a crude psychology and highly simplified rationality on the part of the 'warring party'. It is more likely that a warring faction which is militarily and politically disadvantaged by the actions of a 'peace restoration' or a supposedly impartial peace enforcement mission, will take little comfort from not having been formally designated an *enemy*.[54] Similarly, the assurance that military action directed against a party will not prejudge the political outcome of the conflict, will not have much of an impact if the action itself is not linked to a broader political strategy aimed at bringing the conflict to an end. In Somalia, Aideed viewed Boutros-Ghali as a sworn enemy of the Habr Gidr, intent upon strengthening the Darod clan at its expense and, to this end, using American military might under the guise of a UN operation. Boutros-Ghali's past involvement in the region only reinforced local suspicions and undermined any claims of impartiality. The fact that military action against

Aideed had the direct effect of shifting the local balance of power in favour of his military rivals only confirmed to him and his followers that this was 'war' and not 'peace enforcement'. While Boutros-Ghali's involvement in Somalia may offer a particularly blatant example of partial behaviour, the experience of other operations provides little evidence to suggest that 'peace enforcement' can in fact be conducted impartially. The case of Somalia also raises the broader issue (discussion of which is beyond the scope of this essay) of the challenges of outside military engagement in 'non-Western' societies and cultures, where different 'rationalities' may be at work, and where the State in the Weberian sense is either extremely weak or non-existent.

Finally, those who believe in the feasibility of disinterested and politically neutral 'peace enforcement' may be overestimating the purity of the motives of those charged with restoring the peace, while underestimating the variety of different motives alluded to above – including power political and domestic ones – that influence and constrain governments in their decisions regarding the deployment and use of military force. The situation in central Bosnia in mid-1993 provides a good illustration of this difficulty. Those who have argued in favour of 'active impartiality' as a means of dealing with violations of agreements and resolutions often, and with good reason, refer to the failure to respond to Bosnian Serb military actions against Muslim communities in early 1993 as one instance where force should have been used more readily. 'Active impartiality' as envisaged above, however, would also have required forceful action to be taken against Bosnian Croat forces who, with the active support of late Croatian President, Franjo Tudjman, launched a brutal war against the Bosnian government forces and civilians in Central Bosnia in 1993.[55] Indeed, in a pattern of collusion repeated elsewhere (see Keen in this volume), Croat forces in central Bosnia actually received artillery and other forms of support directly from the Bosnian Serb Army in its war against Bosnian government forces.[56] For a variety of reasons, however, neither the American nor German governments were prepared to sanction military action against Croat forces, even though it was perfectly clear to monitors, observers and peacekeepers operating in central Bosnia at the time that regular Croat forces, taking their orders directly from Zagreb, were active inside Bosnia.[57] This in itself, one might legitimately argue, ought not to have prevented forceful action from being taken against the Bosnian Serbs. The point here is merely that such action would *not* have amounted to politically neutral and disinterested 'active impartiality'. To pretend otherwise would have been to disguise a very different reality.

Another example is provided by Operation *Turquoise*, France's military operation in Rwanda from June to August 1994. This case is of particular interest since it apparently inspired the French military to formalize a doctrine for 'peace restoration' operations. It is also cited in British doctrine as the 'only peace enforcement operation thus far in which force has been used impartially'.[58] While it is clear that public and media pressure for involvement on genuine humanitarian grounds provided part of the background to the French government's decision to send a military force, the claim that the resulting operation amounted to an 'impartial peace enforcement' mission is simply untenable. Indeed, the very suggestion that the operation was in some sense 'impartial' must appear bizarre to observers on the ground at the time, and obscene to those who experienced at close quarter the murderous efficiency with which bands of *interahamwe* continued to work within the French-controlled zone. In fact, the claim to impartiality was fatally compromised at the outset given that France had continued, at least until late May 1994, to provide military support to the *Forces Armées Rwandaises* (FAR). Specifically, it has been established that although an international embargo was imposed against Rwanda on 17 May 1994, at least five French shipments of arms were later delivered to the genocidal regime.[59] As for Operation *Turquoise*, it was far from being simply a disinterested humanitarian operation, even though it did receive the formal blessing of the UN Security Council. The operation had the effect of creating a safety zone into which the 'Hutu Power' leadership and elements of the FAR could and did retreat in large numbers. Indeed, according to Mel McNulty, many French soldiers assumed in advance of deployment that their 'Turquoise brief' implied 'a rearguard action in support of their beleaguered Rwanda allies, to allow them to retreat in good order and regroup'.[60] Philip Gourevitch, in his powerful and deeply disturbing account of the genocide, observes how 'from the moment they [French under Operation *Turquoise*] arrived, and wherever they went, the French forces supported and preserved the same political leaders who had presided over the genocide'.[61] Gourevitch concluded that, 'the signal achievement of the Operation *Turquoise*, was to permit the slaughter of Tutsis to continue for an extra month, and to secure a passage for the genocidal command to cross, with a lot of its weaponry, into Zaire'.[62] Evidence of 'partiality' rather than 'impartiality' has come from a growing number of sources and investigations.[63] The report of the international panel set up by the Organization of African Unity (OAU) to investigate the genocide and 'the surrounding events', released in July 2000, summarizes much of the evidence that has emerged since 1994.[64] While, unlike Gourevitch, it accepts and 'applauds' that some 10,000–15,000 lives were probably saved by the operation, it also concludes that:

> beyond any doubt, their [the French forces] other task was to give support to the interim government. Most of the genocidaire regime, large numbers of high-ranking military officers, as well as thousands of heavily armed interahamwe and the majority of the Rwandan forces

(now called ex-FAR) managed to escape the RPF advance by retreating to the convenience of the safe zone. Indeed, France actually declared that it would use force against any RPF encroachment on the zone. Once it was clear that the RPF could not be halted, however, France took the next logical step and facilitated the escape of much of the Hutu Power leadership into Zaire.[65]

All of this suggests that Operation *Turquoise* provides a very poor model indeed for future operations and, if anything, highlights major difficulties with the French concept of 'peace restoration'. It is simply impossible to isolate the dubious short-term 'tactical' achievements of Operation *Turquoise*, whatever the admixture motives involved, from that of French policy towards the conflict and the region before, during and after the genocide.

Conclusion: The Use of Force and the Necessity of Choice

If these are some of the painful lessons from 'peace support' operations in the 1990s, what are the policy implications for the use of force? The first point to stress is that to question the notion of 'peace enforcement' as a distinct category is not tantamount to opposing enforcement *per se*, and it certainly is not meant to suggest that one should in all circumstances seek to revert to the tried and tested practices of past peacekeeping operations. On the contrary, it only makes the choice of instrumentality starker by stressing that in a number of cases, peacekeeping will *not* be appropriate and hard decisions regarding the use of force will have to be made. By identifying 'peace enforcement' as an area of activity distinct from war-fighting, one in which 'escalation dominance' can supposedly be maintained, advocates of the so-called middle-ground options, whether intentionally or not, are allowing governments to avoid hard decisions about the implications of deploying military personnel. While the advocates of 'grey area' and 'robust' operations usually see these as progressive developments from an earlier and more timid approach, governments – judging from the record of Somalia, Bosnia and elsewhere – tend to see them as a way of limiting involvement and of avoiding the kind of decisions which the nature of the conflict may call for.

The debate on doctrine and the use of force in peace operations was not helped by the introduction of the notion of a so-called 'Mogadishu line'. The idea of such a 'line' gave the misleading impression, easily shot down by critics, that consent was somehow an absolute quality; either you possessed it or you did not. Quite clearly consent is not an absolute quality, and the aforementioned experience of Australian troops in Somalia shows that the margin of consent that does exist in 'messy' or 'grey' operational environments can be enlarged and built upon by an enterprising outside force.

This is not, however, the same as saying that the basic distinction between consent-based operations and enforcement where the logic of war and war-fighting must be accepted, is no longer valid. Asked to comment on a draft of the British Peace Support doctrine in 1997, a highly experienced officer observed that 'in war, however limited the objective or the resources allocated to achieve it, the need to break the will of the opponent and to bear the risk to those resources marks the difference from peace'. Recognizing this distinction has immediate implications which decision-makers will need to think through more carefully than they have been prepared to do in recent years. One is forced back to the initial question of what the use of force or the threat of its use can achieve rather than simply what armed forces can do.

ACKNOWLEDGEMENTS

The author would like to thank Michael Pugh and Adekeye Adebajo for their very helpful comments on an earlier draft of this essay.

NOTES

1. 'The Use of Force in Intervention Operations', seminar presentation, International Institute for Strategic Studies (IISS), London, 1994.
2. Ibid.
3. According to one recent book on the subject, peace operations 'encompass a wide range of different missions, ranging from a handful of unarmed civilians or military observers to combat units with ten thousands of troops'. See Erwin A. Schmidl (ed.), *Peace Operations Between War and Peace*, London and Portland, OR: Frank Cass, 2000, p.1.
4. Report by the Secretary-General, S/25354, 3 March 1993, para. 9.
5. In March 1999, NATO insisted that it was not going to *war* against Yugoslavia but was taking action to weaken the 'ability [of Serb Army and police forces] to cause further humanitarian catastrophe'. Press Statement, Secretary-General Javier Solana, 23 March 1999, NATO.
6. In the UK, the Permanent Joint Headquarters in 1997 issued *Peace Support Operations – Joint Warfare Publication* 3-50, PJHQ (henceforth JWP 3-50). The Swedish doctrine for peace support operations is modelled, if not quite word-by-word, then very closely on UK doctrine. See *Joint Military Doctrine: Peace Support Operations*, Swedish Armed Forces, Oct. 1997.
7. For the French concept of peace restoration, see 'Supplement to An Agenda for Peace, Aide-mémoire by France', A/50/869, S/1996/71, 30 Jan. 1996, UN Document.
8. JWP 3-50, para. 303.
9. John Ruggie, 'The UN and the Collective Use of Force: Whither or Whether?', *International Peacekeeping*, Vol.3, No.4, Winter 1996, p.14.
10. A recent example is provided by the nature of NATO's military action against Yugoslavia in March 1999; an operation that was constrained by measures designed to limit the exposure to danger for aircrews, as well as by a very public ruling out of the use of ground forces. These self-imposed constraints were necessitated by the perceived need to keep the fragile unity of the alliance intact. This was itself a reflection of the political unease that existed in government circles about the depth and durability of public support for a military campaign. The constraints severely limited the effectiveness of the campaign against Serb policies of 'ethnic cleansing' in Kosovo, the disruption of which was NATO's principal campaign objective (see note 5 above).
11. On the reasons for French involvement in Somalia in 1993, Gerard Prunier, a distinguished scholar of the region well-versed in the inner workings of French decision-making on Africa, has observed that 'the main concern of the French authorities had to do with domestic politics

and the fear of any kind of mishap in the field'. Gerard Prunier, 'The Experience of European Armies in Operation Restore Hope', in W. Clarke and J. Herbst (eds.), *Learning from Somalia: The Lessons of Armed Humanitarian Intervention*, Boulder: Westview Press, 1997, p.136.

12. For an early assessment of this trend, see Lori F. Damrosch (ed.), *Enforcing Restraint: Collective Intervention in Internal Conflicts*, New York: Council on Foreign Relations, 1993.

13. Ken Menkhaus, 'International Peacebuilding and the Dynamics of Local and National Reconciliation in Somalia', in Clarke and Herbst (note 11), p.43.

14. General Mohamed Farah Aideed was a member of the Saad sub-group of the Habr Gidr sub-clan of Hawiye, while President Ali Mahdi was of the Abgal Hawiye. For a succinct account of the disintegration of the armed opposition movements to Siad Barre, see Daniel Compagnon, 'Somali Armed Movements: The Interplay of Political Entrepreneurship and Clan-based Factions', in Christopher Clapham (ed.), *African Guerrillas*, Oxford: James Currey, 1998, pp.73–90.

15. Report by the Secretary-General, S/25354, 3 March 1993, paras. 58 and 101.

16. Ibid., para. 91.

17. Ibid.

18. Menkhaus (note 13), p.60.

19. Mark Bradbury, *The Somali Conflict: Prospects for Peace*, Oxfam Research Paper No.9, Oxford: OXFAM, 1994, p.4.

20. See Ioan Lewis, 'Making History in Somalia: Humanitarian Intervention in a Stateless Society', Discussion Paper 6, *The Centre for the Study of Global Governance*, London School of Economics. A trenchant critique along similar lines was also later provided by Mohamed Sahnoun in M. Sahnoun, 'Prevention in Conflict Resolution: The Case of Somalia', *Irish Studies in International Affairs*, Vol.5, 1994, pp.5–11. See also Mohamed Sahnoun, *The Missed Opportunities*, Washington DC: United States Institute of Peace Press, 1994.

21. Menkhaus (note 13), p.54.

22. That is the faction loyal to General Aideed. UNSC Resolution 837, 6 June 1993 (my emphasis). General Aideed established the Somali National Alliance (SNA) in October 1992.

23. S/1994/653, 1 June 1994, 'Report of the Commission of Inquiry Established Pursuant to SC Resolution 885' (henceforth 'Commission of Inquiry'), para. 186.

24. 'Commission of Inquiry', para. 187. Boutros Boutros-Ghali's own account of the sequence of events between the killing of the Pakistani soldiers and the adoption of resolution 837 is misleading since it appears to suggest that Security Council action followed an 'internal UN investigation' which had 'revealed' that Aideed was 'responsible'. See, Boutros Boutros-Ghali, *Unvanquished: A US–UN Saga*, London: I.B. Tauris, 1999, pp.94–5.

25. On the US-led nature of operations, retired Admiral Jonathan Howe served as Special Representative of the Secretary-General (SRSG), while Major General Thomas Montgomery acted as Deputy Force Commander and, more significantly, as commander of US forces in Somalia, reporting to CINCCENT and with sole authority to commit the US Quick Reaction Force. Complicating matters further would be the arrival later that summer of the Ranger Task Force answerable to Major General William Garrison of the US Army Special Operations Command. The complete US domination of the command and control structure in Mogadishu, and the confusion to which multiple chains of reporting gave rise, has been candidly acknowledged in several 'after action' reports by the US military. See 'An Analysis of the Application of the "Principles of Military Operations other than War" in Somalia', *The Army-Air Force Center for Low Intensity Conflict*, White Paper, Feb. 1994.

26. 'Commission of Inquiry', para. 231.

27. 'Commission of Inquiry', para. 153.

28. Mark Bowden, *Black Hawk Down*, London: Bantam Press, 1999, pp.72–4 and pp.358–9.

29. According to Bowden, 'among the elders present at the meeting were religious leaders, former judges, professors, the poet Moallim Soyan, and the clan's most senior leader, Sheik Haji Mohamed Iman Aden.' Ibid.

30. See Elisabeth Drew, *On the Edge: The Clinton Presidency*, New York: Simon & Schuster/Touchstone, 1994, p.274.

31. Bowden, *Black Hawk Down*, p.359.

32. 'US to Leave Somalia with Its Guard Up', *The Washington Post*, 8 Dec. 1993.

33. Gerard Prunier, 'The Experience of European Armies in Operation Restore Hope', in W. Clarke and J. Herbst, *Learning from Somalia*, pp.139–41. For a journalist's perspective on the difference in approach and results, see Richard Dowden's description of the contrast between the 'hope in Baidoa' and 'mayhem in Mogadishu' in July 1993. 'Mortars and Wine in Tale of Two Cities', *The Independent*, 15 July 1993.

34. Robert Patman, *Disarmament in a Failed State: The Experience of the UN in Somalia*, Working Paper No.162, Peace Research Centre, The Australian National University Research School of Pacific Studies, p.33.

35. Boutros-Ghali, *Unvanquished: A US–UN Saga*, pp.95–6.

36. Private interview.

37. Private interview.

38. On the US response to the killing of the Pakistani peacekeepers, see Drew, *On the Edge*, pp.319–20. According to Drew the resolution, which Albright was pressing for, 'was largely drafted at the State Department'. The only other country to abstain on Resolution 836 was Venezuela.

39. The UN forces deployed in former Yugoslavia underwent various name changes in the period 1991–95. UNPROFOR refers here to the forces deployed under the Bosnia Herzegovina Command (BHC), initially headquartered at Kiseljak (1992–94) before moving to Sarajevo (1994–95).

40. The initial NATO plan in March 1999 was for a two-day bombing campaign with daytime pauses to allow Milosevic to back down. The initial target list included only 219 targets and, in the words of one NATO officer involved, the 'prevailing opinion' at NATO was: 'You show them some lead – boom ! boom ! – and they'll fold.' Quoted in Steven Lee Myers, 'Chinese Embassy Bombing: A Wide Net of Blame', *The New York Times*, 17 April 2000. More significantly, at the most senior level of decision-making, Madeleine Albright confidently asserted early on that the air campaign would be a short one: 'I don't see this as a long-term operation. I think this is something – the deter and damage [sic] is something that is achievable within a relatively short period of time.' See, Secretary of State Madeleine Albright, Interview on PBS Newshour with Jim Lehrer, 24 March 1999. For further evidence pointing to an excessively optimistic reading of the likely effects of a short air campaign on Milosevic's resolve, see also 'Kosovo', Foreign Affairs Committee, House of Commons, Volume I, Report and Proceedings of the Committee, 23 May 2000, pp.xxxix–xl.

41. For some of the background and detail on this, see the interesting account in Brendan O'Shea, *Crisis at Bihac: Bosnia's Bloody Battlefield*, Phoenix Mill: Sutton Publishing, 1998.

42. 'With pressure for a ceasefire building, we urged Tudjman to do as much as possible militarily.' Richard Holbrooke, *To End a War*, New York: Random House, 1998, p.191.

43. The UN military observers and especially ECMM teams deployed throughout the area of Croat operations were able to document widespread atrocities in the wake of the offensive. Detailed testimony has also been presented to the ICFY in The Hague. See 'War Crimes Investigators recommend Trial for 3 Croatian Generals', *International Herald Tribune*, 22 March 1999.

44. Force Commander's End of Mission Report, HQ UNPF, Jan. 1996, D-6.

45. For the record, it is worth noting that Richard Holbrooke's account of the events leading up to the start of the air campaign, as well as developments during the campaign itself, are misleading, implying as they do that Holbrooke himself played a key role in making the case for bombing. General Smith took the key decisions in Sarajevo without any consultation with Holbrooke. Smith was able to act in part because his superior, General Bernard Janvier, who had been markedly more cautious on the question of the use of force, was absent. For an account of these critical events, see the interesting and well-researched thesis by Linda Nordin, 'The NATO Strikes over Bosnia-Herzegovina: Why on 30 August 1995?', MA thesis, Stockholm University, Department of Political Science, February 1998. See also Holbrooke, *To End a War*, p.99.

46. Memorandum of SRSG's meeting in Split, 9 June 1995, also quoted at length in David Rohde, *A Safe Area*, London: Simon & Schuster Ltd./ Pocket Books, 1997, pp.419–22, and Nordin, 'The NATO Strikes over Bosnia-Herzegovina', notes 135 and 147.

47. The air strikes on 30 August 1995 started at 02:10 and lasted until little before 05:00. RRF artillery and mortars started at 04:15 against 15 'planned targets' firing over 600 rounds. Air

operations continued to be hampered by poor weather; a limitation which did not affect the use of RRF artillery and mortar.

48. In an exchange of cables, revealing of what the 'Srebrenica report' would later refer to as 'the pervasive ambivalence within the United Nations regarding the use of force', Janvier informed Kofi Annan (head of DPKO) in New York on 7 September that it did not make much sense to distinguish between the 'defensive as opposed to offensive employment of artillery, mortar, or other RRF heavy weapons', and that 'these terms should be avoided'. The cable was in response to a 'note' from Boutros-Ghali's senior political advisor, Chinmaya Gharekan, who on 31 August 1995 had expressed concern that: the 'RRF is still operating in the offensive mode', adding 'I trust that UNPROFOR will use RRF only in responses to attack'. Cable: Janvier to Annan, Subject: RRF Action and UNPF Reporting, 7 Sept. 1995.

49. On the NATO side this was Admiral Leighton-Smith and on the UN side Bernard Janvier. As noted above, however, Janvier's absence on 28 August meant that the decision was delegated to Rupert Smith. Force Commanders's End of Mission Report, HQ UNPF, Jan. 1996, D-9.

50. JWP 3-50, Appendix 1–3.

51. The following draws, in part, on my 'UN Peacekeeping and the Use of Force: No Escape from Hard Decisions,' in Robert Patman (ed.), *Security in a Post Cold War World*, London: Macmillan, 1999.

52. Michael Pugh, *From Mission Cringe to Mission Creep? – Implications of New Peace Support Operations Doctrine*, Forsvarsstudie No.2, 1997, Oslo: Institute for Defence Studies, 1997, p.22.

53. Ibid. As Pugh pointedly adds, the 'concerns about grey area operations cannot be dismissed as a case of academics wishing the world were a less messy place. On the contrary, an appreciation that situations are messy and volatile, leads to a concern that interventions do not create more mess in the long term'.

54. British doctrine speaks of 'corrective actions…taken for non-compliance rather than a desire to support or oppose a particular party'. JWP 3-50, para. 303.

55. For the ferocity and full horror of this war which, especially in the US, never received as much attention as other aspects of the conflict, see S.B. Husum, *At War without Weapons – A Peacekeeper in the Bosnian Conflict*, Shrewsbury: Airlife Publishing Ltd., 1998.

56. ECMM HQ/Info Section, 25 May 1993, Subject: Mission Debrief.

57. The nature and extent of the involvement was brought out clearly in the case of *The Prosecutor v. Tihomir Blaskic* before the International Criminal Tribunal for the former Yugoslavia. See, 'Text Read Out by Judge Jorda during the Hearing', *The Prosecutor v. Tihomir Blaskic*, ICTY, April 2000, para. 28.

58. Appendix 1, JWP 3-50, p.1–5.

59. *Rearming with Impunity: International Support for the Perpetrators of the Genocide*, Human Rights Watch Arms Project, Vol.7, No.4, May 1995, pp.6–7. See also Gerard Prunier, *The Rwanda Crisis: History of a Genocide*, London: Hurst & Company, 1996, especially chapters 7 and 8; and *Rwanda: Death, Despair and Defiance*, African Rights, London, Sept. 1994, pp.670–72.

60. See the excellent and carefully researched article by Mel McNulty, 'France, Rwanda and Military Intervention: A Double Discrediting', *International Peacekeeping*, Vol.4, No.3, 1997, p.39.

61. Philip Gourevitch, *We Wish to Inform You That Tomorrow We Will Be Killed with Our Families: Stories from Rwanda*, London: Picador, 1998, p.158.

62. Ibid., pp.160–1.

63. In my own and more limited number of interviews with observers deployed in Rwanda at the time (including aid workers and UN military observers), I found that the setting up and the running of the French-controlled zone were seen as anything but 'impartial', and that this was not simply a matter of 'perception'. Private interviews.

64. The International Panel of Eminent Personalities to Investigate the 1994 Genocide in Rwanda and the Surrounding Events, set up by the Organization of African Unity and released in July 2000.

65. Ibid. Ch.15, para. 68.

Building Peace through Transitional Authority: New Directions, Major Challenges

MICHÈLE GRIFFIN and BRUCE JONES

In the past 18 months the Security Council has taken the United Nations into uncharted territory in Kosovo and East Timor, with mandates that are broader in scope and ambition than anything that went before. These operations bear little resemblance to traditional UN peace operations[1] and they differ dramatically even from previous transitional administration operations in Cambodia, Eastern Slavonia (Croatia) and Namibia. This shift has occurred not just because the new missions take place in a completely different international and local context, with many new constraints and challenges, but primarily because they entail the UN occupying an unprecedented amount of political and administrative space. The challenges of this situation are complex and manifold; the future of UN peace operations – perhaps even of the UN itself – rests heavily on their success.

The well-known setbacks and over-extension of UN peace operations in the early 1990s, particularly in Somalia,[2] Bosnia,[3] and, most tragically, Rwanda[4] (see Adebajo and Landsberg, and Berdal, in this volume) seemed for some time to have represented the death knell of 50 years of UN peacekeeping. These much-publicized failures ushered in a period of retrenchment, with considerable reluctance on the part of the Security Council to authorize, implement or finance new operations. The total deployment of UN military and civilian peace support personnel fell from a peak of more than 80,000 in 1993 to approximately 14,000 in 1998. In the last years of the twentieth century, it began to seem less and less likely that the UN would ever again be called upon to play any major peacekeeping role. The Security Council became far more modest in the mandates it issued, and the impetus in peacekeeping appeared to shift to the regional level. In an increasing number of cases, the international community instead accepted or even encouraged military actions by multinational coalitions or regional or sub-regional organizations.[5] As a result, the Security Council faced a growing challenge to its authority – not least by some of its own most powerful members – and a discernible decline in its primacy in the maintenance of international peace and security. The final nails in the peacekeeping coffin appeared to come with the sidelining of the UN in the military brinkmanship and eventual air strikes in Iraq in the late 1990s and the diplomatic manoeuvring and subsequent North Atlantic Treaty Organization (NATO) aerial bombardment of the Federal Republic of Yugoslavia over events in Kosovo in 1999.

In light of this apparent decline in confidence in the UN on the part of its most powerful member states, few would have predicted the events of mid to late 1999. In a matter of a few months the Council entrusted the UN with two of its broadest and most ambitious mandates. In Kosovo and East Timor, the UN was vested with executive authority over entire peoples and territories, including all legislative and executive powers and administration of the judiciary.

In fact, this shift is less surprising than it first appears. The drama and setbacks of the 'third generation' peace enforcement operations overshadowed what may well turn out to have been the far more important development in UN peace operations, namely the increased willingness of the Security Council in the latter half of the 1990s to adopt more comprehensive mandates for peace and security operations. Moving away from the narrow political and military-oriented understanding, the Council began to acknowledge the fundamental importance to the maintenance of international peace and security of such factors as humanitarian concerns, peacebuilding, development and structural conflict prevention. This was reflected in an increased number of open thematic debates on topics such as civilian protection, conflict prevention and even HIV/AIDS and in a shift in the balance of tasks and personnel in peacekeeping missions from overwhelmingly military to predominantly civilian. Most noticeably, perhaps, was the assumption in some cases by the UN of far-reaching 'transitional authority' responsibilities, where the Organization began to encroach on areas and activities that have been traditionally understood as being within the purview of governments alone. The first two such operations were in Namibia[6] and Cambodia[7] where the UN personnel engaged in such non-traditional peacekeeping functions as disarmament, demobilization and reintegration of former combatants, resettlement of refugees, police training and supervision, election monitoring and other transitional administrative tasks.

UN Transitions after the Cold War

From April 1989 to March 1990, the electoral component of the United Nations Transition Assistance Group (UNTAG) in Namibia, which oversaw the transition of Namibia to independence, was tasked with repealing any remaining discriminatory or restrictive laws, the release of political prisoners, and facilitating the peaceful return of refugees. The United Nations Transitional Authority in Cambodia (UNTAC), which was deployed from March 1992 to September 1993, had four major components: civilian administration, 'under the direct control of UNTAC',[8] military functions, including demobilization, the verification of the ceasefire, and monitoring the withdrawal of foreign troops; electoral functions, from organizing to conducting elections in Cambodia; and a human rights component, involving the investigation of complaints and developing and implementing a human rights programme. Throughout, it was insisted that 'the focal point of the UN relationship in Cambodia is the Supreme National Council, which, under the Agreement, is the "unique legitimate body and source of authority"', while Article 6 of the Agreement delegated to the UN '"all powers necessary" to ensure the implementation of the Agreement.'[9]

Another such operation – the United Nations Transitional Administration for Eastern Slavonia, Baranja and Western Sirmium (UNTAES) – took place in Eastern Slavonia[10] from 1996 to 1998, with Croatian acquiescence and largely at the insistence of and with strong support from the United States. The Transitional Administrator of UNTAES was given significant power: 'The transitional administrator alone would have the executive power and he would not have to obtain the consent of either the Council or the parties for his decisions.'[11] However, this power was to be devolved to Croatia in a two-phase exit strategy; first the civil administration functions, and second the executive functions, subject to satisfactory performance. A combination of unprecedented power on the part of the Transitional Administrator, a peace agreement accepted by both sides, and, perhaps more importantly, credible military backing from NATO, meant that this operation is generally seen as having achieved some of its main goals.

Clearly these operations were major undertakings, and the responsibilities of the UN in each case were daunting. As the tables below show, however, even by the standards of Cambodia or Eastern Slavonia, there are a number of features that distinguish the operations in Kosovo and East Timor from their 'transitional authority' predecessors. In these two new operations, the UN undertakes sweeping responsibilities unprecedented in scope and complexity for any international institution. The Security Council has, in both Kosovo and East Timor, vested in the UN complete legislative and executive authority over the territories and peoples concerned. In other words, the UN has been asked, as in a 'trusteeship', to be the government and is performing all the tasks one might expect of a government.

Building Peace in Kosovo

Responsibility for Kosovo was not only thrust upon the UN following a period in which the Organization had been actively sidelined, but it was done rather unexpectedly and at regrettably short notice, with the result that the most complex operation in the Organization's history had to be deployed, designed and negotiated (in that order) in under a month. Despite this inauspicious beginning, the enormity of the task at hand and the momentousness of this development for the Organization were widely recognized. Security Council Resolution 1244 of 10 June 1999 set up the UN Interim Administration Mission in Kosovo (UNMIK), encompassing the activities of three non-UN organizations under the UN's overall jurisdiction. This body consists of four substantive components or pillars: UN-led Interim Civil Administration, Humanitarian Affairs led by the UN High Commissioner for Refugees (UNHCR), Reconstruction led by the European Union (EU) and Institution Building led by the Organization for Security and Cooperation in Europe (OSCE).[12] The NATO-led international Kosovo Force (KFOR) provides the international security presence.

Since its deployment, UNMIK has assumed basic civilian administrative functions including: leading commissions in the areas of health, education, energy and public utilities and post and telecommunications; establishment of a legal framework; restoration of public services (including sanitation services, and repair of utilities and transportation infrastructure); humanitarian activities; institution-building (including media, police and political parties); reconstruction; demilitarization; human rights monitoring and institution-building; and the environment. The operation is issuing birth, marriage and death certificates and paying stipends and salaries to public service employees. An annual budget has been approved and UNMIK is now regularly using customs and tax revenues for expenses incurred by the Kosovo administration. A Joint Interim Administrative Structure (JIAS) has been established to allow joint administration by UNMIK and the people of Kosovo until elections can be held.

In December 1999 a controversy over the application of laws by judges and prosecutors was laid to rest with the decision that 'applicable law in Kosovo will consist of UNMIK regulations and the law that was in force in Kosovo before the province was stripped of its autonomy in 1989'.[13] UNMIK has passed over 40 regulations to date in areas such as law and order, legal currencies, customs services, tax collection, the creation of judicial, fiscal and other such institutions, appointments of judges and regional administrators, property rights, import of oil and other petroleum products, post and telecommunications services and the provision of micro-credit loans. The operation has also established a limited postal system and

UNMIK Police has established 42 police stations across Kosovo. Finally, UNMIK has even signed international agreements, such as a cross-border economic cooperation agreement with the former Yugoslav Republic of Macedonia, reached in early March 2000. In other words, UNMIK is functioning exactly like a government.

Building Peace in East Timor

A similar scenario is transpiring in East Timor. On 25 October 1999, the Security Council adopted Resolution 1271 establishing the UN Transitional Administration in East Timor (UNTAET), with the overall responsibility for the administration of East Timor, empowered to exercise all legislative and executive authority, including the administration of justice. The resolution included provisions to: provide security and maintain law and order; establish an effective administration; assist in the development of civil and social services; ensure the coordination and delivery of humanitarian assistance, rehabilitation and development assistance; support capacity-building for self-government; and assist in the establishment of conditions for sustainable development.[14]

UNTAET is under the overall authority of the Special Representative of the Secretary-General (SRSG)/Transitional Administrator and is composed of three pillars, namely a governance and public administration component, including an international police element with up to 1,640 police officers, a humanitarian assistance and emergency rehabilitation component, and a military component of up to 9000 troops and 200 military observers. Unlike UNMIK, in East Timor the UN also has – with the withdrawal of the multinational International Force for East Timor (INTERFET) – full responsibility for the international security presence. In other ways, however, the operations are remarkably similar. Like UNMIK, UNTAET has assumed civilian administration tasks, with the new National Consultative Council, headed by the SRSG, as the primary mechanism through which the East Timorese people participate. UNTAET has passed more than ten regulations including on issues like the central fiscal authority, a central payments office, a new taxation regime, use of currencies, commercial enterprises and transitional legal tender (the United States dollar). Public Service and Judicial Service Commissions have been established and already judges, police and others are being selected and are undergoing training. Public finance in UNTAET includes central bank functions as well as tax and tariff policy, revenue collection and customs arrangements. Talks are underway to allow UNTAET to replace Indonesia in the treaty institutions resulting from the Timor Gap Treaty of 1989.[15]

TABLE 1

UNMIK REGULATIONS, JULY 1999–FEBRUARY 2000

UNMIK regulations 1999 (UNMIK/REG/1999/—)

1. On the authority of the interim administration in Kosovo, 23 July 1999
2. On the prevention of access by individuals and their removal to secure public peace and order, 12 August 1999
3. On the establishment of the customs and other related services in Kosovo, 31 August 1999
4. On the currency permitted to be used in Kosovo, 2 September 1999
5. On the establishment of an ad hoc court of final appeal and an ad hoc office of the public prosecutor, 4 September 1999
6. On recommendations for the structure and registration of the judiciary and prosecution service, 7 September 1999
7. On appointment and removal from office of judges and prosecutors, 7 September 1999
8. On the establishment of the Kosovo corps, 20 September 1999
9. On the importation, transport, distribution and sale of petroleum products for and in Kosovo, 20 September 1999
10. On the repeal of discriminatory legislation affecting housing and rights in property, 13 October 1999
11. On exercising control over payments facilities and services, 13 October 1999
12. On the provision of postal and telecommunications services in Kosovo, 14 October 1999
13. On the licensing of non-bank micro-finance institutions in Kosovo, 16 October 1999
14. On the appointment of regional and municipal administrators, 21 October 1999
15. On the temporary registration of privately operated vehicles in Kosovo, 21 October 1999
16. On the establishment of the central fiscal authority of Kosovo and other related matters, 6 November 1999
17. On the approval of the Kosovo consolidated budget and authorizing expenditures for the period 1/9 to 31/12/99, 6 November 1999
18. On the appointment and removal from office of lay-judges, 10 November 1999
19. On the prohibition of casino-type gambling in Kosovo, 12 November 1999
20. On the banking and payments authority of Kosovo, 15 November 1999
21. On the bank licensing, supervision and regulation, 15 November 1999
22. On the registration and operation of non-governmental organizations in Kosovo, 15 November 1999
23. On the establishment of the housing and property directorate and the housing and property claims commission, 15 November 1999
24. On the law applicable in Kosovo, 12 December 1999
25. Amending UNMIK regulation no. 1999/91 on the authority of the interim administration in Kosovo, 12 December 1999
26. On the extension of periods of pretrial detention, 22 December 1999
27. On the approval of the Kosovo consolidated budget and authorizing expenditures for the period 1/1 to 31/12/2000, 27 December 1999

UNMIK Regulations 2000 (UNMIK/REG/2000/—)

1. On the approval Kosovo joint interim administrative structure, 14 January 2000
2. On excise taxes in Kosovo, 22 January 2000
3. On sales tax in Kosovo, 22 January 2000
4. On the prohibition against inciting to national, racial, religious or ethnic hatred, discord or intolerance
5. On the establishment of a hotel, food and beverage service tax, 1 February 2000
6. On the appointment and removal from office of international judges and international prosecutors

TABLE 1 Continued

7. Amending UNMIK regulation no. 1999/16 on the establishment of the central fiscal authority of Kosovo and other related matters
8. On the provisional registration of businesses in Kosovo
9. On the Establishment of the Administrative Department of Local Administration
10. On the Establishment of the Administrative Department of Health and Social Welfare
11. On the Establishment of the Administrative Department of Education and Science
12. On the Establishment of the Administrative Department of Public Services
13. On the Central Civil Registry
14. On the Extension of Custody of Persons Held Pending the Petition For Extradition
15. On the Establishment of the Administrative Department of Justice
16. On the Registration and Operation of Political Parties in Kosovo

The Unique Cases of Kosovo and East Timor

The level of responsibility thrust upon the UN in Kosovo and East Timor is unprecedented. As the tables above and below illustrate, the nature and extent of the UN's authority in these cases is substantially more than before. In Namibia, the focus was on ensuring 'the early independence of Namibia through free and fair elections under the supervision and control of the United Nations',[16] and in Eastern Slavonia on the 'peaceful reintegration of the region into the Croatian legal and constitutional system'.[17] In Cambodia the UN was tasked with the implementation of the Paris Agreement, 'including...the organization and conduct of free and fair elections and the relevant aspects of the administration of Cambodia'.[18] These operations were undertaken at a time when democracy-promotion efforts by the international community focused almost exclusively on the holding of free and fair elections. In recent years there has been a realization that premature elections neither solve conflicts nor provide easy exit points for the international community; rather they tend to either legitimate perpetrators of war crimes[19] or precipitate another round of violence initiated by the losers. Indeed, the elections in Cambodia were not without their detractors, and observers continue to question the electoral results in Eastern Slavonia. In neither Kosovo nor East Timor, therefore, will there be a rush to conduct premature elections and, as a result, the UN will most likely continue in its executive role for a longer period.

This greater level of responsibility is more than just a function of the legal tasks ascribed to the UN by these mandates. Equally important is that, in each case, the missions are being undertaken in provinces that have never enjoyed independence or functioning indigenous administrations (although there was a ten-year history of Kosovo Albanian parallel institutions that functioned informally and with mixed impact). There are thus no formal governments or officially representative interlocutors with whom to interact (although, in each case, there exist groups that enjoy certain popular legitimacy and work as counterparts to the UN – in some instances presenting political dilemmas for the UN). Moreover, in each case, the mass exodus of people from the territories immediately prior to the UN's assumption of authority means that there are at best rudimentary administrative structures and little indigenous capacity in place.

Thus, unlike in Cambodia, Namibia and Eastern Slavonia, where the UN in essence provided political oversight, legal direction and capacity-building services to a somewhat functional, pre-existing set of administrative institutions, in Kosovo and East Timor the UN has stepped into a political and administrative vacuum. In Cambodia, Namibia and Eastern Slavonia, the UN assumed the role of caretaker of a transition, whereas in Kosovo and East Timor it more closely resembles a midwife to new states.

The transitional authority mandates of UNMIK and UNTAET are in each case for a comprehensive peacebuilding operation with a primary focus on major elements of civilian administration, including development of civil and social services, reconstruction of key infrastructure, rehabilitation of war-affected populations, maintenance of law and order, training of police and judiciary and the establishment of conditions conducive to sustainable development. In each case the UN has been establishing law, deciding which currency is legal tender, signing international agreements and in many other respects performing the functions of a government. This represents a major change from the days when UN peace operations consisted of no more than interposing troops between two previously warring parties. Indeed, the term 'peacekeeping' becomes less and less an accurate rubric under which to understand all the activities in which the UN is engaged. Instead, it represents a subset of the responsibilities assigned to the UN in Kosovo and East Timor. As has been shown above, in addition to traditional security-related tasks, these mandates include major governance and development-oriented elements, as well as humanitarian tasks. Indeed, the only reason that this overwhelming peacebuilding/development orientation does not emerge more explicitly in the Security Council resolutions mandating UNMIK and UNTAET is that this would probably have jeopardized the approval of funding for these operations – particularly by the US Congress – from assessed peacekeeping budgets. However, these developments raise serious questions about the capacity of the UN to meet the challenges it now faces.

TABLE 2

COMPARISON OF TRANSITIONAL AUTHORITY MANDATES

	UNTAG	UNTAC	UNTAES	UNMIK	UNTAET
Enforcement					
Chapter VI	X	X			
Chapter VII			X	X	X
Administrative Authority					
Indirect (after signing of an Agreement and/or in conjunction with a domestic administrative body)	X	X	X		
Direct (imposed by resolution of the SC and not based on a preliminary domestic agreement)				X	X
Judicial Authority					
Repeal existing law	X	X			
Make and repeal electoral and local administrative law			X		
Make and repeal all law (including criminal)				X	X
Electoral					
Monitor and supervise	X	X	X	X	X
Establish electoral system	X	X	X	X	X
Democratization				X	X
Military					
Exercised by PKO in conjunction with existing forces	X	X			X
Multinational force			X	X	
Police					
Assist existing force and capabilities in the maintenance of law and order	X	X	X		
Provide capabilities (transitional police force) to maintain law and order				X	X
Judicial Capacity					
Pre-existing	X	X	X		
Administration of courts, development of legal policy, draft legislation, assess quality of justice				X	X
Human Rights					
Monitor and supervise		X			
Promote and protect			X		
International criminal court/investigate alleged human rights violations				X	X
Humanitarian Assistance					
Oversee the return of refugees and displaced persons	X	X	X		
Ensure the delivery of humanitarian assistance and protect the return and reintegration of displaced persons and refugees				X	X
Economic development					
Assist in economic reconstruction efforts			X		
Design and reconstruct key infrastructure and other economic reconstruction				X	X

TABLE 3

COMPARISON OF MANDATE REACH

Components	UNTAG	UNTAC	UNTAES	UNMIK	UNTAET
Electoral	X	X	X	X	X
Military	X	X	X	X	X
Police	X	X	X	X	X
Repatriation	X	X	X	X	X
Civil administration		X	X	X	X
Human rights		X	X	X	X
Rehabilitation		X	X	X	X
Judicial				X	X
Democratization and institution-building				X	X
Humanitarian assistance				X	X
Reconstruction: economic, financial and development				X	X
Governance					X
Public services					X

New Challenges

The major implications for the UN of these new challenges are as follows:

1. The assumption of these enormous, complex mandates is taking place in a context of huge budgetary and logistical constraints, massive arrears to the UN on the part of some member states, American reluctance to support new peace operations (articulated in Presidential Decision Directive 25), precipitously declining Overseas Development Assistance (ODA), the phasing out of gratis personnel and the apparent decline in the primacy of the Security Council to other regional bodies with respect to international peace and security. These constraints raise serious questions about the capacity of the UN to manage UNMIK and UNTAET.

2. The mandates of UNMIK and UNTAET involve important governance and development-oriented tasks. These are funded in part from the assessed peacekeeping budget, and therefore subject to the constant cycle of renewal and review by the Security Council, which means that the UN is performing development tasks through an entirely new mechanism. In each case, the development-oriented elements of these mandates were devised *ad hoc* and without much reliance on the UN's family of development and specialized agencies, or the tools and mechanisms for in-country coordination of development activities. This raises questions about the relationship between the primary organs of the UN. The world body's development activities have traditionally been overseen by the General Assembly and the Economic and Social

Council, and have not been subject to decision-making by the Security Council. The reliance of UNMIK and UNTAET on governance and development programmes mandated by the Security Council also raises concerns about the issues of continuity at the end of the mandate. The abrupt withdrawal of UNTAC from Cambodia put an end to many ongoing peacebuilding and development-oriented programmes, with negative consequences. A repeat of this action in the UN's new missions would have even more wide-ranging consequences in Kosovo and East Timor. Yet planning for a handover to civilian development actors is patchy at best.

3. In each case, non-UN actors are deeply involved in its missions. In Kosovo, the mandate includes actors like NATO, the EU and the OSCE. Indeed, for the first time the World Bank – which faced obstacles to becoming involved in Kosovo – justified its involvement on the basis of a Security Council resolution (1244).[20] In East Timor the Council recognizes that 'UNTAET will need to draw on the expertise and capacity of Member States, United Nations agencies and other international organisations, including the international financial institutions'. The involvement of other actors, political, economic and military – such as EU, OSCE, international financial institutions (IFIs), NATO and INTERFET – has been substantial from the very beginning of operations.

These factors combine to require three things of the UN that it will be challenged to provide. These relate to internal collaboration, external collaboration, and skill sets.

External Collaboration
The Kosovo mission, and to a lesser extent the East Timor mission, has required an unprecedented form and extent of collaboration with external organizations. In East Timor, the interaction between INTERFET and UNTAET had to be established on an *ad hoc* basis – though by the time INTERFET was phased out, there was little evidence of serious coordination problems. On the fundraising side, a tentative agreement has been reached with the World Bank for common presentation of Trust Funds which are focused on the reconstruction and budgetary issues, and the simultaneous launching of a humanitarian Consolidated Appeal – an untested initiative that could either prove an important innovation or raise unforeseen complications.

These challenges pale beside the complexity of integrating the OSCE, UNHCR and the EU into a UN-led mission structure in Kosovo. Early efforts in this regard required lengthy, detailed and complex political negotiations both at headquarters and in the field. From the outset, it was clear that the major challenge to the integrated mission concept would come from the fact that the different organizations, irrespective of their participation within UNMIK, came to the mission with varying philosophies, different and in some instances divergent concepts of operations, and strong organizational pressures to take on key strategic functions within post-conflict Kosovo. Further, not only do these organizations obviously have different management and political governance structures, there is no established mechanism through which they can solve policy differences at a headquarters level. This diminishes the prospects for achieving and sustaining policy coherence.

Internal Collaboration
While the success to date of the UN reform process has meant the breaking down of traditional barriers to information flow between core UN departments, and an improvement of relations both among UN agencies and between the agencies and the Secretariat,[21] the fact remains that many of these relationships are still characterized more by coordination than collaboration, and have yet to translate into a deep understanding by different elements of the UN system of the purposes, mandates, and capacities of counterpart departments or agencies. Even in the design phase, UNTAET and UNMIK required an unprecedented degree of cross-sectoral collaboration within the UN system. While the relevant departments and agencies, with strong direction from Louise Fréchette, the Deputy Secretary-General, have by and large made a good-faith effort to collaborate on mission design, in support of the Department of Peacekeeping Operations (DPKO), and DPKO itself has deliberately sought inputs from both the humanitarian and development parts of the UN, there are still major limits to the depth and quality of such exchanges. This is likely to be an area of increasing challenge as the missions become fully staffed and begin to perform more substantive functions in the development and governance area.

Furthermore, the integration of humanitarian and development components into these missions poses a new coordination challenge: how to marry pre-existing political, humanitarian and development coordination systems, each of which were developed largely independently and are characterized by discrete structures and reporting lines. Only recently have these mechanisms been called upon to function simultaneously; UNMIK and UNTAET have highlighted the somewhat overlapping purposes and functions of these mechanisms. This new coordination challenge arises from progress – but progress brings its own complications. Further work will be needed to sort out how these various coordination mechanisms will relate to one another in future operations.

Skill Sets and Recruitment

Because these new missions involve such a wide range of operational and planning tasks, the UN has been called upon to perform functions outside its traditional areas of expertise. It is not accidental that virtually all the senior positions in UNMIK are occupied by non-UN staff. This is not simply a function of Security Council politics, although that invariably plays a role in the selection of senior mission staff. Beyond politics, however, the make-up of the senior ranks of UNMIK reflects the fact that UN staff are not traditionally drawn from senior public service or political positions. The ranks of UN staff members with high-level experience in governing provinces or regions are slim. The UN is thus required to recruit, from among member states and agencies, personnel whose experience and qualifications are difficult to judge because they operate in professions with which DPKO and the Department of Political Affairs (DPA) are unfamiliar. Further, there is no established mechanism through which the UN's specialized agencies or the IFIs can assist DPKO in the identification of qualified personnel for the performance of development or administrative functions. (This is less of a problem on the humanitarian side, given both a higher level of regular interaction between DPKO and the Office for the Coordination of Humanitarian Affairs (OCHA) and the far lower numbers of humanitarian staff in both missions.)

The net result of these new developments is that in Kosovo and East Timor, the UN – at a time of unprecedented challenges to its authority, legitimacy, and prestige, with fewer headquarters resources than ever before, with outside personnel it struggles to recruit performing unfamiliar tasks, and in unprecedented and uncertain collaboration with outside organizations – is undertaking the two most ambitious operations it has ever tackled. On the success of this extraordinary challenge rests the future – surely precarious – of UN peace support operations, possibly of the Organization itself.

ACKNOWLEDGEMENTS

This contribution represents the personal opinions of the authors and does not in any way reflect the official position of the United Nations or the United Nations Development Programme. The authors wish to thank Karin Wermester of the International Peace Academy for research support.

NOTES

1. The 50-year evolution of UN peace operations is frequently described in terms of generations, with each successive generation of operations growing in ambition and complexity. 'First generation' operations, characterized by relatively simple post-truce interpositions of peacekeeping forces with the consent of the parties, for example UNDOF (established after the 1973 Middle East war to maintain the ceasefire between Israel and Syria and to supervise disengagement), were followed by a second, more complex generation

in places like UNAVEM in Angola (established by Resolution 626 (1988) in order to verify implementation of the tripartite agreements reached in 1988 between Angola, Cuba and South Africa regarding the implementation of Resolution 435 (1978) on Namibia's independence and the withdrawal of Cuban troops from Angola. With the signing of the Peace Accords for Angola in May 1991, UNAVEM's mandate was extended in order to verify the implementation of the Accords and supervise the holding of free and fair elections. The mission was baptized UNAVEM II, and was established by Resolution 696 in May 1991); ONUSAL in El Salvador (established in July 1991 to verify the implementation of all agreements between the government and the FMLN. It completed its mandate on 30 April 1995) and UNMIH in Haiti (established just after the signing of the Governor's Island Agreement in July 1993, in September 1993 by Resolution 967 (1993), which called on the parties to renounce violence as a means of political expression and implement the Agreement. The Agreement included provision for United Nations assistance for modernizing the armed forces of Haiti and for establishing a new police force. By 1995, after a coup and the subsequent deployment of a multinational force in Haiti in 1994, UNMIH's mandate was extended to include significant police components which included the creation of the new Haitian National Police, and civilian affairs activities ranging from the provision of assistance to the national electricity company, to the development of a disaster response training programme). This new generation of operations was made possible by the fading of Cold War animosities and deployed as part of negotiated political solutions – which the peacekeepers were tasked with implementing – with the consent of the parties. 'Third generation' operations were primarily enforcement operations taken under Chapter VII of the UN Charter without the full consent of the parties, usually in the context of internal conflicts and humanitarian crises and characterized by even more complex mandates with less clear-cut objectives than in previous periods.

2. UNOSOM I (April 1992–March 1993) was mandated to monitor the ceasefire in Mogadishu and to provide protection and security for UN personnel, equipment and supplies at seaports and airports, including escorting deliveries of humanitarian supplies from there to distribution points in the city and its immediate environs. In August 1992, it was strengthened to enable it to protect humanitarian convoys and distribution centres throughout Somalia. In December 1992 (S/RES/1992/794) the Council authorized member states to form the Unified Task Force (UNITAF) to establish a safe environment for the delivery of humanitarian assistance, working in coordination with UNOSOM I. The UNITAF Chapter VII operation (Operation *Restore Hope*) was led by the US with participation by military units from 24 other member states. It was highly successful in its mission. In May 1993 the transition was made from UNITAF to UNOSOM II, mandated to take appropriate action, including enforcement measures, to establish throughout Somalia a safe environment for humanitarian assistance. To that end, UNOSOM II was to complete, through disarmament and reconciliation, the task begun by UNITAF for the restoration of peace, stability, law and order. It was also entrusted with assisting the Somali people in rebuilding their economy and social and political life. Unfortunately, the security situation was unpredictable and unrest ongoing. The deaths of 23 Pakistani peacekeepers led to a revision of the mandate to include the apprehension of those responsible. The disastrous US Rangers raid in October 1993, where a number of US servicemen were killed, led directly to the withdrawal of US troops. The fact that the troops involved in the raid were under US command was obscured by a US Administration deeply alarmed by domestic public reaction to the deaths. UNOSOM II was finally withdrawn in early March 1995.

3. UNPROFOR was established by Resolution 743 on 21 February 1992 as an interim arrangement to create the conditions for peace and security required for the negotiation of an overall settlement of the Yugoslav crisis. Its mandate (subsequently renewed on eight occasions between 1993 and 1995) was initially to ensure that the UN Protected Areas in Croatia were demilitarized and that residents were protected from fear of armed attack. Its mandate was extended to include Bosnia and Herzegovina later in 1992, and was tasked with ensuring the security and functioning of the Sarajevo airports and, under Chapter VII, the delivery of humanitarian assistance (by Resolution770 [1992]). The Council also requested that UNPROFOR 'take all necessary measures' to enforce the 'no-fly zone' by Resolution

816 (1993). UNPROFOR became the guardian of the ill fated 'safe-areas' (Resolution 836 [1993]). In addition, UNPROFOR established a presence on the Macedonian border, essentially as a preventive measure in order to maintain confidence and stability in the region. With the signing of the Dayton Peace Agreement in December 1995, UNPROFOR's mandate was extended until the end of January 1996 by Resolution 1026 in order to ensure the transition to the multinational military implementation force (IFOR).

By S/RES/1031 (15 December 1995) the Security Council, acting under Chapter VII of the Charter, authorized member states to establish IFOR to help ensure compliance with the provisions of the Dayton Agreement. IFOR was composed of ground, air and maritime units from NATO and non-NATO nations and was authorized to take all necessary measures to ensure compliance with Dayton and to defend itself. In December 1996 a smaller Stabilization Force (SFOR) replaced IFOR. SFOR's mandate is to continue the work of IFOR and to maintain a secure and stable environment, actively supporting civilian implementation and the work of the International Police Task Force (IPTF) and the United Nations Mission in Bosnia and Herzegovina (UNMIBH).

4. UNAMIR was originally established to help implement the Arusha Peace Agreement signed by the Rwandese parties on 4 August 1993. With the outbreak of the genocide and the renewed advance of the RPF in April 1994, UNAMIR was disastrously drawn down before public pressure resulted in the Security Council expanding the force and adjusting the mandate so that it could contribute to the security and protection of refugees and civilians at risk, through means including the establishment and maintenance of secure humanitarian areas, and the provision of security for relief operations to the degree possible. Following the ceasefire and the installation of the new Government, the tasks of UNAMIR were further adjusted and its mandate came to an end on 8 March 1996.

5. The practice of so-called subcontracting of peace operations has assumed various forms, with implementation by *ad hoc* coalitions frequently dominated by one member in: Iraq/Kuwait (from 16 January to 28 February 1991, a coalition of UN member states led by the US, acting in accordance with S/RES/678 (29 November 1990) but not under the control of or direction by the UN, conducted Chapter VII offensive military operations – Operation *Desert Storm* – against Iraq to force its withdrawal from Kuwait); Somalia (Operation *Restore Hope* conducted by UNITAF, led by the USA, from December 1992 to May 1993); Haiti (Operation *Uphold Democracy* conducted by a multinational force consisting of 28 countries and led by the USA, from September 1994 to March 1995); Albania (Operation *Alba* was led by Italy from February to April 1997); the Central African Republic (From February 1997 to April 1998 an inter-African force (MISAB) was deployed); Rwanda (the French-led Operation *Turquoise* was only nominally multinational, with token troop contributions by approximately 5 Francophone countries. It lasted from 23 June to 21 August); in East Timor (Australian-led INTERFET intervened in September 1999 and handed over to UNTAET in February 2000); and by regional organizations, in Georgia (CIS peacekeeping operation was deployed to monitor the ceasefire, alongside the pre-existing UN observer mission (UNOMIG)); in Liberia, Sierra Leone and Guinea-Bissau (the ECOWAS Ceasefire Monitoring Group [ECOMOG]), led by Nigeria in all cases except Guinea-Bissau, militarily intervened in the Liberian conflict in 1990, in Sierra Leone in 1997 and in Guinea-Bissau in November 1998).

6. From April 1989 to March 1990, UNTAG's mandate (established by Resolutions 435 (1978) and Resolution 632 [1989]) was to ensure the early independence of Namibia through free and fair elections under the supervision and control of the UN. The electoral component of the mission included the repeal of all remaining discriminatory or restrictive laws, the release of political prisoners, and permitting the peaceful return of refugees. The second, military component of the mission required ensuring the cessation of all hostile acts, demobilizing troops, and aiding in the withdrawal of South African troops. It is widely regarded as one of the most successful UN peace operations.

7. Established to ensure the implementation of the Paris Peace Agreement signed in October 1991, UNTAC's mandate included the organization and conduct of free and fair elections and the relevant aspects of the administration of Cambodia during the interim period. The mission was deployed from March 1992 to September 1993.

8. Annex 1, Paris Peace Agreement.
9. Report of the Secretary-General on Cambodia, S/23613, 19 February 1992.
10. UNTAES, the UN Transitional Administration for Eastern Slavonia, Baranja and Western Sirmium, was established by Resolution 1037 (1996) with the mandate of reintegrating the regions into the Croatian legal and constitutional system, effectively 'governing' the region during the transition via the establishment of a Transitional Council. Under S/RES/1037 (15 January 1996), IFOR was authorized to provide UNTAES with close air support. IFOR – and SFOR, its successor – assisted in the establishment of a safe and secure environment in the relevant area, thus enabling UNTAES to proceed with the implementation of its mandate. The fact that UNTAES was backed by a credible military force is widely regarded as having contributed significantly to the success of the mission. UNTAES was terminated in January 1998.
11. Report of the Secretary-General pursuant to the Security Council Resolution 1025 (S/1995/1028, 13 December 1995)
12. See also on UNMIK 'Financing of the United Nations Interim Administration Mission in Kosovo: Report of the Secretary-General', A/54/494 22 October 1999.
13. Bringing Peace to Kosovo. UNMIK at Nine Months. (http://www.un.org/peace/kosovo/pages/months.html)
14. See also on UNTAET 'letter dated 4 October 1999 from the Secretary-General addressed to the President of the Security Council' (S/1999/1025 of 4 October 1999), and 'Financing of the United Nations Mission in East Timor: Report of the Secretary-General' (A/54/380 of 21 September 1999).
15. See Report of the Secretary-General on the United Nations Transitional Administration in East Timor, (S/2000/53 of 26 January 2000).
16. Resolution 435 (1978).
17. S/1995/1028, 13 December 1995 and Resolution 1037 (1996).
18. Agreement for the Comprehensive Political Settlement of the Cambodian Conflict, (Paris, 23 October 1991) and Resolution 745 (12 February 1992).
19. For example, every election held in Bosnia since 1990 (with a few exceptions at municipality level) has resulted in victory for parties whose appeal is exclusively to voters of a single ethnic group.
20. Authors' discussion with World Bank officials, October 1999.
21. Tools to this effect include: *inter alia* the Strategic Framework, the Resident Coordinator System, the Inter-Agency Standing Committee, the UN Executive Committees, Common Country Assessments, Thematic Groups and improvements to the UN Development Assistance Framework.

Truth Commissions and the Quest for Justice: Stability and Accountability after Internal Strife

CHANDRA LEKHA SRIRAM

In the burgeoning literature of transition after internal strife, sometimes referred to as 'transitology', numerous attempts have been made to justify what is almost universally regarded as the second best outcome, after punishment, in the quest for accountability for past abuses: the truth commission. Scholars frequently argue that while the commission does indeed entail some sacrifice of justice for the sake of stability, it possesses some virtues, in particular the official acknowledgement of wrongdoing. Others have attempted to argue for the inherent moral virtues of these commissions, suggesting that they have the merit of promoting national reconciliation.

This contribution argues that the choice is not a simple one of 'punish or pardon', but rather that there exists a continuum of options available to transitional regimes and international actors who seek to assist them, ranging from complete amnesty through commissions of inquiry and lustration, to wide-ranging prosecutions. Further, each transitional regime's choices are determined by the nature of the peace settlement. The essay delves first into three factors that appear to make accountability more or less possible: the international political and historical context, the history of past abuses, and the nature of civil–military relations and/or the balance of power between the government and the opposition.

While these three factors affect the degree to which accountability is possible, some strategies may be used to achieve greater accountability or, if desired, greater stability. This essay investigates the more nuanced trade-offs of transition, delving into the advances that a nascent democracy may be able to achieve by seeking the third path of a truth commission. The merits of this approach may appear to be obvious: it is generally thought that agreeing to amnesties and seeking the 'truth' rather than 'justice' will reduce the risks of military unrest and coups. This, however, is merely the negative argument. I seek to argue that limiting, though not jettisoning, accountability, may enable transitional regimes (and by extension external aid-givers) to pursue greater levels of reform of the security forces, in particular by cutting their budgets and personnel and by instituting wide-ranging reforms in doctrine and education.

Elsewhere I have examined five case studies in detail in addition to 26 nutshell cases,[1] identifying factors that make accountability more or less feasible in different contexts. This analysis of cases ranging from South America to Southern Europe demonstrates the striking similarity of the options from which transitional regimes may choose. While reformers need not cater excessively to the security forces, recognizing their corporate interests and incentives may enable new, often fragile, regimes not only to avert crises but to institute healthier civil–military relations in the long run.

The Basic Dilemma: Justice vs. Stability

The debate over 'law and lustration', or the treatment of wrongdoers by successor (often democratic) state regimes, has focused on the specific trade-offs faced by these regimes.[2] The basic dilemma is this: the transitional or successor regime is faced with demands to prosecute or otherwise significantly address serious human rights violations or war crimes of a prior regime. That regime, previously authoritarian and frequently dominated by the military, will be reluctant to relinquish authority until key participants are granted amnesty and may maintain sufficient power, often through the continued control of the military, which it can employ to intimidate the successor government.

The majority of the 'peace vs. justice' and 'law and lustration' literature recognizes the practical obstacles presented by recalcitrant elements of repressive regimes, but emphasizes the importance of coming to terms with the past in some form. This literature stresses the importance of revealing the truth, so that future actors cannot deny what occurred or paper over the gravity of their human rights violations.[3] The literature also provides reasons for pursuing punishment: punishing violations serves as a deterrent, and there is some merit in achieving justice in itself.[4] Much of the literature recognizes that compromises are inevitable and that outcomes such as truth commissions combined with amnesties are common.[5] Some of the literature also recognizes the possibility that pursuing justice may be actively harmful to transitional regimes in ways beyond the ill-effects of clashes with recalcitrant militaries.[6]

This literature also adduces moral reasons for prosecution and truth-telling, and places these above arguably utilitarian concerns of stability. This essay does not seek to refute the claim that pursuing lower degrees of accountability entails some degree of moral compromise. It seeks instead to highlight the limits placed on transitional regimes and to demonstrate the benefits which some trade-offs might reap in the realm of institutional, political and military reform, which can, in turn, yield significant benefits for future protection of democracy, stability, and human rights.[7]

Choices of Transition

Much of the existing literature on justice in transitional states consists of case studies documenting the choices made by governments, and following closely their implementation or non-implementation, and their outcomes.[8] These studies often competently examine the agonizing choices faced by successor regimes and the compromises that democratic regimes may make with hold-over militaries in particular. What seems to be missing from these studies, however, is a systematic analysis of the forces that drive these outcomes. Drawing on the literature on democratization and the 'third wave', this essay focuses particularly on the implications of extant civil–military relations, the history of the conflict and past abuses, and the international context for transitional justice.[9]

The factors considered here are the following: first, the protractedness and intensity of the prior conflict or abuses, in other words the nature and extent of repression, human rights abuses, and the impact of war; second, the prior state of civil–military relations, as well as subsequent reform; and third, the effect of international factors and politics on the peace/justice process.

Concerning the nature of human rights violations, it would appear *ex ante* that a long and bloody conflict could either contribute to the prosecution of crimes, or contribute to obstructing their prosecution. Certainly the desire for justice on the part of the victims could increase with the aggregation of abuses;[10] on the other hand, exhaustion from the conflict could lead many to compromise with former abusers and to grant them amnesty. Arguments have been made that the reason for the difficulty in pursuing prosecutions in Argentina, or for the granting of amnesty in Uruguay, was that the sheer number of victims and perpetrators made pursuing justice unwieldy and risky.

Regarding the civil–military relations/'balance of forces' nexus, it seems obvious that where a military establishment has kept a civilian government subordinate, or where the government was a military one, the transition and prosecutions will be more difficult, since the perpetrators will be in possession of the power to obstruct change. Similarly, the degree to which a military has reformed may affect the degree of justice possible. And as noted below, military reform and the pursuit of justice may be traded off against one another while simultaneously recognizing the corporate interests of the military.[11] In addition, the relative strengths of government and opposition/guerrilla groups will be important, as they will affect the amount of leverage each group has in a transition, negotiated or otherwise. Civilian opposition may also be led by political parties or human rights NGOs or church groups, placing pressure at pivotal moments on repressive regimes.

The third factor affecting transitions relates to international involvement in a conflict and its resolution. Shifts in the structure of international politics could also affect the nature of transitions. International factors may be permissive of or more directly manipulative of regime change.[12] Regimes may change because the external environment has changed: for example, a superpower patron may cease to support a repressive regime. This could happen as a result of shifting norms, as a result of examples set by neighbours, in response to pressure such as aid conditionality, or in reaction to the forces of transnational non-state actors.[13] While permissive conditions such as the end of the Cold War[14] are certainly important in that they create unique historical opportunities for change, such changes are rare and difficult to predict.

The Players in Transitions

Two distinct sets of actors may be involved in framing strategies for transitions: international actors such as the United Nations (UN) or strong actors like the United States and former Soviet Union, and the transitional states themselves. International actors can have significant effects on transitions in several ways. First, they could pressure regimes to liberalize, or warring factions to negotiate, through 'good offices' or more active negotiations such as those undertaken by the 'Friends of the Secretary-General' in Cambodia and El Salvador. Such actors can condition aid on altered policies. These actions may help tip the 'balance of force' if not in favour of the opposition, at least in favour of negotiation. Finally, these international actors can provide funds for mechanisms of accountability, such as the significant contributions made to the Salvadoran Truth Commission by the UN, and in particular member states like the US. The democratizing regimes themselves may wish to develop strategies to pursue accountability. However, they will most likely also be concerned with maintaining stability. This will, of course, be more important where there has been significant military involvement in or domination of politics. Militaries may be eased out of power only with certain guarantees which will be discussed below.

Nature of the Conflict and Violations

The duration and intensity of a conflict may affect the choices available to a transition in a number of ways. An intense conflict may reach a stalemate in which, out of exhaustion, the parties are more amenable to political compromises. Simultaneously, however, a prolonged conflict may mean that there are a large number of victims and perpetrators, such that while the demand for accountability may be intense, the obstacles to judicial or other action may also be greater. It has been argued that the vast extent of the violations in Argentina hampered accountability while the lesser extent in Honduras made accountability more feasible; only mixed evidence supports this claim.[15]

Compromises are more likely to be achieved when the parties reach a 'hurting stalemate': the conditions are most 'ripe' for a peace accord when parties to a civil conflict have reached a point where both sides have become exhausted and neither side can 'win'.[16] Stalemates may take some time to be reached or recognized: both sides need to have lost faith in the possibility of a military victory and seek a way to cut their losses through a negotiated compromise.[17] In such situations, parties may find the use of third party mediators especially helpful.[18] Many have argued that El Salvador in late 1989 had reached such a stalemate, so that international mediation was more likely to yield results. Alternatively, exhaustion may even incite an authoritarian regime not faced with a strong military opponent to initiate transition. However, prolonged conflicts also frequently generate more victims, making a reckoning significantly more risky. Victims and their families may clamour for punishment, but where there are a large number of powerful perpetrators objecting, repression may also have pervaded society and collaboration with the perpetrators of abuses may have been widespread.[19] In such cases, an approach like the selective prosecutions in Argentina might be pursued. Thus accountability may be particularly hard to seek in instances where repression was prolonged and/or intense. The form the repression took also matters: disappearances may be more difficult to overlook because of the trauma felt by not knowing the locations of loved ones; outright killings may be brutal, but at least this issue is in some ways resolved.

Pressures on a transitional regime may derive from a regional and/or international organization and/or a superpower. Transitional regimes may be subject to the influences of either a regional power or a great power: in Latin America, this was frequently the United States. The influence of a great power may cut both ways: the United States was heavily involved in the domestic and military politics of its Latin American neighbours, frequently to the detriment of human rights.[20] Nonetheless Congressional opinion occasionally led American policy to emphasize human rights. While this latter policy was not always successful, or of a high priority, the political landscape changed significantly with the end of the Cold War.[21] Washington's conceptualization of its interests in the region changed significantly: it no longer saw communism as a global geo-strategic threat, and thus concerns that regional allies and military aid recipients were non-democratic or abusive of human rights came to the fore. This shift in interests or the conception of interests meant that American influence was, in many cases, changing dramatically to encouraging peace accords and promoting human rights.

Institutions may help promote peace agreements and/or human rights accountability in two related ways. First, they may help lower transactions costs and thus facilitate negotiations,[22] while acting as guarantors of peace agreements through monitoring and implementation bodies (for example, the peace negotiations in El Salvador created the transitional body COPAZ [Commission for the Consolidation of Peace]).[23] Second, institutions may help induce agreements by altering the incentives of the parties. Through the skilful use of carrots and sticks such as aid or the denial of it, external actors may manipulate parties. Institutions such as the UN may have fewer direct aid dollars to use as carrots or sticks, but may still be important in creating programmes and funnelling aid dollars into post-conflict development. The global spread of the norms of human rights and democracy may play a subsidiary role, but are not dealt with in detail here.[24]

Balance of Forces, Civil–Military Relations and Corporate Interests

It is tautological to say that regimes where militaries are subordinate to civilians are regimes where militaries do not intervene in politics. Of greater interest is why, after soldiers have intervened in politics, directly or indirectly, they might choose to withdraw. At issue is what sort of resistance from below might push a military to withdraw from politics and how much opposition the military brass hats will allow. This can be treated in terms of the balance of forces and the corporate interests of the military.

The 'balance of forces' level of analysis itself contains two elements: civil–military relations and the relative strengths of state security forces and resistance (for example, guerrilla) groups. The view that there is something unique about militaries in comparison to other institutions, even highly disciplined and hierarchalized state structures, is now widely accepted. The military, so the conventional wisdom goes, is separated from the rest of society by virtue of its education, socialization and training, by the values assumed by its members, and by its extremely rigid and vertical hierarchy.[25] However, while this separation and specialization can make for 'good' professionalism in some countries, it can make for 'bad' or praetorian professional militaries in some developing countries.[26]

In many (although not all) developing countries, particularly in Latin America, the traditional isolation of the military from society was compounded by the effects of the so-called Doctrine of National Security (DNS). The DNS can be seen as a direct result of the ideological and geopolitical struggle between the superpowers in the Cold War era. The US came to perceive a security threat as deriving not simply from external attack but from internal, inevitably viewed as 'communist', subversion. American security policy with respect to Latin America was, therefore, concerned with aiding local governments and militaries in combating such perceived internal subversion.[27] This strategy resulted in a series of mutual defence pacts and training by the US military of various local militaries,[28] and the provision of aid to local armies to face local conflicts and subversion.[29] Despite some shifts in application, the doctrine remained intact into the Ronald Reagan administration between 1980 and 1988.[30] The content of the DNS itself helped structure much of the repression that many of these regimes undertook in the name of 'security'. The communist threat was thought to be everywhere, and could even come from internal subversives.[31]

Guerrilla groups are not the only actors that might oppose military or otherwise repressive regimes. Civilian opposition may come in the form of human rights and other NGOs, opposition political parties or other social networks of resistance. Civic traditions and various civilian interactions and organizations might serve as a shield against authoritarian rule, or help eventually to topple it.

Even before authoritarian and/or military regimes step down, the question of the relative strengths of government and opposition is a salient one. Elites do not operate in a vacuum; their hold on power will depend on the degree to which they have consolidated and institutionalized it and the degree of opposition offered by other societal forces. Regimes may not simply choose to leave power, but rather, the transition may be initiated by the shifting nature of domestic politics and power alliances.[32]

Where a military/authoritarian regime has actually been ousted, it will be in a particularly weak position vis-à-vis the forces of reform. However, most transitional situations are more nuanced. Even where the military remains relatively strong within an authoritarian regime, it may not necessarily oppose a democratic transition: it might even lead the transition if it views such a transition as being in its interests.[33]

Nonetheless, the military will be concerned to protect its own interests: this will affect the level of accountability for past abuses that can be achieved, and may also limit the extent of other reforms that civilians can implement. Thus while the factors enumerated here will be examined for their role in making accountability more or less feasible, a more dynamic approach is also needed which recognizes that the achievable level of accountability is partly manipulable. Strategies of transition entail some degree of trading accountability for goods that might make stability more likely.

Stability, Transitions and Reform: Addressing and Preventing Abuses

While nearly all transitional regimes have experienced some sort of truth-telling/investigatory effort, this does not mean that prosecutions and other efforts at accountability have been entirely jettisoned, but rather that they have frequently been limited procedurally or through other means. Thus the truth-telling effort has generally been the most wide-ranging effort to address the past, while other efforts at accountability may be limited as other features of reform are pursued.

If, then, one seeks to sacrifice some measure of justice to some measure of accountability, what does this entail? What sorts of reform measures might enable the nascent regime to entrench itself more deeply? Not surprisingly, these sorts of measures are the type that elements of the old regime will resist, such that other measures, like extreme accountability, may have to be curtailed.

Obviously, where a military establishment has kept a civilian government subordinate, or where the government was a military one, the transition and prosecutions will be more difficult, since the perpetrators will be in possession of the power to halt change. Furthermore, reform of the military and the pursuit of justice may be traded off against each other. The 'corporate interests' of the military are likely to be protected in at least one of three ways: the protection of members of the armed forces from prosecution, the maintenance of large military budgets, and the defence of institutional autonomy. Progress may be achieved on one or two, but probably not on all three fronts.

Strategies of Transition

The array of concerns that must be addressed in developing strategies for transitions generally remain relatively constant: how can the new regime ensure stability, institute reform to prevent future abuses, *and* be responsive to the demands for accountability for past violations? In many societies, both the perpetrators of abuses and the principal obstacles to reform and accountability are the security forces. The literature on military intervention, the factors that encourage militaries to go 'back to the barracks', and democratization all help to illuminate the issues at stake for new regimes and militaries.[34] Militaries are most concerned about their 'corporate interests'; this fact holds in times of transition. Alfred Stepan sees three issue-areas of concern: how the new regime handles the legacy of human rights violations, how it deals with the organizational mission, structure and control of the military, and how it handles the military budget.[35] A closer examination of cases reveals the compromises that transitional regimes must make in arenas of deep concern to militaries. Encroachment on one traditional area of military power (say, the budget) will likely be simultaneous with significant compromise in another area (say, accountability).

Militaries and Transitions

Militaries take care to protect their corporate interests during periods of transition. Thus, one would expect them to take measures to ensure their continued institutional autonomy, sufficient budgets and the protection of members of the armed forces from retribution for past deeds.[36] However, some militaries may be more concerned about some of these interests than others. In Argentina, Honduras and El Salvador, members of the military were at various points subject to some degree of retribution for past behaviour. At least part of the explanation may be that concern for corporate interests does not extend to all members, but generally pertains to the interests of the elite. Thus, the military itself is left intact, and many officers are left unpunished, while a few low-level individuals may be called to account for crimes of a prior regime, though Argentina is an interesting exception to this trend.[37] In Argentina, junta leaders were tried, and five were convicted, although they were later pardoned by a civilian president.

Trade-offs may be made among the three sorts of interests held by the military: institutional autonomy, treatment of its members and budgetary allocations. As Stepan argues, 'In a democratizing regime the degree of articulated contestation by the military is strongly affected by the extent to which there is intense dispute or substantial agreement' concerning the three issue areas listed above.[38] New regimes may be able to force compromise on some or all of these issues, but will often have to compromise as well. In order to force long-term institutional reform, punishment might be sacrificed. Alternatively, budgets might be maintained at an unnecessarily high level so that some form of reckoning with past abuses can take place.[39]

Conclusion

This contribution has examined three factors which affect the level of accountability that can be attained by transitional regimes: the international context, the balance of forces and the nature of past abuses, largely a function of the duration or intensity of the conflict or repression. Through an examination of 26 cases in Central and South America, southern and eastern Europe, Asia and Africa[40] some of which have been mentioned in this essay, I found that the first two factors appear to have been considerably more important than the third, which has largely anecdotal evidence to support it.

International factors seem to have worked to encourage transitions and frequently some level of accountability. First, the international context can create a permissive environment for political change. Such a historical moment occurred at the end of the Cold War, with the waning of the bipolar rivalry between the superpowers having a profound effect on states in their orbit. In the American sphere of influence, many states that had dogmatically followed the Doctrine of National Security, suddenly lacked an external bogeyman to justify internal repression. At the same time, the US became less supportive in military and economic terms, of some of its abusive client regimes. Washington began to push its former clients to change their behaviour, threatening to withhold crucial military aid if necessary. Moscow became even less supportive of its former clients, as many of its former repressive satellite regimes were toppled. International organizations like the UN and the Organization of American States (OAS) also played a central role in some of these transitions. In some of the Southern European cases, a desire to join NATO and/or the European Union (then the European Community) encouraged transitions and some limited redress of past abuses. International organizations have played a greater role more recently, as have NGOs, by embarrassing regimes for their poor human rights records, playing more active roles in negotiating peace accords and monitoring the implementation of these agreements.

In terms of the balance of forces between military and transitional regimes, it seems obvious that where a military remains strong and has no serious opposition, guerrilla or military, it will be in a stronger position to set the terms of its own withdrawal from power. Clearly this control extends to the matter of accountability, which is why self-amnesties by outgoing military dictatorships occur. This may not yet bar all prosecutions, as enterprising courts can occasionally find loopholes to enable them to pursue some measures of accountability. Attempts at such accountability, however, will likely be threatened by a military that refuses to stay in its barracks. What matters, therefore, is not only the balance of forces prior to and at the moment of transition, but the balance of forces shortly after the transition when such crucial decisions are being made.

Regarding the nature and extent of past abuses, it has been suggested, based on anecdotal evidence, that the extent of conflict or severity of repression may have some impact on the degree of accountability that is ultimately attained. However, the logic of these arguments frequently points in contrary directions. Some argue that having few violations would make pursuing prosecutions easier while numerous violations that beget numerous prosecutions tend to generate instability and ultimately fail to achieve their goals of justice. Others suggest that the very fact of extensive abuses generates a societal demand for action and forces accountability. However, upon closer examination of 26 cases, support for these claims remains anecdotal at best.

Claims about the ways that extant factors drive near-term outcomes run the risk of being not only static but overly deterministic. Further, they do not reflect the full nature of the choices that regimes actually confront. Instead, regimes and those who seek to assist them have some options with regard to transitional policies.

Militaries will be concerned not only with whether or not their members (especially officers) face punishment, but also with the continued maintenance of high military budgets and retaining control over doctrine, institutional structure and education. Not surprisingly, these areas of 'corporate concern' to the military are all areas where transitional regimes will try to take action. While the virtues of achieving 'justice' are obvious, we have also seen that there are perils both practical and normative. Furthermore, other goods like the entrenchment of stability and democracy might be furthered with measures such as the reduction of military forces and budgets, and educational and doctrinal reform that emphasizes the purely defensive role of the military, the subordination of the military to civilian leaders, and human rights norms.

This is not to say that accountability ought to be abandoned in pursuit of these other goods, but that regimes often rightly strike a delicate balance among several goods, seeking accountability and reform simultaneously. Lowered levels of one good will generally be necessary to achieve elevated (or any) levels of another good.

A somewhat surprising discovery arises from an examination of the outcomes in the various cases. Prosecution occurs much more frequently than the 'punish vs. pardon' debate would lead us to believe. It also occurs in tandem with other measures such as commissions of inquiry or lustration.

However, this does not mean that prosecution is both widespread and successful: many countries saw prosecutions curtailed by amnesties and other political and procedural roadblocks.

In the realm of transition, we see that all three of the issues which are traditionally of 'corporate' concern to militaries were subjects of action or significant debate by new regimes. In particular, reforms of institutions dealing with security were common, as well as accountability, if only at the lowest level in the form of 'naming names'. Budgetary levels appear to have been less salient, both in terms of actual change or salient governmental debate about them, although they were not completely insignificant.

The case studies do not provide us with strict causal logic, such as 'greater international involvement yields greater accountability'. They can only point out salient factors, as the substantive content of each affects the outcome. For example, one must know not only that international actors are involved but what their goals are. Causal arguments would be further muddled by the presence of an important intervening variable: the strategies that the regime (and international actors who seek to assist it) deploys with regard to the security forces. However, several important conclusions can be drawn from examining cases of countries in transition.

The key general lesson that one might draw from this examination of the dilemmas that transitional regimes face is that there is a continuum of options with no definitive one 'right' answer. At a practical level there is a continuum of options from which transitional regimes might choose. While their options may well be constrained by their particular circumstances, they are generally not completely without choices. The factors that this essay has discussed – international actors, the nature and extent of abuses, and the balance of forces – all play a role, but need not completely determine a country's fate.

Instead, a government may make strategic choices about what values it wishes or needs most to pursue. Extensive legal justice may not be accomplished in some cases, but only lesser measures of accountability like truth-telling or lustration/purification. However, at the same time a regime may pursue measures that will help entrench a new democracy, provide for future stability and safeguard human rights, through the reduction and reform of the security forces, so often the source of the most heinous human rights abuses.

One cannot generalize with any certainty, much less make predictions of law-like regularity, what 'type' of transitional situation results in what 'level' of accountability, because each state has a distinct history, culture and set of political problems. However, one can identify issues, factors and strategies of particular salience for transitional regimes, from which one can deduce likely policy choices. One can also identify salient factors that are permissive factors or barriers to greater accountability: the most important of these being international factors and the balance of forces, a less clear one being the nature of past abuses. These factors may be permissive or inhibitive. One cannot simply assume that because, for example, international players are involved in a transition then more accountability will automatically result. Instead, one must examine not just the fact that particular factors are salient but also the content of these factors, and one must ask what policies international actors are advocating and what resources they are contributing to these efforts. Similarly, we see that there are a number of 'goods' that regimes may wish to pursue, but that they may need to strike a delicate balance among these goals. Again, we cannot predict exactly what balance a state will or should strike but rather claim that some balance will have to be struck and identify the sorts of goods that will be exchanged in trade-offs (accountability, reform, budgetary levels).

This essay has sought to challenge the common treatment in the transitional justice literature of the peace/justice trade-off as overly simplistic, if not a false dichotomy. It has sought to illustrate the more nuanced set of choices that regimes face, and to describe the contexts and strategic choices that make accountability more or less possible. What we find through this examination is that there is a real continuum of options that dichotomies obscure. There are many practical options that transitional regimes may choose short of full prosecution, although these options will be somewhat constrained by the context. Regimes may have to make certain strategic trade-offs to achieve more or less accountability or stability, though this does not mean that one goal must be completely jettisoned in favour of another.

ACKNOWLEDGEMENTS

The author would like to thank Michael Doyle and Adekeye Adebajo for their invaluable advice and comments. Any mistakes are, of course, the sole responsibility of the author. The research underpinning this article was made possible by grants from SSRC-MacArthur, Princeton University, and the Institute for the Study of World Politics.

NOTES

1. Chandra Lekha Sriram, 'Truth, Justice, and Accountability: The Way that Transitional Regimes Address the Human Rights Violations of Previous Regime', PhD Dissertation, Princeton University Department of Politics, 2000.

2. See, for example, the papers in 'Symposium: Law and Lustration: Righting the Wrongs of the Past', in *Law and Social Inquiry*, Winter 1995, Vol.20, No.1, esp. Peter Siegelman, 'The Problems of Lustration: Prosecution of Wrongdoers by Democratic Successor Regimes'; Stanley Cohen, 'State Crimes of Previous Regimes: Knowledge, Accountability, and the Policing of the Past'; Luc Huyse, 'Justice after Transition: on the Choices Successor Elites Make in Dealing with the Past'; Margaret Popkin and Naomi Roht-Arriaza, 'Truth As Justice: Investigatory Commissions in Latin America'; and Lynn Berat and Yossi Shain, 'Retribution or Truth-Telling in South Africa? Legacies of the Transitional Phase'. See also Naomi Roht-Arriaza (ed.), *Impunity and Human Rights in International Law and Practice*, Oxford: Oxford University Press, 1995. Finally, for an excellent compilation of case studies, documents, and general considerations of the normative issues, see Neil J. Kritz (ed.), *Transitional Justice: How Emerging Democracies Reckon with Former Regimes*, 3 vols., Washington, DC: United States Institute of Peace Press, 1995.
3. Cohen (n.2 above), pp.12–22.
4. Cohen (n.2 above), p.22; see also Naomi Roht-Arriaza, 'State Responsibility to Investigate and Prosecute Human Rights Violations in International Law', *California Law Review*, Vol.78 (1990), p.449.
5. Huyse (n.2 above), pp.52–3. El Salvador is an excellent example of this sort of compromise. See Popkin and Roht-Arriaza (n.2 above).
6. Huyse (n.2 above), pp.57–64.
7. Another facet of the literature that I do not address here is that discussing whether there is a duty under international law to pursue prosecutions. See, e.g., Nigel S. Rodley, 'The International Legal Consequences of Torture, Extra-Legal Execution, and Disappearance', and Ellen L. Lutz, 'After the Elections: Compensating Victims of Human Rights Abuses', in Ellen L. Lutz, Hurst Hannum, and Kathryn J. Burke (eds.), *New Directions in Human Rights*, Philadelphia: University of Pennsylvania Press, 1989. See also Carlos S. Nino, 'The Duty to Punish Past Abuses of Human Rights Put into Context: The Case of Argentina', *The Yale Law Journal*, Vol.100, 1991, pp.2619–21; Diane Orentlicher, 'Settling Accounts: The Duty to Prosecute Human Rights Violations of a Prior Regime', *Yale Law Journal*, Vol.100, 1991, pp.2537–615.
8. See n.2 above.
9. See Sriram (n.1 above) 'Truth, Justice, and Accountability', chapter 2 for greater detail. See generally Samuel P. Huntington, *The Third Wave: Democratization in the Late Twentieth Century*, Norman, OK: University of Oklahoma Press, 1991, pp.112–61; Huntington, 'How Countries Democratize', in *Political Science Quarterly*, Vol.106, No.4, 1991–92, pp.579–616; Jose Zalaquett in Neil J. Kritz (ed.), *Transitional Justice*, Vol.1, pp.18–19; Terry Lynn Karl, 'Dilemmas of Democratization in Latin America', *Comparative Politics*, Vol.23, October 1990, pp.1–21 and also Alexandra Barahona de Brito, *Human Rights and Democratization in Latin America: Uruguay and Chile*, Oxford: Oxford University Press, 1997.
10. Berat and Shain (n.2 above), p.176. Alfred Stepan, *Rethinking Military Politics: Brazil and the Southern Cone*, Princeton: Princeton University Press, 1988, p.64.
11. This I call generally institutional reform.
12. See Philippe C. Schmitter in 'The International Context of Contemporary Democratization', *Stanford Journal of International Affairs*, Fall/Winter 1993, pp.1–34.
13. I am grateful to Alexandra Barahona de Brito for this point.
14. On the role of the end of the Cold War, see generally Sriram (n.1 above), chapter 2.
15. Sriram (n.1 above), chapters 5 and 6.
16. I. William Zartman (ed.), *Elusive Peace: Negotiating an End to Civil Wars*, Washington, DC: Brookings 1995; Fen Osler Hampson, *Nurturing Peace: Why Peace Settlements Succeed or Fail*, Washington, DC: United States Institute of Peace Press, 1996, pp.11–21, 23, and passim.
17. Zartman (n.16 above), p.18.
18. Zartman (n.16 above), p.19.

19. This problem, compounded with serious concerns about the rule of law and retroactive justice, pervaded the Eastern European transitions.

20. See my discussion, in particular, of the impact of the Cold War and the Doctrine of National Security in the region, infra.

21. See Richard L. Millett, 'The Limits of Influence: the United States and the Military in Central America and the Caribbean', in Louis W. Goodman, Johanna S.R. Mendelson, and Juan Rial (eds.), *The Military and Democracy: The Future of Civil–Military Relations in Latin America*, Reading, MA: Lexington Books, 1990, pp.123–40. See also Hampson (n.16 above).

22. Robert O. Keohane, *After Hegemony: Cooperation and Discord in the World Political Economy*, Princeton: Princeton University Press, 1984. See Hampson (n.16 above), p.23, and on the Salvadoran case, pp.129–37.

23. Hampson (n.16 above), pp.221–22.

24. Schmitter (n.12 above), pp.22–3. Samuel P. Huntington, 'Reforming Civil–Military Relations', in Larry Diamond and Marc F. Plattner (eds.), *Civil–Military Relations and Democracy*, Baltimore: Johns Hopkins University Press, 1996, pp.3–11.

25. Morris Janowitz, *The Professional Soldier: A Social and Political Portrait*, Glencoe, IL: Free Press, 1960, pp.175–95; Samuel Finer, *The Man on Horseback: the Role of the Military in Politics*, Boulder, CO: Westview, 1962. See also Juan Rial, 'The Armed Forces and the Question of Democracy in Latin America', in Goodman *et al.*, *The Military and Democracy*, p.15; Barry Rubin, *Modern Dictators: Third World Coup-Makers, Strongmen, and Populist Tyrants*, New York: McGraw-Hill, 1987.

26. Michael Desch, 'Threat Environments and Military Missions', in Diamond and Plattner (n.24 above), pp.12–29.

27. Ernesto Lopez, *Seguridad Nacional y Sedicion Militar*, Buenos Aires: Editorial Legasa, 1987, pp.41–50; Frederick M. Nunn, *The Time of the Generals: Latin American Professional Militarism in World Perspective*, Lincoln, NE: University of Nebraska Press, 1992. See also Consejo Episcopal Latinamericano, *La Seguridad Nacional: Doctrina o Ideologia?*, Bogota: CELAM, no date given, pp.16–18.

28. Lopez (n.27 above), pp.55–63. See also Simon Lazara, *Poder Militar: origen, apogeo y transicion*, Buenos Aires: Editorial Legasa, 1988, p.29; Carina Perelli, 'The Military's Perception of Threat in the Southern Cone of Latin America', in Goodman *et al.*, *The Military and Democracy*, pp.94–101.

29. Moises Chernavsky, *La Seguridad nacional y el fundamentalismo democratico*, Buenos Aires: Centro Editor de America Latina, 1993, p.13.

30. Chernavsky (n.29 above), pp.13–20, discusses the DNS over time.

31. Lazara (n.28 above), pp.35–7; Juan Rial, 'Armies and Civil Society in Latin America', in Diamond and Plattner (n.24 above), pp.47–65; Perelli (n.28 above), pp.96–101; Virginia Gamba-Stonehouse, 'Missions and Strategy: The Argentine Example', in Goodman *et al.*, *The Military and Democracy*, p.165.

32. Gerardo L. Munck, *Authoritarianism and Democratization: Soldiers and Workers in Argentina*, 1976–83 University Park, PA: Pennsylvania State University Press, 1998.

33. Gabriel Aguilera, 'The Armed Forces, Democracy, and Transition in Central America', in Goodman *et al.*, *The Military and Democracy*, pp.24–31.

34. For key works, see Janowitz, *The Professional Soldier; Samuel Finer, The Man on Horseback: The Role of the Military in Politics*, Boulder, CO: Westview, 1962, 1988; Samuel P. Huntington, *The Soldier and the State: The Theory and Politics of Civil–Military Relations*, Cambridge, MA: Belknap/Harvard University Press, 1964; Stepan (n.10 above); Munck, *Authoritarianism and Democratization*; Lopez (n.27 above); Frederick M. Nunn, *The Time of the Generals: Latin American Professional Militarism in World Perspective*, Lincoln, NE: University of Nebraska Press, 1992; Lazara (n.28 above); Perelli (n.28 above); Aguilera (n.33 above), pp.24–31; David Pion-Berlin, 'Military Autonomy and Emerging Democracies in South America', *Comparative Politics*, Vol.25, No.1, October 1992, pp.83–102; Philip J. Williams and Knut Walter, *Militarization and Demilitarization in El*

Salvador's Transition to Democracy, Pittsburgh: University of Pittsburgh Press, 1997; Eric A. Nordlinger, *Soldiers in Politics: Military Coups and Governments*, Englewood Cliffs, NJ: Prentice-Hall, 1977, pp.66–71; Christopher Clapham and George Philip (eds.), *The Political Dilemmas of Military Regimes*, Totowa, NJ: Barnes and Noble Books, 1985; Constantine Danopoulos (ed.), *From Military to Civilian Rule*, London: Routledge, 1992; Guillermo O'Donnell and Philippe C. Schmitter, *Transitions from Authoritarian Rule: Tentative Conclusions about Uncertain Democracies*, Baltimore, MD: The Johns Hopkins University Press, 1991, Huntington (n.9 above); Myron Wiener, 'Empirical Democratic Theory and the Transition from Authoritarianism', *PS*, Vol.20, Fall 1987, p.864; Merilee S. Grindle, 'Civil–Military Relations and Budgetary Politics in Latin America', *Armed Forces and Society*, Vol.13, No.2, Winter 1987, pp.255–75.
35. Stepan (n.10 above), pp.68–9; Aguilera (n.33 above), p.32.
36. Stepan (n.10 above), pp.68–9.
37. See, e.g., Huntington (n.9 above), pp.211–12.
38. Stepan (n.10 above), p.68.
39. Grindle (n.34 above).
40. See Sriram (n.1 above).

Protégés, Clients, Cannon Fodder: Civilians in the Calculus of Militias

MARIE-JOËLLE ZAHAR

There are approximately a dozen major civil wars currently raging around the world. These conflicts are characterized by unusually high numbers of civilian casualties. The striking feature of contemporary warfare is the use of non-combatants as instruments and objectives of warfare. Whereas international law helped shield civilian populations during inter-state wars, often one or more combatant faction in internal conflicts is not party to the international legal covenants that regulate conduct in war.

External observers, both practitioners and academics, are thus increasingly concerned with humanitarian assistance and protection of civilian populations. But intervention in civil wars can and has been construed as a violation of the principle of sovereignty. The absence of clear guidelines as to how and when to intervene in internal conflicts creates a particular set of challenges for potential interveners. First, most international law and conventions on the conduct of war have been elaborated in the context of inter-state wars. This means that concerned third parties have little or no leverage on the combatants to force the respect of international conventions. Second, internal conflicts typically pit a state against part or parts of its society. This often limits the access of outsiders, either because state authorities resist what they see as external interference in an internal matter or because the non-state actors block access to areas under their control. Finally, when outsiders manage to secure access, they have few if any specific guidelines on how to convince combatants to protect civilian populations and abide by international conventions to this effect.

Concerned outsiders face a dilemma. They can reach agreements with the combatants for access to, and protection of, civilians, but in the process they risk becoming or being perceived as 'complicit' with the armed factions. Critics note, for example, that international humanitarian assistance allows combatants to shirk their responsibilities towards civilians. At most, this assistance is an unwilling collaborator in the reprehensible actions of combatants.[1] Dialogue with belligerent groups may even legitimize such actors. Humanitarian assistance can also be diverted to other aims and in the process it can allow combatants to prolong conflicts.

In spite of this growing concern over the fate of civilian populations, there is little systematic research on the crucial topic of civil–militia relations. This contribution uses the term militia as a generic label that includes all non-state actors who resort to violence in order to achieve their objectives. The incentives of these belligerents[2] either to respect or violate the rights of civilians are little understood and even less systematically studied. What factors shape relations between these two groups? Can these factors point to ways of alleviating the humanitarian crisis and encouraging militiamen to abide by legal and customary obligations towards civilians in war? Do they provide the international community with tools that improve access to civilian populations?

The horrors of ethnic cleansing and other violence targeted at civilians often overshadow other aspects of civil–militia relations. They obscure the fact that these relations are complex and nuanced:

- They vary depending on the nature of the groups involved.

- They change over time.

- They can be, if not moulded, at least influenced by the actions of the international community.

Bearing this in mind, this essay has two main objectives: to detail and group into distinct categories several considerations that affect the nature of civil–militia relations; and to develop a typology of civil–militia relations, ranking warring groups from most to least challenging in terms of their expected compliance with the letter and the spirit of the provisions of the Hague conference, the Geneva conventions, and other related international humanitarian laws.

A Working Definition of Militias

The working definition of militias used in this essay covers a wide range of groups. At the most fundamental level, the various groups that fall under this label share one characteristic: these are armed factions resorting to violence to attain their objectives. Though they may be *de facto* forces in the political landscape of the countries where they operate, militias are usually illegitimate in spite of potential connections to established and recognized political forces.

In recent times, the label 'militia' has been used loosely to describe the private armies of pro-regime strongmen and the paramilitary formations that organize in defense of the political order in a given country.[3] In Togo for example, Emmanuel Eyadéma, one of President Gnassingbé Eyadéma's three sons, established his militia in Lomé in the early 1990s. Likewise, in

Rwanda, the Interahamwe were intimately connected to the regime of President Juvénal Habyarimana. The word 'militia' has also been used in connection with states where the central authority has been considerably weakened to describe the formations established by warlords, tribal or regional strongmen, drug lords, and the like. In Lebanon and Bosnia, for example, paramilitaries were often referred to as militias.

Militias can vary in terms of military structure (more or less similar to regular armies), connection to central authorities, and membership (ethnic vs. ideological for example). The word militia is therefore used in lieu of, and in reference to:

- Guerrillas: Guerrilla warfare refers to hit-and-run operations carried out by small bands of irregulars.[4] Guerrilla tactics have been used in the fight against enemy occupation, as illustrated by Tito's Partisans in Yugoslavia during the Second World War. Guerrilla warfare has also been the centrepiece of a number of internal wars such as the conflicts in Angola and Mozambique. The term guerrilla has often been used to refer to insurgents espousing left-leaning ideologies, especially in Latin America.

- Revolutionary armies: While some groups adopt guerrilla tactics and remain small and loosely structured, others develop along the lines of conventional armies. The word revolutionary army brings China and Vietnam to mind. In both instances, Communist insurgents engaged in regular army operations as well as in guerrilla warfare.[5]

- Insurgents: Insurgents use violence to challenge the power of the state. In Northern Ireland, for example, this is the main difference between the Irish Republican Army and the Ulster Defence Forces.

- State proxies fighting on behalf of, but not at the behest of, the state. This distinction is important because many regimes (the Duvaliers in Haiti, Somoza in Nicaragua) are highly personalized but their armed supporters still do not qualify as militias. Yet there have been numerous instances in which states cultivated militias as adjuncts of state power, the paradigmatic case being the Interahamwe in Rwanda.

- Ethnic armed formations: Some militias form along ethnic divides. This type of militia has become increasingly common with, though not exclusively connected to, the resurgence of ethno-national conflict in the former Soviet Union and Eastern Europe. The Bosnian Serbs fall under this category. So do Chechen, Abkhaz, and other ethnic groups currently engaged in civil wars in the Caucasus and Central Asia.

- Warlords: The absence of collective, versus private interest, is said to be 'a major distinguishing feature of warlord politics'.[6] Warlords may mobilize followers along tribal, clan or family lines, as was the case in Somalia. However, narco-terrorist warlords in Colombia and Southeast Asia operate differently, usually attempting to control peasant/rural populations in their areas of operations.

As mentioned earlier, there are not only similarities but also differences between a revolutionary army, an insurgent group, and an ethnic militia. These differences ought to be investigated because they are consequential for civil–militia relations.

Dimensions of Civil–Militia Relations

Analysts typically evaluate civil–militia relations almost exclusively in terms of identification vs. control. In summary, the assumption is that a militia that identifies with a population will treat civilians well. Where no such identification exists between the militia and civilians, the *modus operandi* of civil–militia relations will be control. This hypothesis though intuitively logical is only one element of a larger and more complex explanation. Both identification and control are complex factors that need unpacking. Furthermore, it would be erroneous to think of them as polar opposites. Identification with a civilian population does not automatically imply that militias will refrain from attempting to control this group or community. Control, for its part, should not be thought of as pure military imposition. There are less obvious ways in which a militia can control civilian populations, such as the creation of civilian dependence on the militia for sustenance and economic relations. In this section, I discuss two dimensions of identification and control that are relevant to a typology of civil–militia relations.

Defining Membership: In-Groups and Out-Groups

Civil–militia identification matters: the first and most obvious consideration is the difference between the treatment of one's in-group and the treatment reserved to out-groups. Identification of in-groups and out-groups can be driven by societal constructs–ethnic, religious, linguistic, tribal, or clannish. Hence, in Somalia, membership in the various militias was a function of one's clan lineage. In Bosnia, nationality (ethnic and religious: Serbs are also Orthodox, Croats are Catholics, Bosniacs are Muslims) often determined membership. Identification can also be economic in the sense that civilians identify with the economic grievances of the combatants, or political in the sense that they share a common ideological creed. An example of economic identification would be the support that Chiapas inhabitants provided to the Ejercito Zapatista de Liberacion Nacional (EZLN).

Whereas militias routinely violate the human rights of out-group non-combatants, these same combatants are often involved in the protection and promotion of the rights of their own civilian populations. The same groups that practice ethnic cleansing and engage in kidnapping, torture and indiscriminate shelling of non-combatant populations will simultaneously claim that their actions are in defense of the rights of their 'aggrieved' communities. A cynic would probably dismiss these arguments as convenient justifications, but extensive interviewing of militiamen in Republika Srpska and Lebanon suggests that many believe that they are or were fighting for a 'just cause'.[7]

* Lebanon's Hizballah [Party of God] provides a striking example of this dichotomy. Hizballah was committed to forcing the Israel Defense Forces out of occupied South Lebanon and to the implementation of UN Security Council resolution 425. The militia (turned party in 1990) has resorted to guerrilla methods including the shelling of civilians inside Israel. Hizballah has also been involved in the abduction of civilians, the use of booby-trapped cars, and other actions clearly contravening the provisions of the Hague convention. Hizballah has simultaneously upheld a tradition of providing social services to the poorest strata of the Shi`a community of Lebanon. Its efficient and responsive organization has earned it wide social support mainly in the Biqa` Valley and in southern Lebanon.[8] In the words of one Lebanese political analyst, 'here... Hizbullah is seen primarily as a social movement, a defender of the poor.'[9]

Membership is an important factor in improving access to civilian populations in internal conflicts. The wider the 'constituency' of a militia, the more it will be responsive to arguments about the need to improve the fate of civilians. The narrower a militia's 'constituency', the less likely this group will be to exhibit concerns for the civilian population at large.

This is not to say that militias will necessarily treat in-groups well. Social identification with a militia does not automatically imply that civilians share its economic or political stances. Indeed, there may be economic or political differences between members of the same ethnic or religious group. Members of the same class may also split over ethnic tensions. In other words, social, economic, and political cleavages are not always reinforcing. They can be crosscutting. For example, contrary to common perceptions, not all Bosnian Serbs agreed with the extremist views of the leadership in Pale, in spite of their shared 'ethnicity'. Likewise, economic civil–militia cohesion may be torn asunder by ethnic tensions or political differences that emerge at a later point in a given conflict.

*   Factionalism among the various branches of the Sudan People's Liberation Army (SPLA) is a good case in point. In general, southern Sudanese of all stripes agreed on their opposition to the political, economic, and developmental pre-eminence of the North. However, this opposition did not prevent serious factionalism to develop among the southern resistance movement along linguistic, tribal, and other lines. Factionalism has been considered one of the most important factors in understanding the functioning (or lack thereof) of the SPLA.[10]

The treatment of civilians also depends on other factors including the objectives and structure of the group (discussed below) and its economic ties to the population.

The Economic Dimension of Civil–Militia Relations

Militias often depend on civilian populations for two essential resources: fighters and revenue. Both are necessary to sustain the military effort. Militias may also find independent sources of revenue through external patrons or by selling commodities on the international market. Various types of economic relations have different impacts on the militias' propensity to uphold international norms of conduct *vis-à-vis* civilians. The more dependent the militia on the civilians over whom it has control, the more likely it will be to avoid harming them. Moreover, militia dependence on the population provides a space for civilians to negotiate the terms of militia conduct *vis-à-vis* non-combatants.

Sources of Militia Revenue: Militia revenue can come from different sources. It can be domestically generated or externally garnered. Some militias try to induce the populations under their control to provide resources willingly. Others force the populations to sustain their needs. These relations range from parasitical to symbiotic. Parasitical fundraising refers to the steady yielding of income through extortion, licensing fees, theft of international aid, or 'revolutionary taxation'. Symbiotic fundraising refers to militia efforts to promote certain types of activities in exchange for a share in the outcome. In this case, the economic development of the area and the economic well being of the population are relatively dependent on the provision by the guerrilla group of security and infrastructure.[11] Likewise, part of the militia's income depends on the population's ability to continue to conduct economic exchanges without fear of extortion. Below are the various sources of militia revenue:

- Extortion: A common source of combatant revenue in civil wars. Armed men take advantage of their weaponry to engage in theft, looting, and other exactions. They take advantage of the population's fear and helplessness to prey upon readily available resources. Extortion can generate substantial amounts of revenue but the supply side is not inexhaustible.

- Theft of international aid: Aid taxation can be imposed on the aid-recipients, at distribution sites, or at the source. In the latter case, aid convoys are either hijacked and their contents sold for profit, or a protection cost is imposed to secure the delivery of the aid to its intended recipients. Though a common feature in civil wars, the integration of aid in conflict dynamics was probably most publicly discussed in the Somali case.[12]

- Licensing fees: When they control territorial enclaves, militias often impose fees on entry to and exit from their zones of control. These fees apply equally to individuals and merchandise. In Republika Srpska, a substantial amount of revenue was thus generated by issuing exit visas to Bosnian Muslims who sought official assurances that they would be allowed to leave the Bosnian Serb areas safely.

- Revolutionary taxation: An independent resource base usually involves some form of revolutionary taxation. As early as 1976, barely one year into the Lebanese conflict, the Lebanese Forces established the 'national treasury' a highly organized financial department, responsible for generating revenue for the war effort. More recently, the Kosovo Liberation Army (KLA) established an international fund, 'Homeland Calls', as an essential element of its effort to secure independence for Kosovo from Serbia.

- External assistance: Militias turn for support to external actors who sympathize with their cause. For example, in its early days, 'much of the support for the IRA came from the United States, where there are about 15 million Americans of Irish descent. ... Irish-Americans collected funds and weapons for the Provos. The New York-based Irish Northern Aid Committee (Noraid) became the largest American source of cash. In addition, machine guns, rifles, pistols, grenades, and ammunition were sent to help the underground fighters.'[13] Militias also seek external patrons willing to finance their war effort because of shared ideology or for strategic reasons. The Lebanese Forces turned to Israel for assistance; Belgrade extended lines of supply and financial support to the Bosnian Serbs.

• Economic re-organization of the relations of production: Militias can divert some of their revenue into non-military activities and develop economic relations with the population of the territories under their control. In Latin America, insurgents tended to buy supplies from local peasants at prices well above market rates.[14] Involvement may even mean a total reorganization of the relations of production. For example, Peru's Sendero Luminoso typically altered the economic base of areas under its control by establishing cooperative forms of agriculture. In the Philippines, the New People's Army implements land reform and attempts to replace capitalism with a cooperative parallel economy.[15]

• Guaranteeing the 'rule of law': Militias, not unlike states, can sometimes provide security and infrastructure to underpin normal economic exchanges. In return, they receive a part of the population's income. In Lebanon's Christian enclave, the Lebanese Forces (LF) established an elaborate infrastructure to regulate the conduct of commerce and other economic activities. This involved customs duties, harbour facilities, a price control commission, a body of law-like regulations on the conduct of business, as well as the provision of internal security within the militia's zone of control. This infrastructure was instrumental in allowing the population to conduct business and maintain relatively normal economic activities. In return, the LF collected taxes and excise duty on goods and services.

• Business empires: In some cases, the involvement of militias in the economy is so diversified and complex that it becomes difficult to separate the grey economy from the legal market economy. The militias not only replace the state in the provision of a framework for the conduct of economic exchanges, they also form business empires often with connections to international markets. This is most evident in the case of narco-terrorist militias.

Parasitical Economic Relations: In the case of parasitical militias, civil–militia relations are similar to the relations of protection rackets with prospective 'protégés'. The militias are in essence undertaking to ensure civilians' 'security' in return for financial retribution. Militias rule through fear and they do not care much for the population's evaluation of their performance.

• In Lebanon, militias on all sides of the conflict imposed direct and indirect taxes on citizens, commercial establishments and industries, as well as at public facilities (harbours and customs). 'Militias demanded outright ransoms from industrialists, merchants, or wealthy investors (easily totaling U.S. $500 million since 1975).'[16]

• In Republika Srpska (RS), the Bosnian Serb leadership took the real and movable property of Muslims away from them. Terrorized Muslims would sign 'official' documents 'willingly' giving up their material property in return for the right to leave, itself often made official by the issuance of a departure 'visa'.[17] These practices were not simply limited to the 'out-group'. Real property was awarded to the 'war municipality' or 'crisis committee' of the particular town. Close associates of the local leaders got first pick; state officials used the remainder to control the Serb population. In Bijeljina, for example, one of the officials in charge of the 'ethnic cleansing' campaign retooled in security services and real estate. He would '[shake] down local businessmen and [offer] incoming Serb refugees their pick of "abandoned" homes, provided that they could come up with the requisite sweetener'. In Prijedor, Simo Drljaca, the police chief who played a leading role in setting up the notorious Serb concentration camps 'was known as Mr. Ten Per Cent, because of the kickbacks and extortion payments he squeezed from almost every enterprise in town'.[18]

Symbiotic Economic Relations: Parasitical relations, based on the might of the gun and the fear factor, are not the only kind of economic exchange in militia-controlled territories. In fact, there are many more examples of situations where militias have, for a wide array of reasons, sought to reshape economic relations in their areas of control. While some have totally transformed the mode of production from capitalism to socialism, others have interfered in the economy in a different way, providing security, infrastructure and the rule of law necessary for the orderly conduct of economic exchanges in return for a percentage of the profit made by the population.

Apart from reorganizing the relations of production in the areas under their control, militias have often been known to provide a full array of social contract services to the local populations.[19] It is interesting to note that, in several cases, the civilian populations have come to perceive the combatants as governments.

• There is massive evidence that insurgents in Cuba, Venezuela, Colombia and Guatemala, among others, sought to provide civilian populations with social contract services. A Venezuelan peasant summarized this situation by distinguishing 'the guerrillas' gobierno de arriba, or government up in the hills, from the normal government down in the towns, or gobierno de abajo'.[20]

- In Ethiopia, the Eritrean People's Liberation Front (EPLF) sought to apply its Maoist message of social transformation. The EPLF established 'a reciprocal process: in order to move freely through the rural areas, the population of the latter was necessary for support of the armed bands, and as a source of recruits, sustenance for armed guerrillas and intelligence.' In Sahel, for example, where the Ethiopian state was absent, one nomadic clan leader referred to the EPLF in 1977 as a *hukuma*, the Arabic word for government.[21]

It is also extremely important to note that civil–militia economic relations can change over time. In Lebanon and Republika Srpska, early parasitical relations developed into (and sometimes coexisted with) the provision of collective goods, a centrepiece of the relations between the militia and the population.

- In the Republika Srpska, the Bosnian Serb leadership controlled imports and exports, delivering licenses to traders, providing a 'legal' framework for the conduct of business, and receiving payment in return. This infrastructure remained one of the main sources of Bosnian Serb revenue, especially as the imposition of economic sanctions by the international community provided an opportunity for enrichment through sanction busting. However, the leadership also put in place 'war municipalities' that provided, among other things, relocation and gainful employment to Serb refugees.

Independent Sources of Militia Revenue: Some militias obtain most of their revenue from external sources. Thus the economic dependence between them and the civilian populations over which they rule is extremely lopsided. Although civilians may need to work for the militia to earn their livelihood, the militia itself is not really dependent upon its workforce but upon its connections to global markets where its products (precious stones, drugs, and the like) are sold.

- During Liberia's civil war between 1989 and 1997, the political economy of Charles Taylor's power relied on independent connections to global markets and regional non-state actors. The resources of Taylor's National Patriotic Front of Liberia derived from its control of diamond smuggling, logging,[22] rubber production and iron-ore mining.[23]

- In Angola, UNITA (the National Union for the Total Independence of Angola) initially used the illicit sale of ivory and rhino horn abroad as a means of financing its weapons' acquisitions. By 1993, the movement controlled 'an estimated $1 billion in annual earnings from gemstone exports'.[24] UNITA's stake in Angola's diamond industry is estimated at between $300 million and $1.5 billion in annual revenues.

Finally, it is important to note that civil–militia relations are not merely relations between an agent (the militia) and its target (civilian populations). Civilian populations have agency in shaping these relations as well. When militias depend on the civilian population for logistical support, manpower and/or funding, civilians have some means at their disposal to renegotiate the terms of their relations to the combatants. The relationship between combatants and host societies may also be one of common interest whereby the population supports the insurgency which, in turn, represents popular aspirations.[25]

The Nature of Militias and Its Impact on Civil–Militia Relations

Apart from their identification with, and the economic ties linking them to, the populations that they control, there are a number of militia-specific factors that play a role in shaping civil–militia relations.

Militia Objectives: The calculus of belligerents should be understood in the larger context of their objectives. A group seeking international legitimization will approach civil–militia relations differently from a radical organization. A group seeking separation will also evaluate the cost-benefit of transgressing human rights differently from one that seeks inclusion in the political system.

Whether they seek to secede or to renegotiate the role of their community in the future polity, militia leaders typically want their voices to be heard.[26] Often facing authoritarian regimes, militias seek to attract international attention to their plight in an attempt to modify an unfavourable internal balance of power (the KLA in Kosovo is a case in point). But what starts as a tactical move often turns into an intrinsic militia objective. This is a direct consequence of the organization of the international system into states, which makes the resolution of civil conflict particularly arduous.[27] It also means that international actors tend to privilege 'legitimate interlocutors' and that legitimacy is usually associated with statehood.

In practice, this often means that states will play on the illegitimacy of insurgent movements to attempt to exclude them from peace negotiations. The international community has adopted this logic in a number of instances. In the Bosnian war, the international community elected to negotiate with President Slobodan Milošević rather than deal with the Bosnian Serbs. This phenomenon is not restricted to militias. Even regimes that are not considered 'legitimate' will often be discounted as negotiating partners. In the Shaba crisis of 1977, for instance, America's inability to treat Angola's MPLA (the Popular Movement for the Liberation of Angola) regime as anything other than a Soviet puppet was to blame for the failure of negotiations.[28]

Militias thus face a conundrum. They may become *de facto* forces with which local and international actors are forced to reckon but this in itself does not secure their legitimization or their inclusion in future negotiations. When such non-state actors become more visible and draw more support, they risk being portrayed as 'mavericks threatening international legitimacy'. Hence, militias are particularly concerned with the issue of being 'heard, perceived, and recognized by nation-states and international organizations'.[29] This predicament has a direct impact on militia development. Whether or not militias intend to establish a separate state, it is not uncommon for them to look increasingly like quasi-states or to develop governments-in-waiting. The adoption of proto-state characteristics becomes an end in itself. Militias thus appropriate the forms and procedures of states in a bid to achieve the ultimate objective of gaining legitimacy and recognition.

• The Palestine Liberation Organization's (PLO) struggle for recognition is illustrative of this conundrum and of its dynamics. In an effort to mount a successful guerrilla war against Israel and to gain autonomy from often-constraining allies, the organization underwent a process of institutionalization. Although the Arab League recognized the organization as the sole legitimate representative of the Palestinian people, this legitimization was neither universal nor unproblematic. Instead, the PLO's growing capacity and visibility were instrumental in heightening the threat perception of not only its foe, Israel, but even some of its allies, namely Jordan and Lebanon. In both countries, embattled regimes perceived the increasingly complex and powerful organization as a threat to their own stability and they acted militarily to contain this threat. In spite of its increasing organization as a proto-state, the PLO continued to be viewed as a terrorist group – though a more dangerous group in view of its growing capabilities – by the United States and Israel. It was not until the negotiations leading to the 1993 Oslo accords that the US and Israel extended official recognition to the PLO and brought it within the fold of peace talks. This recognition followed a number of signals that indicated that the PLO would behave in a 'state-like' manner, including but not limited to a public renunciation of terrorism. Whereas the PLO shift towards moderation can be traced back to 1974, it still took until 1993 for the organization to be officially accepted as an interlocutor in peace talks.

Militias thus seek to gain recognition from external observers and potential mediators or interveners. This affects militia decisions relating to organizational form and development which, as we will see in the next section, also have an impact on civil–militia relations.

As earlier noted, objectives can also shape militia incentives either to uphold or violate the rights of civilians in a more straightforward manner. A group with a universal message of solidarity will act differently towards civilians than a group with ethnically based objectives. A group seeking secession will evaluate its relations with civilians partially through the prism of its need for territory.

* In Bosnia, control over territory was central to the Bosnian Serbs 'to consolidate ethnically pure territories that would vote correctly in a referendum on sovereignty and in future elections and to justify government administration by their national group'.[30] Bosnian Serbs knew from experience that a majority could easily ignore a minority's objections in a referendum. Their own wishes to remain within Yugoslavia had been brushed aside by Bosnian Muslim and Croat parliamentarians in early 1992. Hence, it was not sufficient to control territory militarily; you had to ensure that the territory's inhabitants would vote in line with your wishes in any upcoming referendum. In this instance, the critical need to gain control of territory shaped Bosnian Serb attitudes towards non-Serb civilian populations. These needed to be driven out of Srpska, hence originated the policy of 'ethnic cleansing' that turned the Bosnian war into such a humanitarian and moral nightmare.[31] Ethnic cleansing was the instrument through which Republika Srpska acquired its territorial definition and through which the Serbs achieved their objective of controlling territory.

* Consider the case of Biafra as a counter-example. During the Biafra civil war, the Nigerian government paid particular attention to the fate of civilians because of its ultimate objective to reintegrate Biafra into the larger Nigerian polity.

In summary, militia objectives can affect civil–militia relations directly by determining the militia's position *vis-à-vis* the population under its control. The militia's objectives also affect civil–militia relations indirectly by shaping the way combatants seek to be perceived by the international community.

Militia Structure: The various militias listed above differ in their organizational complexity and coherence. Whereas some groups are loosely structured, others are highly organized along military lines (revolutionary armies for example). Others still have developed beyond the military realm and established their own social and economic departments earning, in the process, the label of quasi-states or *de facto* states. The structure of these groups is important because it can either impede or assist in the development of norms of conduct towards civilians.

For example, one would expect that the more structured a group, the easier it would be to determine the chain of command and control and therefore to attribute responsibility and accountability for violations of the rights of civilian populations. Where a group is loosely structured, where the membership is fluid, and norms of conduct under-developed, it becomes more difficult for outsiders and leaders alike to enforce standards of conduct and develop enforcement and retribution mechanisms.

*   In Bosnia, responsibility for ethnic cleansing undertaken between 1992 and early 1993 is more diffuse than after that period, when the Srpska Demokratska Stranka [or SDS, the Serb Democratic Party of Radovan Karadžić] unified the small bands of irregulars under the banner of the Vojska Republike Srpske [Serb Army].

*   In the Sudan, the growth of the Sudanese People's Liberation Army (SPLA) Civil Administration was instrumental in the development of institutions to regulate civil–militia relations. In 1983, the SPLA enacted its Penal Code, a disciplinary code confined to the military. The Code prescribed the death penalty for a number of crimes committed by military personnel, including looting and rape. In 1984, the Penal Code was amended to include a disciplinary law for the army, a general penal code and a code of procedures. The 1984 laws recognized the application of customary law in each community within SPLA-controlled territory and established three tiers of military courts. However, the application of these norms and procedures remained arbitrary.[32]

A Typology of Civil–Militia Relations

This section integrates the various considerations that come into play in determining civil–militia relations into a typology.

Militia-Specific Considerations

In spite of their many differences, the various groups described above belong on a continuum of non-state forces that resort to violence in the pursuit of their objectives. They can usefully be conceptualized as varying along two axes (though it ought to be understood that groups can actually move along both axes during the course of a conflict). The first plots the nature of militia objectives.

- The more general the militia's objectives (in the sense that they seek to improve society at large) the more likely it will be that the international community will find a way to engage the militia on the issue of civilian protection.

- The narrower the militia's objectives, the less receptive they are likely to be with respect to pleas for the respect and protection of civilian populations writ large.

The breadth or narrowness of militia objectives may, of course, be a function of the type of militia that we are dealing with. Indeed, an ethnically based group is expected to have narrower objectives than a guerrilla movement espousing a radical ideology of social change.

The second axis plots the degree of organizational complexity of a militia (otherwise discussed as militia structure). Structure implies a certain degree of responsibility by clarifying command and control. It also allows the group to establish rules of conduct towards civilian populations and to develop enforcement mechanisms to this effect. However, structure and the development of institutions and procedures do not automatically imply compliance with the norms of conduct at the heart of this discussion. Therefore, structure is at best an enabling condition. It is not necessary nor is it sufficient to secure that civil–militia relations are in harmony with the letter or spirit of the Hague and Geneva conventions.

TABLE 1

MILITIA-SPECIFIC CONSIDERATIONS FOR DIFFICULTY OF NEGOTIATIONS

	Loose structure	Clear structure
Narrow objectives	Most challenging	Moderately challenging
Broader objectives	Moderately challenging	Least challenging

In terms of humanitarian access negotiations, militias can usefully be divided into four ideal types. The militias that seek the improvement of general societal conditions and which possess clear lines of command and control are expected to be the least challenging interlocutor because they have both an interest in, and the capacity to, engage the issue of civilian protection. In contrast, militias with very narrow objectives and with a loose structure are expected to be the toughest interlocutor because they lack the motivation and the capacity to improve civilians' conditions.

Non-Militia Specific Considerations

Having provided a rough typology of militias, we can integrate other considerations into our characterization of civil–militia relations.

FIGURE 1

CIVIL–MILITIA RELATIONS, A TYPOLOGY

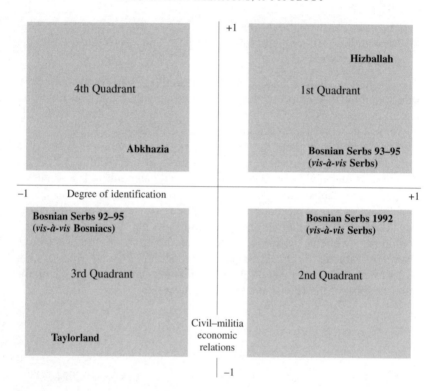

The horizontal (x) axis represents the degree of identification between civilians and the militia. As discussed earlier, the higher the perceived identification between a militia and the civilian population that it controls (in-group), the lower the likelihood is that the militia will hurt this population. In the diagram, in-groups are assigned the arbitrary value of +1 while out-groups are assigned the arbitrary value of −1. Of course, these two labels represent ideal types and there is potential for variation on this axis. As discussed earlier, in-groups are not always treated well by combatants who identify with them. Likewise, out-groups can be treated well by militias.

- For example, in the Abkhazian case, the combatants negotiate security bargains across the demarcation line. These bargains benefit parties on both sides financially. They allow internally displaced people to return periodically for the harvest season. These policies result in the manipulation of refugees into cycles of migration. Nevertheless, during the harvest season – albeit for financial considerations rather than out of loftier motives – militias treat out-groups better than is otherwise the norm.[33]

The vertical (y) axis represents civil–militia economic relations. The higher a militia's symbiotic dependence on the civilian population, the less likely it is that the militia will harm the civilians. Going back to our discussion of civil–militia economic relations, we can collapse the various types of relations into three broad categories:

- *Independent militia sources of revenue*: the militia depends largely on external trade connections for survival and for income generation, examples include Taylorland under the NPLF [assigned the value –1].

- *Parasitical civil–militia relations*: the militia extracts resources from civilians by force; a good illustration is the relationship between the Bosnian Serb militias and the Bosniac population [assigned the value 0].

- *Symbiotic relations*: the militia contributes largely to the economic well-being of the population. It is involved in the economy in positive ways. Lebanon's Hizballah approximates this type of civil–militia economic relations [assigned the value +1].

In this figure, Quadrant 1 represents the most propitious civil–militia relations. The militia not only identifies with the civilian population over which it rules, but it has also become positively involved in the economy of the territories under its control. Quadrant 4, by comparison, represents the most difficult set of cases where the militia not only rules over an out-group but civil–militia economic relations are either non-existent or predatory.

Some Practical Implications

This contribution has identified two broad classes of factors that influence civil–militia relations. The first set includes militia-specific considerations, notably the impact of militia objectives and structure. In this respect, we hypothesize that inclusive objectives are more likely to generate sensitivity to issues of civilian protection than narrow interests. We also expect higher degrees of control and command to enable militia leaders to enforce norms of conduct *vis-à-vis* civilians and to hold violators accountable. However, a tighter structure does not automatically bring about concern for civilian protection.

The second set of factors relates to potential ties between the combatants and the population. In this respect, we discussed the potential impact of identification. In general, it is expected that militias will treat in-groups better than out-groups. Economic ties can also influence militia attitude towards civilian protection. The heavier a militia depends on the population it controls, the more likely it will seek to limit the harm done to this population.

Quadrant 1: In this grouping, militia identification with the civilian population and symbiotic economic relations provide the international community with opportunities to engage the militia on issues of humanitarian assistance. A militia that depends in part on the population for support and sustenance may find it in its interest to cooperate with the international community to improve humanitarian access and enforce certain norms of conduct towards civilians.

Here, the challenge emanates from the type of militia with which the international community is dealing. If the militia has command and control, it will be able to shoulder responsibility for its commitments to the international community. However, if the militia is weakly structured, chances are that the leadership cannot speak for individual militiamen, nor can it vouch for their compliance.

As mentioned earlier, larger, more organized groups often set up networks of organizations to regularize relations with the populations of the areas they control. They build elaborate infrastructures to provide collective goods to communities. For militias that seek the right to represent a given community at eventual peace negotiations, the establishment of patrimonial relations is one way of securing *de facto* legitimacy through the creation of clientelist networks. These groups tend to see themselves as either governments-in-waiting or as potentially independent political entities. Either way, they seek legitimization. Therefore, when they cannot engage their domestic adversaries, they commonly turn to the international community to seek redress for grievances. This conjuncture provides the international community with an opportunity to engage the groups on issues of treatment of civilians. It also provides civilian populations with leverage over militias.

• In the early to mid-1980s, the Christian Lebanese Forces militia (Lebanon) used resources garnered in the course of legal and illegal economic activities to develop para-statal institutions and provide collective goods to the population of the Christian enclave. The establishment of services such as a subsidized public transport network, garbage collection, a police force, and a legal system, among others, reinforced perceptions of the militia as 'of and for the people', a policy the success of which was reflected in the population's perception of LF militiamen.[34] However, there was also intermittent exasperation with abuses committed by individual militiamen. This exasperation grew as the LF became a complex and coherent organization endowed with the means to put an end to such abuses. In time, the abuses committed by militiamen – in spite of efforts by the leadership to impose sanctions on transgressors – reinforced the stereotype of militiamen as brigands.[35] The growing estrangement of a population tired of the war system dominated the popular evaluation of the militia.[36]

Quadrant 2: In this cluster, the militia identifies with the population. However, civil–militia economic relations are predatory. This is a particularly challenging quadrant because, on the one hand, the population may exhibit strong identification with the militia; on the other hand, the economic relations between both are such that the militia does not hesitate to take advantage of non-combatants if need be.

The strong identification factor may lead outside observers to believe that sanctions imposed on the community as a whole might bring the militia into compliance with the norms of conduct towards civilians on the opposite side of the conflict. This is often not the case. Rather, it may lead to a deterioration of the conditions of non-combatants over whom the militia rules. A thorough understanding of the nature of civil–militia economic ties is important to assess the kind of sanctions to be imposed as well as their potential efficacy.

• The imposition of economic sanctions on the Serbs worsened the condition of civilians in Republika Srpska. A few months into the war, an extremely lucrative black market economy developed.[37] Local commanders organized some of this black-market activity for personal benefit. In Republika Srpska, the black market was 'run by the [SDS] party and delegated to people that it trusts, upon which it takes a percentage of the gains… After Serbia imposed sanctions on the RS, criminality increased.'[38] For black-market profiteers, the embargo provided an excellent opportunity for enrichment. They could increase their activities by selling goods not only to Bosnian Muslims and Croats but also to ordinary Serbs that the sanctions affected most directly. General consumption goods became a source of financial gain as core SDS people traded these goods tax-free in return for contributions to their 'bosses' in the state structure. Petrol station owners had to pay racketeers on a monthly basis.

Quadrant 3: This is by far the worst situation that international observers concerned with the fate of civilian populations can face. Not only does the militia have control over a population with which it does not identify, civil–militia economic relations deprive the population of effective means of leverage on its 'rulers'. When the militia does not have totally independent sources of revenue, it resorts to looting, revolutionary taxation, and other predatory economic practices.

In such cases, it is extremely doubtful that the international community will be able to affect the nature of civil–militia relations short of imposing measures that cut off the militia's external sources of support. This is where it becomes crucial to understand the international financial networks in which militias are inserted, be it in the case of the diamond trade of Sierra Leone or the drug trade of the Colombian warlords. The notions of social responsibility increasingly adopted by multinational enterprises are, in my opinion, the most fruitful way to put pressure on these militias. Recent UN efforts to sanction the sale of 'conflict diamonds' are also encouraging. Only by depriving them of the sources of their revenues will such militias even consider discussing the fate of civilians.

Quadrant 4: In this cluster, the militia will not be persuaded by humanitarian arguments that it should care for the civilian populations under its control. Indeed, there is no strong bond between the civilian populations and their rulers. However, civil–militia economic relations may provide a venue to engage the militia on issues of civilian protection as militias depend at least in part on the population for sustenance and economic resources.

It should however be noted that once again the nature of the militia ought to be given utmost attention. Under the impact of international pressure, some groups are likely to move from Quadrant 3 to Quadrant 4, while others may move to Quadrant 1.

Conclusion

The ultimate objectives of combatants, their internal organizational structure, and their belief-systems all affect civil–militia relations. Civil–militia degree of identification and the nature of civil–militia economic ties are also variables in this equation. Unless they are scrutinized and understood, policymakers will not be able to make effective recommendations to limit the humanitarian disasters associated with civil wars.

Finally, I would argue that we 'sin by omission' when we fail to grasp the dynamics that shape civil–militia relations. When external mediators do not understand the complex calculus at work within militia groups, we tend to dismiss the militia too easily as fanatics who will not settle their conflicts. By so doing, the international community is often complicit in the failure to bring conflicts to a speedy end. And when it comes to the fate of non-combatant populations, it is essential to stop the killing.

ACKNOWLEDGEMENTS

A version of this essay was originally published in *Civilians in War: Global Norms, Local Contexts*, edited by Simon Chesterman, Boulder, CO: Lynne Rienner Publishers, © 2001. Used with the permission of the publishers. Stanford's MacArthur Consortium Program at the Center for International Security and Cooperation and the UN Office for the Coordination of Humanitarian Affairs provided funding for this research. The author would like to thank Bruce Jones for comments on an earlier draft of this essay. Thanks are also due to participants in the IPA-Carnegie conference on Civilians in War: 100 Years after the Hague Convention.

NOTES

1. Accusations that Dutch UNPROFOR soldiers actually helped the Bosnian Serbs commit the massacres of Srebernica are an example in point.
2. This essay focuses on non-state actors. However, it will implicitly and sometimes explicitly make reference to and compare non-state actors with state actors.
3. Comi M. Toulabor, 'Sur un continent en quête de stabilité: La "bataille finale" du général Eyadéma au Togo', *Le Monde Diplomatique*, March 1993, pp.18–19.
4. For a comprehensive review, see Walter Laqueur, *Guerrilla: A Historical and Critical Study*, London: Weidenfeld & Nicolson, 1977.
5. Early on in the Red Army's existence, guerrilla operations were 'on the whole subordinate to regular army activities'. Mao denounced the use of such tactics arguing that the army should not be dispersed but that it should instead 'establish and consolidate revolutionary bases'. The Long March proceeded largely along regular military lines but the Red Army reverted to guerrilla tactics after the massive defeat that it incurred at Kuang Chang in April 1934. In the first Vietnam war, Vietnamese Communists set up a regular army early on. But in the beginning the war was 'mainly guerrilla in character'. The guerrillas built a counter-state, one in which they 'levied taxes, collected rice, recruited soldiers and disseminated their propaganda'. It was not until 1950 that major units of the Communist regular army entered the battle. Laqueur (n.4 above), pp.246–66.
6. William Reno, *Warlord Politics and African States*, Boulder: Lynne Rienner, 1999, p.3.
7. The interviews were conducted as part of my doctoral dissertation research. Marie-Joëlle Zahar, 'Fanatics, Brigands, Mercenaries…and Politicians: Militia Decision-Making and Civil Conflict Resolution', McGill University, Montreal, 2000.
8. For example, on the morrow of the Israeli 'Grapes of Wrath' onslaught in April 1996, Hizballah 'claims to have repaired 5,000 Lebanese homes, rebuilt many roads, and paid compensation to 2,300 farmers'. According to outside observers, the figures are not exaggerated and they compare favourably with government aid to the victims. 'Lebanon, Hizbullah in Politics', *The Economist*, 7 September 1996.
9. Ibid.
10. See for example, Douglas Johnson, 'The Sudan People's Liberation Army and the Problem of Factionalism', in Christopher Clapham (ed.), *African Guerrillas*, Oxford: James Currey, 1998.
11. R.T. Naylor, 'The Insurgent Economy: Black Market Operations of Guerrilla Organizations', *Crime, Law and Social Change*, Vol.20 (1993), p.21.
12. See Daniel Compagnon, 'Somali Armed Movements: The Interplay of Political Entrepreneurship and Clan-Based Factions', in Christopher Clapham (n.10 above), p.86. See also, John Prendergast, *Frontline Diplomacy: Humanitarian Aid and Conflict in Africa*, Boulder: Lynne Rienner, 1996.
13. Louis Snyder, *Global Mini-Nationalisms: Autonomy or Independence*, Westport: Greenwood Press, 1982, pp.58–9.
14. Timothy Wickham-Crowley, *Exploring Revolution: Essays on Latin American Insurgency and Revolutionary Theory*, New York and London: Sharpe Inc., 1990, p.40.
15. Naylor (n.11 above), p.16.
16. Georges Corm, 'The War System: Militia Hegemony and the Reestablishment of the State', in Deirdre Collings (ed.), *Peace for Lebanon? From War to Reconstruction*, Boulder: Lynne

128   MANAGING ARMED CONFLICTS IN THE 21st CENTURY

Rienner, 1994, p.217.
17. Laura Silber and Alan Little, *Yugoslavia: Death of a Nation*, New York: Penguin, 1997, p.246.
18. Lawrence Weschler, 'High Noon at Twin Peaks', *The New Yorker*, 18 August 1997, pp.29–30.
19. Wickham-Crowley (n.14 above), p.39.
20. Norman Gall, 'The Continental Revolution', *The New Leader*, Vol.48 (12 April 1965), p.5 cited in Wickham-Crowley (n.14 above), p.39.
21. David Pool, 'The Eritrean People's Liberation Front' in Clapham (n.10 above), p.30.
22. 'Taylorland' was reportedly France's third largest African supplier of logs. *Marchés Tropicaux*, cited in *Economist Intelligence Unit*, Vol.3 (1992), p.33.
23. William Reno, 'The Organization of Warlord Politics in Liberia', in *Warlord Politics and African States* (see n.6 above), pp.79–111.
24. Al J. Venter, 'Mercenaries Fuel Next Round in Angolan Civil War', *International Defense Review*, Vol.29, No.3 (March 1996), p.65; Al J. Venter, 'Executive Outcomes Mercs and MiGs Turn Tide in Angola', *Soldier of Fortune* (January 1996), pp.31–76. Both cited in William Reno (n.6 above), p.76.
25. For more detail, see the discussion in Christopher Clapham (n.10 above), pp.12–14.
26. Militias engaged in civil wars typically seek to champion the cause of their community. The groups' objectives can range from re-negotiation of the current political system to secession. Attempts to secure re-negotiation suggest that militias want guarantees that other groups in the polity will respect their community's political and other rights. Attempts to seek secession or independence indicate a belief that such rights can only be secured through the establishment of an independent nation-state.
27. Martha Finnemore, 'Norms, Culture, and World Politics', *International Organization*, Vol.50, No.2, p.332.
28. I. William Zartman, *Ripe for Resolution: Conflict and Intervention in Africa*, New York: Oxford University Press, 1989, p.256.
29. Mohammad Selim, 'The Survival of a Non-State Actor: The Foreign Policy of the Palestine Liberation Organization', in Bahgat Korany and Ali Hillal Dessouki (eds.), *The Foreign Policy of Arab States: The Challenge of Change*, Second edition, Boulder: Westview, 1991.
30. Susan Woodward, *Balkan Tragedy: Chaos and Dissolution after the Cold War*, Washington, DC: The Brookings Institution, 1995, p.242.
31. See Susan Woodward (n.29 above), pp.236–246.
32. Douglas H. Johnson, 'The Sudan People's Liberation Army and the Problem of Factionalism', in Clapham (n.10 above), pp.68–9.
33. Catherine Dale, oral comments, Conference on The Uses of Refugees: The Manipulation of Human Suffering by Warring Groups, Stanford University, 4 November 1999.
34. The term *shabab* literally means 'the young ones'. It is socially used with reference to adolescents within one's familial and close social networks.
35. A strong man known for committing such abuses, Commander Abu Jawdeh would become a high-profile LF military official. His military prowess and the fact that his units managed to secure `Ayn al-Rummaneh, one of the most dangerous areas along the demarcation line, could not offset the resentment of the local population against his frequent excesses. The population of the locality would thus migrate en masse to the ranks of supporters of General Michel `Awn in 1989. Interview data, Summer 1993 (not for attribution).
36. By 1988, a German study revealed that all militias had lost as much as 50 per cent of their 1984 support. Theodor Hanf of the Arnold Bergstraesser Institut in Friburg conducted the study. It is quoted in Ghassan Tuéni, 'Peut-on refaire le Liban?', *Politique Etrangère*, Vol.2 (Summer 1990), pp.344–5.
37. All the illustrations are taken from Tim Judah, *The Serbs: History, Myth and the Destruction of Yugoslavia*, New Haven, CT: Yale University Press, 1998, pp.247–51.
38. Branko Perić, Editor-in-chief, Alternativna Informativna Mreza [Alternative Information Network], Banja Luka, author interview, 5 September 1998.

Messiahs or Mercenaries?
The Future of International
Private Military Services

DOUG BROOKS

Private companies that provide military services worldwide are flourishing, especially in Africa. Widespread conflict means that firms prepared to provide explosives disposal, robust security for resource extraction operations and even protection for humanitarian NGO operations are finding lucrative contracts. The same conflicts may also provide opportunities for companies prepared to do combat operations on behalf of states, international or regional organizations. However, widespread international bias against these companies means that their potential for peacekeeping, peace enforcement and humanitarian rescue missions could very well remain tragically untapped. Ironically, *not* using legitimate private firms will probably lead to a resurgence of uncontrollable individual freelance mercenaries who will flock to satisfy the profitable demand for military expertise, but who have far less regard for the legitimacy of their clients.

Definitions

Defining the international private military services industry has always been problematic. For the purposes of this essay, the focus is on any firm or individual that provides international services traditionally provided by national militaries.

In terms of organized private companies, this essay will differentiate between Private Security Companies (PSCs) and Private Military Companies (PMCs). Both PSCs and PMCs provide military services and generally operate in regions or countries experiencing armed conflict. While the definitions are still very much debated, for the purposes of this essay 'PSC' will refer to companies that provide passive security in high-risk conflict environments – predominantly to private companies. 'PMC' will refer to companies that provide more active services such as military training or offensive combat operations, generally to individual states or international organizations such as the United Nations (UN). There is obviously some blurring between the two terms, and a number of companies offer services that fit into both categories, but it is helpful to think of PSCs as passive defensive/protective companies with private clients and PMCs as more active military companies that cater to state contracts.

The most common and recognized services include:

TABLE 1

SERVICES PROVIDED BY PRIVATE SECURITY COMPANIES AND/OR PRIVATE MILITARY COMPANIES

Activity	PMC or PSC
1 Offensive combat operations (pulling triggers)	PMC
2 Armed security services in unstable states to private clients	PSC
3 Armed security services in unstable states to public or international clients, including law and order operations	PMC
4 Humanitarian protection, operations, and support	PMC/PSC
5 Military surveillance, strategic advice and intelligence	PMC
6 Demining	PSC
7 Military and police training	PMC/PSC
8 Logistics and supply for military operations	PSC
9 Hostage situation advice and/or rescue operations	PMC/PSC

Most PMC/PSCs use retired personnel from national militaries (it should be remembered that soldiers who serve for 20 years in a state military might be as young as 39 or 40 when they retire). They have recognizable company structures based in legitimate states and operate using standard international business practices. They avoid clients that are internationally condemned since that would adversely impact on their long-term viability. PMC/PSCs are rewarded for quality and efficiency in the form of future contracts and they strive for international respectability.

The term 'freelance mercenaries' refers to private individual soldiers that offer military services on the open market to the highest bidder. Freelance mercenaries are very different from PMC/PSCs in terms of operations, clients, accountability and the capacity of the international community to regulate their activities. Private soldiers prefer to work as contractors with organized companies, which provide dependable income, organized support and benefits such as emergency medical care and evacuation. Most private soldiers would not resort to becoming freelancers. Nevertheless, when employment in a private company is not an option then some may look to less reputable sources for employment. Thus, freelance mercenaries have an inverse economic relationship with PMCs, in that they thrive in areas of armed conflict where the more legitimate PMCs are usually absent.

It is important that PMC/PSCs should be differentiated from freelance mercenaries. Freelance mercenaries are individuals that generally exhibit few of the inhibitions that influence companies to maintain a degree of ethics in their operations. Companies fear retribution by their home governments for illegal or unethical operations, and recognize that a bad corporate reputation could result in the loss of future contracts to their competitors. Freelance mercenaries thus find lucrative work with countries or military groups that are facing international sanctions for their activities. Their motivations range from financial gain to idealism, to mere adventure. Freelance mercenaries have fought on the side of a number of internationally condemned organizations and individuals, such as Sierra Leone's Revolutionary United Front (RUF), Angola's National Union for the Total Independence of Angola (UNITA) and Liberia's president Charles Taylor.[1] While legislation can influence and channel the operations of legitimate companies, there is little chance it will affect the behaviour of freelance mercenaries.

What makes PMC/PSCs viable is their ability to offer military services more efficiently, more rapidly, and much more cheaply than state militaries or non-military companies could do themselves. PMC/PSCs tend to be more innovative, more flexible and more pragmatic and they allow state militaries to focus on their core missions and give multinational corporations (MNCs) the ability to operate in militarily unstable regions that would otherwise be unfeasible. In Angola, the government actually stipulates that MNCs operating facilities in the country provide their own security, a policy that frees up soldiers for the war with UNITA.[2]

However, the contrast in quality and efficiency is most stark when PMC services are compared to UN operations – PMCs can do military tasks for a fraction of the costs of typical UN operations. A case in point is Sierra Leone, where the South African company Executive Outcomes, along with Sierra Leone army units and *Kamajor* militia, forced the Liberian-backed RUF rebels to the point of defeat in 1995–96 for a cost of less than $40 million.[3] Currently, UN peacekeepers are trying to resurrect a negotiated peace in an operation that is costing almost $50 million a month and will ultimately cost much more.[4] At some point in the near future, the cost-effective benefits of using private companies will become too obvious to ignore, and the UN will be forced to reconsider its current policies against using PMCs.

In fact, these UN policies mean that PSCs who wish to work with the UN and other humanitarian clients must maintain 'squeaky-clean' operations and are scrupulous about their activities so that they are not 'tainted' by any hint of 'mercenarism'. Thus, they are keen not only to emphasize what services they *do* provide, but also to emphasize what services they *do not* provide.[5] James Finnell of Defence Systems Limited (DSL), a division of ArmorGroup,[6] writes:

> A note of caution. Commercial security organisations need to be seen as separate from 'Military Companies' who are often engaged to assist in the prosecution of aggressive actions. In military jargon, their utility is to assist in the 'taking and holding of ground'. Commercial security organisations are not involved in such actions. Indeed, for my company Defence Systems Limited (DSL), a division of ArmorGroup, involvement in such activities would preclude us from working for many of our major clients.[7]

The policy appears to be effective since ArmorGroup has apparently far more government, UN and NGO clients than any other PSC.[8] But while ArmorGroup does provide (lightly) armed security services, there are some PSCs that even shy away from going into any sort of security at all, but still provide military services.

Companies that engage in demining (for example Minetech of South Africa) and those engaged in logistics (such as Brown & Root of the United States) tend to focus only on their particular specialties, despite the fact that they use much the same pool of ex-military personnel as regular PMC/PSCs. Demining companies are considered humanitarian entities and the majority of their contracts come from NGOs, states and international organizations such as the UN. Logistics companies that supply and support state militaries, often in war situations, are also careful about how they are perceived. Although both provide specialized military services, demining and logistics are accepted as more legitimate vocations than other PMC services, and thus benefit from disassociating themselves from services that their clients could label as 'mercenary-related'.

Growth of an Industry

The rapid growth of the industry in the 1990s came about as a result of demand and supply resulting from the end of the Cold War. Three factors were particularly important. First, the end of the global bipolar struggle meant that many states and dictators once propped up by superpowers were now allowed to fail. The large numbers of small conflicts that resulted created a demand for private security to fill the superpower void. Second, the post-Cold War demobilizations of armies after civil conflicts and the end of the apartheid military structure in South Africa also created a large pool of available military talent. Finally, economic globalization has led to greater profits from investments in natural resource extraction operations in less developed countries. Even countries suffering from armed conflict offer impressive opportunities for profits and thus spur increased investment by MNCs. To counter the obvious risks to their operations in conflict situations, many MNCs turn to private security services. As a result, demand for private military services is strongest from the private sector, but the potential is greatest in the public sector.

In Africa, Western multinational companies are still finding profitable niches in natural resource extraction even in countries that have been suffering from conflicts for decades. Investment has been drawn in by new oil discoveries in Nigeria, Angola and Sudan, which continue to require adept security services capable of fending off heavily armed dissidents and guerrilla forces. Increased economic activity worldwide has also increased the profitability of mineral extraction ventures, making investment in even highly dangerous war zones profitable despite the healthy sums paid to PSCs for security. Thus unless there is a dramatic turnaround in the levels of stability in the developing world, PSCs have a lucrative future.

Consolidation and Legitimization

The international private military services industry is still an infant industry in a state of flux. Essentially, the bulk of the industry has only existed since the end of the Cold War. There are a few large established companies and a great number of small new companies. While some smaller companies have found useful and profitable niches, such as advising corporations on security, specialty transportation or other fields, many other smaller firms essentially offer menus of services similar to the larger companies. As the industry matures it is likely that most of the smaller companies will be acquired by the larger companies or forced out of the market in the face of the greater efficiency of their bigger competitors. The giant American company Armor Holdings has been at the vanguard of this acquisition of the industry 'minnows'.

Armor Holdings represents the future of the legitimate military services industry. Based in Jacksonville, Florida, Armor originally specialized in body armour, industrial security systems and non-lethal weapons. Although founded in 1969, it suffered through lean years, but recently was named one of Fortune magazine's 100 fastest-growing US companies.[9] Between 1996 and 1998, Armor acquired no less than 15 smaller companies, ranging from rivals in the non-lethal weapons market, to security consulting firms.[10] As a result, Armor quadrupled its revenue from security services between 1996 and 1999, and is now earning more than $150 million a year.[11] Armor

Holding's rate of growth shows every sign of continuing. In just a one week period in March 2000, Armor picked up three new companies.[12] These acquisitions have allowed Armor Holdings to move beyond its American home base and offer a full menu of security-related services and products on a global scale.

Perhaps their most interesting acquisition to date has been the British company, Defence Systems Ltd. (DSL), acquired in April 1997.[13] DSL had been founded by former Special Air Service (SAS) soldiers and had a reputation for working closely with the British government in executing many of their contracts. Its acquisition by an American company raised eyebrows on both sides of the Atlantic, and many observers felt that the secretive nature of so many PMC/PSCs could not survive the scrutiny that comes with being a subsidiary of a company listed on the New York Stock Exchange.[14] DSL, however, appears to have thrived since its acquisition. Currently the company is one of the few PSCs that have contracts with the privatization-shy United Nations.[15] With its 'foot in the door', and with the acquisition of so many other companies that DSL can call on – including demining and computer security firms – additional UN contracts are very likely in the future.

Privatized Peacekeeping

The full potential for PMCs, on the other hand, may have to wait several years, if ever, to be realized. The demand is as strong as ever for peacekeeping, peace enforcement, military assistance and humanitarian rescue operations, especially in Africa. Unfortunately, the supply of such services from the developed world has been drastically reduced since the Cold War. Fewer and fewer state militaries are capable of full-scale military interventions due to post-Cold War downsizing. In addition, the political willingness to undertake such interventions waned dramatically after the tragic events of the UN's Somalia intervention between 1992 and 1995. (See Adebajo and Landsberg, and Berdal in this volume.) The genocide in Rwanda in 1994 was clear proof of this lack of interest in future military interventions. Without the worldwide threat of the Cold War, former colonial powers such as Britain and France have shown less interest in stabilizing their former colonies and have given up much of their 'strategic reach' capabilities – their ability to intervene militarily in distant locations. Essentially, no matter how critical a crisis, intervention requires the direct assistance of an increasingly reluctant United States military with its massive and unparalleled air and sealift capabilities, and its large, combat-ready forces.

In an era of world-wide privatization, it would seem that private companies would be ideal to fill this gap. But unfortunately the international community has not been enthusiastic about using PMCs despite their proven military successes in Angola and Sierra Leone.[16] In fact, PMCs have often been exemplary in their behaviour, their cost-effectiveness and their capabilities, and would seem ideal for providing the stability necessary for establishing long-term peace agreements, state building and internationally acceptable democratic governments. The fact that PMCs often use elite troops from the best-trained militaries in the world allows them to field extremely competent forces that are fully capable of confronting the much larger but poorly trained armed groups so common in conflict zones in the developing world.

Oddly, what worries the international community enough to shy away from utilizing PMCs is the *potential* harm that they could do, not any particular past incident.[17] In addition, PMCs are frequently categorized with the less-respectable mercenaries of the 1960s and 1970s who fought in Africa, creating an unmerited bias against them. To many analysts it is unconscionable that the only military forces capable *and willing* to do humanitarian interventions are thus ignored.

Nevertheless, this bias against PMC/PSCs will probably last until the problems faced by current UN peacekeeping operations in Sierra Leone and the Democratic Republic of Congo (DRC) are played out. These two operations could make or break standard UN peacekeeping policies. Current indications are that those operations are not likely to meet with long-term success in light of the complex situation and quality of the peacekeeping participants (or likely participants in the case of DRC). Without substantive participation by a first-rate military, ideally the American military, the cards are stacked against the peacekeepers. Nelson Mandela publicly recognized this fact recently when he stated,

> The United States has the biggest and strongest military force in the world, and it is for this reason that we hope the US can give us more help... We are going to need a strong military force in the Congo because we are dealing with a dangerous and complex situation. But without support from the United States, it is going to be very difficult for us to make progress and create an environment in the Congo where peacekeepers can move freely without threat of violence.[18]

And even the US military is not always a decisive factor as events in Somalia proved. Furthermore, states that have publicly committed themselves to peacekeeping in DRC are qualifying their commitments. South African Minister for Defence, Mosiuoa Lekota, said that his country's troops would not participate in DRC peacekeeping if there were any chance they might be involved in combat.[19] Such sentiments may make a desperate international community take a closer look at the use of PMCs in the future.

The Questions of Legislation and Regulation

A key wildcard affecting the shape and growth of the private security industry is the uncertainty about legislation designed to regulate or even outlaw the trade in military services in countries that host PMCs. This is especially true in Britain, where a much-anticipated Green Paper outlining the basic focus of government policy towards PMCs has yet to be released more than six months after its original due date. Thus far, the relevant sectors of the British government have made it clear that they will not be consulting with industry representatives, which is an ominous sign for those who desire a constructive policy.[20]

Much of this antipathy dates from the 'Arms to Africa' affair which began in 1997 when the PMC, Sandline International, shipped arms to Sierra Leone to help support efforts to restore elected president Tejjan Kabbah to power after a military coup. The shipments had the full knowledge and blessing of some officials in the Foreign Office, including Peter Penfold, Britain's High Commissioner to Sierra Leone. Unfortunately, others in the Foreign Office were ignorant of Sandline's actions including, embarrassingly, Foreign Secretary Robin Cook.[21] The scandal was the first to seriously blemish Cook's 'ethical' foreign policy, and some analysts believe that this may adversely influence the government's Green Paper.

South Africa has already passed some especially restrictive and arbitrary legislation, but to date it has not been effectively tested.[22] Rumours abound about South African PMC/PSCs that have skirted such legislation rather than submit their foreign contracts to the vagaries of the law as it is currently written. In addition, South Africa has perhaps the largest pool of willing and available military talent that non-South African PMC/PSCs call on to execute many of their contracts in the rest of Africa. A change in South African legislation easing restrictions might actually improve the country's control over these private contractors who apparently continue to ply their trade.

While PSCs have shown that they can thrive in the current regulatory environment through private and humanitarian contracts, the future of PMCs depends very much on regulation. There are a number of PSCs that would be willing to compete as PMCs for peacekeeping/peace enforcement contracts should that role become legitimized through national legislation.

For the time being, however, few PMCs are prepared to do elaborate planning or investment in an industry that could see its current legitimacy endangered by sudden changes in policies, policy interpretation or overzealous enforcement.

Nevertheless, while the essential goal of legislating private military services is restrictive, legislation can also offer companies clear boundaries within which they can operate. In effect, such laws would end the uncertainty and allow companies to focus their efforts on military services that would thus be officially 'legitimate'. For NGOs and regional organizations such as ECOMOG (the Ceasefire Monitoring Group of ECOWAS, the Economic Community of West African States), legislation could allow them to utilize the services of PMC/PSCs without having to justify the moral position of whether the companies are actually 'mercenaries' or not. Most PMC/PSCs have publicly welcomed moves towards increased regulation in the industry, believing that the increased legitimacy will bring with it new clients, and also because regulations are a 'barrier to entry' that helps to keep out new competition.[23] Enlightened legislation could do much to give the international community a new tool to use for humanitarian rescue, peacekeeping and peace enforcement.

Military Services Worldwide

For the past decade, private military services have been a growth industry around the world. However, the United States Department of Defense (DoD) has gone the furthest in privatizing many of their traditional tasks. Such privatization has allowed the DoD to focus more of its resources into the combat arms and streamlined its logistics and supply lines. While post-Cold War defence changes have been financially harmful to many of the equipment suppliers, service companies have been doing well working with the Pentagon both in the United States and supporting American missions abroad.[24]

In the Balkans, private firms are often used instead of regular military units for training, demining, policing, supply and logistics, minimizing the commitment and exposure of US military personnel. Increasing American involvement in drug interdiction and the Colombian civil war has included the use of DynCorp for training, aerial surveillance and intelligence.[25] International observers provided by the United States to high-risk multinational operations in the future are as likely to come from private companies as the regular military, as was shown in Kosovo in 1998 shortly before the war.[26] While much of the military-industrial complex has suffered from downsizing and consolidation since the end of the Cold War, the military services industry has been blossoming. Companies like MPRI[27] and Pacific Architects and Engineers (PA&E) have taken advantage of increasing worldwide opportunities to supply and train foreign militaries. PA&E and their subcontractor, International Charters Inc. of Oregon (ICI), provided extensive logistics services for ECOMOG forces operating in Liberia and Sierra Leone, while MPRI recently began a training program in newly democratic Nigeria to professionalize the military and encourage better civil–military relations.[28] This project is substantially funded by USAID.

Other states are recognizing the utility of private military companies. Post-Cold War military downsizing has drastically diminished the combat readiness of Western militaries (see Finlay and O'Hanlon in this volume). While overall size has been reduced, more significantly the proportion of the militaries that are actual combat units has also been reduced. The war in Kosovo revealed to European NATO members how embarrassingly inadequate the combat arms of their militaries are compared to the United States. American aircraft did well over 90 per cent of the bombings, and European militaries were painfully stretched even in providing the few necessary ground units for occupying Kosovo once Serbia had capitulated and withdrawn. To be able to field more combat units, European militaries will have to follow the American lead and increasingly turn over their logistics and supply operations to private companies so that they can focus their militaries on combat arms. The United Kingdom is a notable holdout against the privatization of their military services, purportedly on ethical grounds. But this policy is rapidly evolving and, in any case, would almost certainly not survive a change of government.

Beyond strictly military activities, many companies are finding a lucrative security market in unstable states, as previously discussed. Globalization has opened up new opportunities for MNCs to expand into countries with marginal security situations. To protect their facilities, these corporations usually turn to private security firms since state militaries are often unwilling or unable to provide the necessary security. The PSCs offer specialization, experience and flexibility that would not be possible if the MNCs were to provide their own security. The increasing numbers of PSCs offering services in this area make security contracts for MNCs highly competitive, bringing security costs down and encouraging MNCs to expand their operations in areas of conflict.

Africa

Africa, especially South Africa, will see the greatest proportionate growth in the private security industry. While MNCs will increasingly use private firms to protect valuable assets such as mines and oil facilities, regional and international organizations such as ECOMOG and the UN are likely to turn to private firms for expertise and services that member states are unable to provide. Any future African peacekeeping operations that take place in the DRC or Angola will require the services of private firms for logistics at the very least. The South African government has been highly critical of its international private military services industry, but since South African troops are likely to be significantly involved in future African peacekeeping missions, this policy will most likely be modified. The ANC government already tried to use two South African PSCs to provide security for 'Xanana' Gusmao, the East Timorese leader with whom it has close ties. South Africa's *Mail & Guardian* newspaper found out about the plans and embarrassingly revealed them, indicating that Pretoria saw the utility of PSCs and was willing to ignore its own legislation regarding selling military services abroad. Once publicly revealed, the plans were quietly dropped.[29]

If Western militaries are used in African peacekeeping operations, they will bring private companies with them in the form of support services. There will also be many opportunities for African PMCs to gain contracts supporting such a force, and it is likely that many new African PSCs will be created for just such tasks, and existing companies expanded to provide the necessary services. Although up until now the UN has been reluctant to work with private military companies, the global security situation will require a more nuanced policy in the future since some interaction with private companies will be useful, cost-effective and probably unavoidable. It is also likely that the UN will face political pressure to use African companies to supplement the few Western PSCs already under contract.

MNCs that have extensive operations in Africa are likely already to be using African PSCs to provide the necessary security for their facilities. In many countries, security firms are required to have a percentage of 'local content'. In some cases, the deal that MNCs make with the governments requires the use of locally owned and operated private security firms. Sometimes MNCs also form partnerships with locally owned firms to get around restrictive legislation.[30] Even Western-based PSCs executing contracts in Africa usually provide little more than management personnel, while the bulk of their employees are recruited and trained locally. Due to the nature of most African wars, these security firms are often exposed to direct attack by rebel forces. Therefore, while they may be perceived as private 'police', the reality is that many of these firms are by necessity trained and armed not only to prevent theft but also to repel military attacks. As earlier noted, the presence of these private, defensive armies protecting valuable economic facilities frees up national militaries to concentrate on regular military operations and enhances localized security especially at sites of strategic economic importance.

It is ironic that African states that have suffered from recent wars have a comparative advantage in the globalized world because of their experiences with conflict which have created useful military skills applicable to conflicts worldwide. Notably, demining companies based in Zimbabwe and South Africa are already cornering much of the world market in this area. Few Western companies can match their experience, skills, technology or even their prices.[31] Mozambique also has a number of demining companies which are currently employed in extensive domestic operations but could eventually market their services internationally. These companies have a great deal of experience in the field and have a large potential market for their services.

Trends and Predictions

Before concluding this essay, we identify six trends and predictions related to the future of private security firms.

- Around the world PMC/PSCs will increasingly take over military tasks such as training, intelligence, surveillance, demining and logistics from state militaries. This growth will be especially prevalent in the militaries of less developed countries.

- With the mounting numbers, size, scope and complexity of peacekeeping operations, PMC/PSCs will eventually be called upon by regional organizations and even the UN to assist with humanitarian efforts, military logistics, intelligence, supply and all forms of peacekeeping support. Within five years, PMCs may take prominent and active roles in peacekeeping and peace enforcement.

- Although a few firms have made clear their willingness to participate in offensive combat operations, there is no opportunity for such action on the immediate horizon (although individual freelance mercenaries will continue to sell specialist war services such as piloting combat aircraft). Nevertheless, PMC/PSCs will increasingly engage in combat roles providing security for industrial sites in war zones, leading peacekeeping support and protecting humanitarian operations. Should the UN or regional international organization decide to 'legitimize' the use of PMCs for combat operations, then there will be a rapid growth in the number of PMCs, mostly as subsidiaries of established PSCs.

- MNCs like oil companies and mining firms with operations in unstable states will increasingly contract out to PSCs to protect their facilities. Outsourced security will be preferred due to the high levels of specialization required, the complexity of such operations, and the need to provide a degree of separation from any ugly security 'incident'. Employing PSCs cushions MNCs from potentially disastrous public relations situations and allows them greater flexibility in their response to such incidents.

- PMC/PSCs from developing countries that have recently emerged from war will increasingly offer essential military services on the world market. These companies can utilize the skills left over from their conflicts to provide inexpensive military services more cheaply than established Western military service companies.

- The private security industry will experience increasing consolidation. While there are a great number of small companies that appear and disappear almost daily, they will not be able to compete effectively with the larger companies that have name recognition and proven reliability. Perhaps due to a lack of regulation and legitimization, the industry has too many firms claiming to provide too many services. Whether such companies can provide the services they claim to offer is unknown, but MNCs, states, NGOs and the UN are more likely to patronize only those companies that have a reputable track record.

Conclusion

The international private military services industry is still in its infancy. It is an industry where reputation means everything as evidenced by the dominance of a few large firms. The bulk of the revenues of these companies come from the private sector, but the greatest opportunity for future contracts comes from the public sector. While the UN and NGOs have only used PMC/PSCs in limited roles, they are increasingly likely to use their services for humanitarian, peacekeeping and even state-rebuilding operations in the future. The increasing numbers of public sector contracts will result in a 'legitimization' of the industry, which will include a standardization of regulation and oversight to ensure that humanitarian standards are maintained. For newer PMC/PSCs, the key to accessing these future international contracts will be to develop rapidly stellar reputations for efficiency, ethics and humanitarianism. In Africa, which currently suffers from many of the world's conflicts and has many of the least trained national armies, the trend towards privatization of military services – with their potential to end violent wars, provide effective peacekeeping and peace enforcement, and force warring parties to the negotiating table – can only be a positive development.

NOTES

1. There have been numerous accounts about the use of freelance mercenaries in all these cases. For some good references, see 'Foreign Mercenaries Who Fought with RUF Threat to ECOWAS'; Inter Press Service, 10 Feb. 1999; also with regard to UNITA's use of mercenaries, see Enrique Bernales Ballesteros, 'Report on the question of the use of mercenaries as a means of violating human rights and impeding the exercise of the right of peoples to self-determination', UN document E/CN.4/1994/23 submitted to the UN Commission on Human Rights, 12 Jan. 1994, para. 40.
2. David Isenberg. 'Soldiers of Fortune Ltd.: A Profile of Today's Private Sector Corporate Mercenary Firms', *Center for Defense Information Monograph* (November 1997), Center for Defense Information.
3. Most sources claim the cost was closer to $35 million or $36 million. The actual cost of EO's operations in Sierra Leone has been disputed by many, with some sources indicating that companies related to EO received mining concessions as partial payment. Nevertheless, EO used less than 220 soldiers for its operations, while the UN currently has about 13,000 peacekeepers. It is obvious that EO ran a substantially more cost-effective operation than the UN is able to. PMCs make a strong claim that they could do peacekeeping for much less than what it currently costs the UN.
4. Norimitsu Onishi, 'Anger Still Fires the Hell That Was Sierra Leone', *New York Times*, 31 March 2000. Onishi attributes the figure of $90 million to Oluyemi Adeniji, the United Nations' Special Representative in Sierra Leone.
5. 'Companies such as Armor Holdings, or Control Risks, a consultancy based in London, are always keen to stress what they do not do. Although they approach the business of managing risk more directly than, say, an insurance firm, their employees do not don uniforms or wield guns. They are not, in other words, to be confused with Executive Outcomes, a defunct South African firm that could provide anyone who was rich enough to pay with machinegunners and fighter-pilots who had plenty of combat experience.' 'Corporate Security: Risk Returns', *Economist*, 20 November 1999.
6. ArmorGroup is a London-based subsidiary of the American company Armor Holdings, described in more detail later in the essay.
7. James Fennell, 'Private Security Companies: The New Humanitarian Agent', Presentation to the Conference on Interagency Co-ordination in Complex Humanitarian Emergencies, 19 October 1999 at Cranfield University/Royal Military College of Science, Shrivenham, UK. Abridged document can be found on the ArmorGroup web page (http://www.armorgroup. com/mainframe.htm) or the full version can be requested by emailing info@armorgroup.com.
8. Ibid. Fennell lists as DSL clients: 'Our client list is remarkably similar to the list of major governmental and corporate donors to International NGOs and includes UN agencies, the Governments of the United Kingdom, USA, Switzerland, Sweden, Japan and Canada among others, the European Commission, ECHO, USAID, DFID, the International War Crimes Tribunal, the European Union Human Rights Office, the ICRC and NGOs such as IRC, CARE and Caritas.'
9. 'America's Fastest Growing Companies' *Fortune*, 6 September 1999.
10. Nicole Ostrow, 'Armor Holdings an Industry Leader', *Florida Times Union*, 3 September 1999, found on Armor Holding's web page, http://www.armorholdings.com.
11. 'Corporate Security: Risk Returns', *The Economist*, 20 November 1999; 'America's Fastest-Growing Companies', *Fortune*, 6 September 1999; 'Armor Holdings, Inc. reports fourth quarter earnings', PRNewswire, 19 March 2001.
12. 'Armor Holdings Acquires Special Clearance Services: Expands Capability in Landmine Clearance Operations and Gains Extended Contracts in Balkans', *Company Press Release, Armor Holdings, Inc., PRNewswire*, 23 March 2000; 'Armor Holdings, Inc. Completes Acquisition of New Technologies, Inc. and Acquires Safeback Technology from Sydex, Inc.', *Company Press Release, Armor Holdings, Inc., PRNewswire*, 31 March 2000.
13. Kevin O'Brien, 'Freelance Forces: Exploiters of Old or New-age Peacebrokers?', *Jane's Intelligence Review*, 1 August 1998. For a rather apocalyptic view of DSL and the merger with Armor Holdings, see Pratap Chatterjee, 'Guarding the Multinationals: DSL and the

International Private "Security" Business', *Multinational Monitor*, March 1998.
14. On the NYSE Armor Holdings is listed as 'AH'.
15. David Isenberg, 'Combat for Sale, The New Post-Cold War Mercenaries', *USA Today Magazine*, 1 March 2000.
16. Although a number of analysts have questioned the military capability of PMCs, notably Alex Vines of Human Rights Watch, most concede their military usefulness, while often questioning their long term effects. Christopher Clapham writes: 'Efficient armies...can have an impact well beyond their numbers. Quality differentials among the various assemblages of human beings engaged in conflict in Africa...are very high indeed. The capacity of EO [the South African PMC Executive Outcomes] in Angola, and of EO in collaboration with local *Kamajor* militias in Sierra Leone, to stabilize a previously crumbling government military situation provides the clearest evidence.' Christopher Clapham, 'African Security Systems', in Greg Mills and John Stremlau (eds.), *The Privatisation of Security in Africa*, Johannesburg: South African Institute for International Affairs and United States Institute of Peace, 1999, p.43.
17. Laurie Nathan of the Centre for Conflict Resolution makes many of the classic arguments against PMCs in his article, 'Trust me, I'm a Mercenary' (full citation below). However, his main argument is that PMCs do not have the same controls as state militaries and thus they *could* abuse their authority. In fact, there are remarkably few examples of PMCs abusing their authority, and this indicates that while PMCs may not have the *same* constraints as state militaries, like any other private firm they do face *different* constraints. PMCs still fear legal action from their home states, do in fact try to maintain a clean record in order to attract future clients, and, thus far, have proven to be far more observant of international laws of war and human rights than the forces they have faced in combat. Laurie Nathan, '"Trust Me I'm a Mercenary": The Lethal Danger of Mercenaries in Africa', Seminar on the 'Privatization' of Peacekeeping, Institute for Security Studies, 20 February 1997.
18. Spokes Mashiyane, 'U.S. Military Backing Sought: Mandela Predicts War Could Escalate', Reuters News Agency, found in *Washington Times*, 17 February 2000, p.13.
19. Steven Mann, 'SA Troops Will Stay Out of Hostile Territory', *Mail & Guardian*, 7 April 2000. With South Africa as one of the strongest backers of sending peacekeepers to DRC, this statement makes one wonder which country *is* expected to do the peacekeeping in the more dangerous regions.
20. This was made eminently clear at the Wilton Park conference in November 1999 when industry representatives were first invited, then disinvited, indicating government confusion but also a clear bias against PMCs. Sandline International published a letter describing the incident in detail on their web site (www.Sandline.com) and also online on the 'PMCs' discussion group (www.egroups.com/group/pmcs) on 20 October 1999. For access to the discussion group and its archives contact the author at hoosier84@aol.com.
21. For a good synopsis of the 'Arms to Africa' affair, see Baffour Ankomah, 'How the Good Guys Won', *New African*, July 1998.
22. The best evaluation of this legislation was actually written before the legislation was passed in hopes that it would influence the final product. Unfortunately, the proposed legislation was apparently not much impacted by the critique and many have criticized its current form. See Mark Malan and Jakkie Cilliers, 'Mercenaries and Mischief: The Regulation of Foreign Military Assistance Bill', *Institute for Security Studies*, Occasional Paper No.25, September 1997. Additional information on the effect of the South African legislation came from discussions with representatives of the South African National Conventional Arms Control Committee and various South African PSCs.
23. This phenomenon is investigated at length in Jeffrey Herbst, 'The Regulation of Private Security Forces', in Mills and Stremlau (eds.), *The Privatisation of Security in Africa*.
24. For an excellent article on 'frontline' PSCs, see A. Craig Copetas, 'Corporate Soldiers Advance in Balkans', *Wall Street Journal*, 14 April 1999, p.21.
25. Tod Robberson, 'Contractors Playing Increasing Role in U.S. Drug War', *Dallas Morning News*, 27 February 2000.
26. Rick Rigazio (ed.), 'A New Approach to Honoring American Military Commitments – Hiring Mercenaries', *Balkans Chronology*, Vol.1 Issue 24, 26 October–1 November 1998,

http://www.nwc.navy.mil/balkans/sumo26n1.htm

27. MPRI used to be 'Military Professional Resources Inc.' but has since officially simplified the company name to just the acronym.

28. Peter Andersen. Untitled news item reported from Liberian Star Radio, *Andersen Web Page*, 30 May 1998, http://www.sierra-leone.org/; 'U.S. Hopeful of New Relations with Nigeria', IPS, 29 November 1999; Ed Soyster (Vice President, International Operations, MPRI), interview by author, 16 March 2000, Alexandria, Virginia, USA.

29. Paul Kirk and Ivor Powell, 'Private SA force for East Timor conflict', *Mail & Guardian*, 29 October 1999.

30. David Shearer, 'Outsourcing War', *Foreign Policy*, Fall 1998, p.68.

31. Conversations with Gareth Elliot, Researcher and demining specialist, South African Institute of International Affairs, 1999–2000.

NATO's Underachieving Middle Powers: From Burdenshedding to Burdensharing

BRIAN FINLAY and MICHAEL O'HANLON

As the world's sole remaining superpower, the United States possesses the unique capability of projecting military power with relative impunity anywhere around the globe. With annual defence budget outlays of some $290 billion supporting an active armed force of just under 1.4 million men and women, along with unrivalled airlift and sealift capabilities, the United States is far and away the most potent military force in the post-Cold War world.

With American forces stationed in significant numbers around the globe, and as the only state capable of swiftly and decisively undertaking large-scale military operations in times of crisis, the United States naturally becomes the focal point of international attention whenever military crises or humanitarian emergencies erupt. However, while American participation in these missions is often indispensable to their success, Washington is frequently villified as being self-promoting, unilateral and arrogant – the imperial hegemon, or 'hyperpower' (in the words of French Foreign Minister, Hubert Védrine) once again foisting itself, its military and its values on the rest of an international community that is incapable of resisting.

Some of these criticisms are well-founded. But while many critics, who include a significant percentage of America's North Atlantic Treaty Organization (NATO) allies, continue to castigate the United States for 'unilateral' and 'interventionist' policies, there has yet to be a large-scale mobilization of resources by NATO allies to rival, or even significantly complement, America's unique military capabilities. Such a development would sometimes allow Washington to step aside in times of crisis – and perhaps even reduce some of its overseas military deployments.

Since the end of the Cold War, NATO's European members have cut defence spending by less than the United States. Their aggregate real military spending declined about 17 per cent between 1985 and 1998, while US outlays were cut by 28 per cent. However, their original spending levels were much less robust, and their allocation of defence resources is generally too skewed towards maintaining large standing armies rather than building deployable armed forces. Despite the myriad of new initiatives aimed at 're-shaping the [European] security architecture,' including most recently NATO's Defence Capabilities Initiative designed to improve the quality and usability of members' armed forces, few new capabilities have yet been developed which are suited to future security challenges.

Not all of America's allies are equally guilty of what economists might describe as a 'free-rider problem'. Britain notably provides NATO's only rapidly-deployable corps headquarters, and its forces form the core of the Allied Command Europe (ACE) Rapid Reaction Corps (ARRC). The British army also has the capability to deploy and sustain a division-sized force of 20,000–25,000 personnel in a major theatre war – perhaps more, if reservists are mobilized, as was envisioned for a possible ground war against Serbia in 1999. These capabilities were demonstrated in miniature in the British intervention in Sierra Leone to support UN peacekeepers in the spring of 2000. Under the premiership of Tony Blair, London has been seeking to improve these capabilities further by restructuring its forces and acquiring more strategic lift. The French are in the process of establishing a Rapid Action Force (FAR) designed for rapid response in both European and overseas contingencies. Likewise, Germany is standing up a Rapid Reaction Force of some 53,000 fully-equipped troops from the Army, Navy and Air Force – though it is doubtful that most of it will be quickly transportable overseas given ongoing cuts in Germany's defence spending (cuts since 1985 already exceed 35 per cent and are continuing).

If progress has been modest in western Europe's three largest countries, it has been barely perceptible in the small and medium-sized states within NATO. While European allies continue to slash spending on defence, they have failed to adequately consolidate their major defence industries and to downsize significantly their bloated land forces. As a result, European armies continue to lack funds for major initiatives aimed at reducing the technological and strategic transport and logistics disparities with the United States.

In Canada, the issue is somewhat different but on the whole even worse. There, defence spending presently sits at approximately US$7 billion, down about 40 per cent from the 1985 level. Even after adjusting for the relative size of the two populations, this figure represents only about a quarter of what Americans spend to finance the Pentagon. This has sometimes left the Canadian Forces hard pressed to maintain even their low-intensity peacekeeping deployments in places like the Balkans and Africa. Since 1991, Ottawa has slashed military spending by 23 per cent, and some members of the current government have actively advocated a further 30 per cent reduction in the country's military budget. Moreover, the number of active duty personnel in Canada has fallen from 84,000 to 59,000 since the end of the Cold War.

The military imbalance between the US and its NATO allies, even if it is presently fiscally convenient for America's allies and politically desirable to some policymakers in Washington for the status and influence it affords the country abroad, is extremely unhealthy for the long-term future of the Western alliance. Continued US preponderance in multilateral operations abroad ultimately reduces the influence of American allies in how those operations are conducted. It also lessens the prospects that future American-led operations will receive enough international backing to gain strong legitimacy in the eyes of the global community. At home, the disproportionate military burden borne by Americans in NATO risks a strong public backlash against engagement and in favour of isolationism. An America disengaged from international affairs is clearly not, as the experience of the period between the two world wars starkly revealed, in the best interests of the United States or of the world.

The Plan

The NATO debate over 'burdensharing' – defence lexicon for the division of costs and responsibilities within the alliance – is as old as the alliance itself. Recent events, notably NATO's 1999 war against Serbia, but also Operation *Desert Storm* in the Gulf in 1991, have highlighted the burgeoning capability gap between the US and its alliance partners. While it would be unrealistic to expect the allies to replicate America's military might, NATO's underachieving middle powers could become more deeply engaged, shoulder a heavier military burden, gain greater global influence, and thus help attenuate America's perceived bullying dominance over the alliance.

While NATO's non-American armies are highly competent in basic military skills, they also tend to feature several crippling deficiencies. For example, most of these armies, with the partial exception of Britain, are unable to deploy independently and rapidly in theatres of conflict. Few of them can engage in the type of military campaign that today's technology affords, particularly in air warfare and joint operations.

This essay proposes that America's NATO allies should develop high-technology and strategic transport and logistics capabilities for what might be called a 'one major theatre war' effort. (Throughout the 1990s, the United States has tried to have the capability to fight two such wars, most likely against Iraq and North Korea.) We provide a case study of the Canadian army below as an illustration of how this can be achieved.

Middle powers like Canada, Spain and the Netherlands should contribute to the proposed force at a level amounting to about one-third of the contributions of Germany, France and Britain. Italy might aspire to contribute about half as much as NATO's European 'big three' – a realistic goal, given its current capabilities and defence budget (a straight GDP analysis might argue for even more Italian strength, but that would not be politically realistic). Smaller countries like Belgium could contribute less than Canada and the other middle powers.[1] With this approach, a middle power like Canada would require about 7 to 10 per cent of a major theatre war force – or about 30,000 to 50,000 deployable, well-equipped combat troops. That translates into up to a division of ground forces and a wing of combat aircraft – though even two brigades of ground forces and two squadrons of aircraft would be a worthy contribution to the proposed force.

This proposal of a one-war capability force is, of course, an artificial construct. It is not meant to imply that non-American forces should plan to defeat Iraq or Iran on their own without US assistance. This proposal would mainly ensure that NATO allies which participate in a future conflict would, in conjunction with the United States, do more militarily in any future war than they did against Iraq in 1991 or Serbia in 1999.

Nor is the one-war construct meant to suggest that countries like Canada, which often prefer to play a complementary role to the US in global affairs rather than simply recasting themselves in Uncle Sam's image, would need to view their militaries only as traditional war-fighting instruments. More deployable and combat-capable NATO forces would be useful for a host of missions, from muscular peacekeeping in the Balkans, to halting genocides like the one in Rwanda in 1994, to patrolling ceasefires like those that the UN now hopes to help consolidate in the Democratic Republic of Congo (DRC) and Sierra Leone. In many cases, such capabilities could also help countries like Canada lead military missions in which Washington wishes to play – or should play – a minimal role. Canada had agreed to lead such a humanitarian intervention into eastern Congo in November 1996, before the plans were overtaken by events on the ground. The precedent of Australia's successful intervention in East Timor in 1999 is, however, particularly noteworthy in this regard.

The Military Imbalance Today

As witnessed in the skies over Kosovo in 1999, the degree of US military supremacy, even over its Western allies, is overwhelming. Not only does Washington spend five or six times more on defence than any other country in the world, it also spends its money better, producing a far more effective return on its investment than any of its major NATO allies – again with the partial exception of Britain. Among the military advantages that the US has over most other states, even in proportionate terms, are in the realms of long-range strategic transport, mobile logistics, advanced precision-guided weaponry, stealth technology and global surveillance and communications systems.

One might think that NATO's European states, which, in aggregate terms, spend two-thirds as much on defence as the United States and maintain even more people under arms, might have at least 50 per cent of the actual capability of the US armed forces. Although they may attain or even exceed this figure on European territory, NATO's European armies do not come close to the US beyond their borders. In fact, beyond their own continent, the European allies and Canada, in aggregate terms, would do well to keep up with the US Marine Corps, which makes up just 12 per cent of total American military strength and an even less fraction of US defence spending.

While not revealing much about relative ground-combat capabilities, Operation *Allied Force*, the air campaign over Yugoslavia in 1999, served as a wake-up call to both the United States and its NATO partners. A quick look at the statistics is revealing: the United States flew 71 per cent of all support sorties during the multinational operation, American pilots conducted 53 per cent of all strike sorties – not an unreasonable share – but dropped 80 per cent of all precision munitions and launched 95 per cent of all cruise missiles. Also, 90 per cent of all of the electronic warfare aircraft used in the air campaign were American.[2] Meanwhile, the United States had about 250,000 troops based or deployed in other parts of the world, while the NATO allies, in aggregate, were managing about half of that number outside their own territories.[3]

But one must also give America's allies their due: they have been providing the lion's share of the peacekeeping forces in Bosnia throughout the last decade and in post-war Kosovo since the war ended there in June 1999. In each place, the share of the non-American NATO forces has typically exceeded 75 per cent. And in the early 1990s, countries like Britain and France lost dozens of soldiers in the UNPROFOR mission in Bosnia, while the United States, scarred by Somalia, stayed on the sidelines. But the Balkans are the exception, not the rule.

The glaring defence imbalance within NATO is clearly on the minds of American officials. General Wesley Clark, who ran NATO's air war against Serbia, has repeatedly warned that the Allies run the risk of becoming junior partners within the alliance. Even before the Yugoslavia campaign of 1999, American Secretary of Defense, William Cohen, had warned that allied countries run the risk of falling so far behind the United States that future multilateral operations may be jeopardized by interoperability problems. Then US Under-Secretary of Defense, Jacques Gansler, and America's Joint Chiefs of Staff Chairman, General Henry Shelton, likewise commissioned a Defence Science Board study on the topic of American-led coalition operations, out of deep concern that advanced technologies could make such operations even more difficult to run in future.[4]

The Canadian Example

Despite shrinking from 87,000 service personnel in 1990 to some 58,000 today, the Canadian Forces – like other middle powers within the Alliance – have never been more active on a global scale. By October 1999, Canada had 4,500 military personnel on 22 overseas missions, the largest commitment of troops overseas since the Korean War of 1950–53.

While European militaries have the ability to share costs due to their close proximity to one another, Canada represents something of a special case. Geographically isolated from its non-American NATO allies, combined training, transport and logistics operations have proven to be inconvenient. Canada has focused increasingly on peacekeeping missions, which, together with coastal patrols, preclude a significant contribution to traditional air and ground combat forces – at least at current defence-spending levels.

Moreover, the former Canadian Minister for Foreign Affairs, Lloyd Axworthy, succeeded in pushing a so-called 'human security' policy agenda that will potentially imply even wider military or quasi-military peace engagements. While Axworthy and others assumed that the end of the Cold War and the rise of non-traditional threats to security would portend the need for more lightly-armed and rapidly deployable national forces – with hard military power becoming all but tangential to global order – this has not proved to be the case. Delivering humanitarian aid often takes place in unstable areas and stretches concepts of traditional peacekeeping missions beyond breaking point. As is still evident in post-war Kosovo, the fine line between peacekeeping and peace enforcement is increasingly blurred (see Berdal, and Wermester and Malone in this volume). Kosovo also proves the need to maintain a combat-capable military force able to back up diplomatic posturing. Moreover, traditional UN peacekeeping missions in places like Angola and Rwanda in the early 1990s have sometimes failed, for lack of political will and military capability on the part of international forces, when ceasefires or peace agreements have broken down (see Adebajo and Landsberg in this volume). The human toll from renewed conflict in these places was enormous.[5]

At the end of the day, traditional military might often remains crucial to providing security and ensuring stability in conflict situations. The sharp end of the military continues to be vital to the success of many peace operations – this is as true for the US as it is for Canadian forces or other mid-level NATO powers.

Canada's annual defence spending amounts to just over one per cent of the country's GDP. Among the 15 members of NATO assessed in the US Department of Defense's 1999 study, *Report on Allied Contributions to the Common Defense*, Canada ranked second to last – ahead of only Luxembourg – in annual defence spending. As the Pentagon baldly puts it, Canada's contribution to common defence is little more than half the NATO average of 2.1 per cent, and about a third of the US level by the same measure.

Problems with the Canadian Forces' inventory of equipment comprise both obsolescent items and shortages. After losing almost a quarter of its budget over the last decade, Canada's Department of National Defense is struggling with financial pressures that are felt in every area of the defence programme. There is a compounding deficit of funds available for operations and training; and, most serious of all, there is a severe shortage of people. According to the Conference of Defense Associations, an Ottawa-based non-profit lobby, personnel shortages are particularly severe in the army, which has only 65 per cent of the staff it needs to fulfil Canada's increased commitments to multilateral peace operations in the post-Cold War era. Canada's over-commitment of forces abroad, peaking in 1999 at around 4,500 men and women, produced an unsustainable OPTEMPO[6] for the Forces. As a result of this, the Canadian contingent was forced to begin withdrawing from East Timor prematurely in February 2000, and Ottawa reduced its military commitments in Kosovo in order to consolidate positions in Bosnia.

This over-tasking has generated serious quality of life and readiness problems for the Canadian Forces. Last year, while en route to East Timor, a Canadian Forces transport plane was forced to turn back three times due to malfunctions with its compass and tail rudder. Another Canadian C-130 aircraft was forced to make the trip flying below a 10,000-foot ceiling due to a malfunctioning cabin-pressurization system. Transporting equipment across the Pacific to Indonesia also posed difficulties, since the Canadian Navy has little transport capability and was forced to use one of its only two supply ships to service the entire fleet. In late 1998, an ageing Canadian Labrador search and rescue helicopter crashed in Quebec during a training flight, killing all six crew.

Canada's 31 Maritime Sea King helicopters, which are 36 years old, require 40 hours of maintenance for one hour of flight time – twice that required for a new helicopter.[7] In the key area of strategic lift, the Canadian Forces maintain only 32 Lockheed C-130 Hercules and five Airbus *Industrie* CC-150 Polaris transport aircraft. At sea, the Canadian Forces have only two auxiliary oiler-replenishment ships available. The picture presented here is hardly one of an equal partner bearing its fair share within the Western Alliance.

The NATO allies are clearly concerned about Canada's meagre defence budget. In 1999 Gordon Giffen, the American Ambassador in Ottawa, took the unusual step of criticizing Canadians for going too far with defence budget cuts and for neglecting their international responsibilities. On his inaugural trip to Ottawa as NATO Secretary-General, Lord George Robertson said: 'When called upon, Canada has always been there – strong in Bosnia, strong in Kosovo – but...still languishes in terms of spending per unit of national wealth just above Luxembourg.' While Canada performed well in Kosovo, deploying 18 CF-18 fighter aircraft equipped with infra-red sensors and laser designators for precision-guided weapons,[8] that number was only one-fortieth the total number of American aircraft. The Canadian army remains deeply lacking in key capabilities. To its credit, Canada was able to participate in 10 per cent of the strike sorties in Kosovo in 1999, but did much less in other areas. For example, well before the air campaign over Yugoslavia in 1999, the Canadian military was obliged, due to lack of funds, to retire its entire fleet of electronic warfare aircraft, crucial to any aerial conflict.

For the first time in a decade, it is now expected that spending on national defence in Canada will finally increase. The Canadian military has outlined ten critical procurement programs, worth more than US$4.5 billion, which are expected to begin within the next four years. Additional funding will help finance 32 new Maritime helicopters, upgrades to 18 Aurora maritime patrol aircraft, further upgrades to CF-18 fighter aircraft,[9] a satellite communications system,[10] 290 new armoured combat vehicles and an Afloat Logistics Sealift Capability. A new Joint Space Project will develop a surveillance system to detect land, sea and air targets on or approaching the North American continent. Canada's Department of National Defense also intends to replace the Army's main battle tank, the Leopard, beginning in 2004. The 1994 Defense White Paper has called for the modernization of Canada's Hercules transports, the replacement of logistics ships, and establishment of new army command and control systems.

In keeping with its continued commitment to peacekeeping, Canada is also establishing a rapid-reaction force capable of deploying anywhere

TABLE 1

CANADIAN DEFENSE MODERNIZATION

Purchase/Upgrade	Cost (Canadian Dollars)	Initial Operational Capability
Maritime Helicopter	2.2–2.8 billion	2004
CF-18 Fighter Aircraft	1.2 billion	1999
Afloat Logistics Sealift Capability	more than 1 billion	2007
Aurora Patrol Aircraft	1 billion	1999
Armoured Combat Vehicle	800 million	2007
Canadian Military Satellite Communications System	700 million	2006
Joint Space Project	624 million	2010
Armoured Personnel Carrier Replacement	400 million	2000
Naval Command and Control Air Defense Replacement	N/A	2001–2005
Strategic Air-to-Air Refuelling	N/A	2006

Source: Department of National Defense, *Defense Planning Guidance 2000*, Ottawa, 5 August 1999, and David Pugliese, 'Canadians Target Broad Equipment Upgrade Scheme', *Defense News*, 27 September 1999.

around the globe within 30 days – half the time currently required. The force will be composed of 1,000 troops, military helicopters, armoured personnel carriers and, when required, navy frigates to patrol coastal areas. Although this rapid-reaction initiative is in the right spirit, it is about a factor of 10 short of what is truly required in size.

The Canadian Forces plan to finance this modernization by increasing the percentage of the annual defence budget for procurement to 23 per cent over the course of the next five years – up from just 18 per cent in the fiscal year 1999 budget. This increase, however, will be insufficient to fund fully each of these equipment procurement initiatives. In an April 1998 report, Canada's Auditor General noted that the Canadian military's future equipment needs far exceed its budget. In fact, Ottawa's capital budget will be short by some CDN$4 to 6 billion over the next ten years.[11] Even with projected increases, Canada's annual defence budget is to increase by only about half a billion dollars, after declining nearly ten times as much since 1985.[12]

While the focus of Canadian defence modernization remains in the field of peacekeeping and peace support operations, budget cuts have led to a degradation of capabilities needed to conduct conventional military operations – or even difficult humanitarian interventions that may involve some combat. Without additional resources, Canada's role within the NATO alliance will be severely undermined.

Preparing the Defence Shopping List

For the NATO allies, the post-Cold War restructuring of their respective militaries has been difficult. NATO members must focus more on their deployable capabilities and realize that the defence of national territory should no longer be the sole, or even necessarily the primary, focus of military planning in the post-Cold War era. Having the capacity to transport only a few tens of thousands of relatively lightly armed soldiers quickly to a trouble spot (in aggregate), and needing many months to send significant amounts of armour, is grossly inadequate to deal with the sorts of contingencies facing the NATO alliance today.

Despite spending two-thirds of what the United States does on defence, other NATO countries have only some 10 per cent of the transportable defence capability for prompt long-range action (more than half of it British).[13] To play a major partnership role with US forces, the allies do not need to develop an independent 'forced-entry' capability that could fight its way onto enemy territory with large numbers of amphibious ships or air assault units. Nor do they require major initiatives in reconnaissance assets, theatre missile defences (TMDs) or several other key support areas. By focusing on strategic transport, deployable logistics, munitions stocks and several key 'Revolution in Military Affairs (RMA)'-type systems, they could develop roughly half as much rapidly deployable military capability as the United States for a total of about $100 billion over the next seven to ten years or so.[14] Although large in total amount, this figure represents an average of no more than 10 per cent of projected defence budgets over this time period.

In Europe, this initiative could be funded within projected resource levels simply by reducing the size of the unnecessarily large European force structures. Smaller, better equipped forces would be much more useful, at the same overall budgetary price, in theatres where the Western alliance faces its most likely future tests.

In Canada, increased defence spending is clearly required, given the severity of recent budget cuts and the extremely low level of current defence spending. However, the amount of the increase need not be crippling if the money is well spent.

Keeping up with High Technology

NATO's non-American members must make targeted investments in key technologies in order to remain interoperable within the Western Alliance. This does not mean however, that the alliance's middle powers must adopt wholesale the dubious notion that a revolution in military affairs is under way, or bankrupt themselves in the process of modernizing.[15] If it were so hard and expensive to keep up with trends in high technology, the US Marine Corps would surely be shut out of the action. Although it admittedly has direct access to various American military satellites, strategic transport and other critical enabling technologies that other services or joint military programs purchase, its own funds are quite limited. At $10 billion a year, with only about $1 billion set aside for procurement, the US Marine Corps has a budget that is only about 25 to 35 per cent of the size of several of America's bigger-size allies, and comparable to those of NATO's middle powers like Canada. Yet the Marine Corps is a major player in military innovation – just as allied forces can be.

To see just how affordable the so-called RMA should be for major US allies, one can consider the following shopping basket of RMA technologies listed below. Although admittedly not a comprehensive list, it is nevertheless an extensive one. It might be within the purchasing power of the three large European countries, Germany, France and Britain; for NATO's middle powers like Canada, a list of roughly one-third as ambitious would be more appropriate.

- Advanced radios, computers and identification-friend-or-foe (IFF) devices for all major vehicles and aircraft in three modern ground divisions;

- Advanced radios, avionics, data links, bomb racks and designators for precision-guided munitions, and helmet-mounted displays in three air wings;

- A dozen ground stations, some fixed and some mobile, to integrate and disseminate data and commands, with electronics and computers similar to those of the joint surveillance and target attack radar system (JSTARS) aircraft;

- A fleet of 50 UAVs of various sizes, ranges, and payloads similar to those operated by the United States;

- 1,000 cruise missiles;

- 5,000 short-range munitions, including an assortment of laser-guided bombs, Maverick, and Hellfire-like ordnance;

- 500 advanced air-to-air missiles, a mix of beyond-visual-range radar-homing missiles and short-range infrared missiles; and

- A squadron of stealth aircraft to map out an enemy's radar defences and lead any attack, particularly in the first days of battle.

This basket of capabilities includes most of the types of advanced sensors, computing and communications grids, and precision firepower needed to detect, target and destroy military assets on the future battlefield. In rough numbers, the costs of this system of systems would be approximately $15 billion – or perhaps one-third as much for a scaled-down version for Canada. That is hardly an inexpensive price tag. Yet it is the equivalent of less than two years of procurement spending for most non-US NATO countries. Averaged out over a decade, it would equal about 15 to 20 per cent of the weapons acquisition budget of the typical allied nation. Generally speaking, there would be few – if any – additional operating costs, since these systems would replace existing assets rather than require the formation of new units. Moreover, some of these capabilities are already in the hands of the middle powers and many, such as Canada, already intend to upgrade their capabilities under existing plans. That should further reduce the need for additional spending.

Making Forces Deployable

Price tags for buying sealift, airlift and mobile logistics assets for this notional one-theatre-war capability are roughly comparable. For a large European NATO country, they might total $15 billion. The largest elements would be in long-range airlift (perhaps 20 C-17 aircraft or the equivalent), mobile logistics capabilities such as equipment repair facilities and hospitals and construction assets, refuelling aircraft (again, perhaps 20 planes), and sealift (perhaps three large roll-on/roll-off ships). For Canada or a similarly-sized country, these numbers could be scaled back accordingly.

Adding in the costs of improving their power-projection capacities in areas such as long-range transport and mobile logistics, the total defence restructuring price tag would not exceed 30 per cent of the typical middle power's acquisition budget. Since most European militaries are at least 30 per cent larger than they need to be, that price tag is hardly beyond the realm of the possible. For Canada, increased spending on defence will be needed, perhaps restoring its budget level to a midway point between the 1985 level and today's much lesser amounts.[16]

Admittedly, this list of technologies and deployment assets does not push all types of possible military innovation equally rapidly. It focuses on information warfare, not on stealth or speed, and on bulk transportation rather than on amphibious or air assault capabilities. Pursuing stealth across the board would be extremely costly. Not only combat aircraft but also transport helicopters, ships and armoured vehicles might have to be designed and built from scratch to profit fully from technologies reducing radar, acoustic and other signatures. However, these types of improvements are not at the core of the current electronics-led defence modernization wave. They are generally areas in which radical improvements in capability are unlikely to be necessary – especially in light of the absence of sophisticated and wealthy potential adversaries to Western security interests. Nor is it necessary for non-American NATO countries to obtain every type of 'forced-entry' asset or reconnaissance capability possessed by the United States. Fiscal constraints are clearly real and cannot be ignored.

Doubtless, in many European countries and in Canada where public attitudes are deeply imbued by pacifist sentiments, plans to reconfigure and enhance the capabilities of national war-fighting instruments will be unpopular. However, in a changing world where traditional territorial defense is less prevalent, and where difficult peace operations and humanitarian interventions are more plausible and increasingly necessary, Western militaries will be forced to reconfigure to manage global peace and stability. In the wake of Somalia, Rwanda, Bosnia and Kosovo, it is no longer NATO's choice to intervene, it is NATO's duty. Too many lives are at stake for the Western world to stand by. Moreover, American forces cannot and should not be asked to bear the burden of global security single-handedly – nor should the international community be prepared to let the United States do so.

How the Allies Should Cooperate

Perhaps more than ever before, close collaboration between NATO's allies is crucial to maintaining interoperability in the information age. For example, with regard to radios, it is not only a matter of agreeing to common frequencies, but also of using common software that allows radios to encrypt, frequency hop and share bandwidth in synchronicity. Similar challenges have prevented NATO from establishing common standards in computer hardware and software to date. America's NATO allies may need to acknowledge US leadership in information technology and advanced munitions, in some cases, and be willing to buy US systems. But the United States may sometimes need to buy European or Canadian technology – or at least enter into relatively equitable collaborative ventures. The chances are that the first network-centric information systems will be designed and built in the United States, given the Pentagon's four-to-one edge over US allies in defence research and engineering spending as well as the strength of the US computer industry. Still, the Pentagon should try to find ways to purchase upgrades or certain follow-on systems from its NATO partners, or team up increasingly with allied firms in joint ventures to do so.

If such a spirit of allied collaboration can be established, money should not be a major constraint on developing an integrated, interoperable, and militarily deployable high-technology NATO alliance. Once they are developed in research laboratories and test ranges, the prices of purchasing most relevant technologies should generally be modest. Innovations in electronics at the turn of the century are characterized as much by declining prices as by increasing capacity and power. Improvements to munitions, avionics, sensors, computers and communications systems can be made relatively inexpensively as well.

Conclusion

In concluding, it is important to reiterate the point noted at the beginning of this essay: NATO allies cannot fairly criticize the United States for overbearing international behaviour while expecting it to shoulder the burden of maintaining a stable international environment from East Asia to the Persian Gulf to the airways over Serbia. Nor should any of the allies, American and non-American alike, have clear consciences over their collective neglect of Africa in recent times.

Nor is the present imbalanced state of defence burdensharing within the Western alliance healthy for NATO. Even countries like Canada that are eager to help usher in a different kind of international environment, with different and generally lesser demands for traditional military forces, cannot claim that these aspirations obviate the need for viable combat capabilities today. The first decade of the post-Cold War era, with wars against Iraq and Serbia as well as a number of demanding humanitarian missions around the world, shows that force is still needed – even for those who wish to use it principally to save lives on humanitarian missions.

Fortunately, despite a good deal of talk to the contrary, it is not beyond the budgetary means of Canada and other like-minded countries to play a much greater role in global security affairs. Most NATO countries can do their part simply by reordering defence spending, reducing manpower while simultaneously making the remaining forces more deployable and sustainable abroad, and equipping these forces with advanced sensors, munitions and communications systems that take full advantage of new trends in electronics and computer technology. Canada, which has allowed itself to become too much of a defence laggard, needs to increase its military spending – but it need not do so by inordinate amounts, if it is sensible in allocating funds.

Even for a country like Canada, which is not a member of the European Union and therefore not privy to its evolving defence mechanism and architecture, there will be ample opportunity to participate in coalitions of the willing under UN or NATO auspices in the future. In 1999 in East Timor, Australia showed that a medium power can sometimes lead missions itself, and do so in support of the types of democratic and humanitarian values that Canadians hold dear. With a deployable military force worthy of its size, status and wealth, Canada could become a true global power, even if not a superpower. NATO's other underachieving middle powers must also start carrying their fair share of the military burden if the alliance is to be effective in defending its interests and promoting its values in the new millennium.

NOTES

1. In its most basic form, national military capability would be based upon the relative size of each ally's economy. In 1998, the Gross Domestic Product (GDP) of various NATO allies in billions of US dollars were as follows: Canada, $629.1; France, $1,389; Germany, $2,073.2; Italy, $1,142; Spain, $534.2, United Kingdom, $1,366.
2. William S. Cohen, Statement to the Senate Armed Services Committee's Hearing on Operations in Kosovo, July 20 1999.
3. International Institute for Strategic Studies, *The Military Balance, 1999/2000*, Oxford: Oxford University Press, 1999.
4. Greg Sherman, 'U.S. Warns of Risk to Defence Ties', *The Australian*, 31 July 1998; Bryan Bender, 'U.S. Worried by Coalition "Technology Gap"', *Jane's Defence Weekly*, July 29 1998, p.8.
5. See Stephen John Stedman, 'Spoiler Problems in Peace Processes', *International Security*, Vol.22, No.2, Fall 1997, pp.5–53.
6. Operations tempo refers to the pace of a military operation or operations in terms of equipment usage – aircraft 'flying hours', ship 'steaming days' or 'tank [driving] miles'. Obviously, the average 'optempo' of a country's overall military force increases with the intensity of and number of operation.
7. See Joel Baglole, 'Canada Confronts its Military Weakness – U.S. Cheers Plan to Reverse a Decline in Spending that Dates Back to '91', *The Wall Street Journal*, 15 February 2000, A23.
8. Canada was one of only five countries participating in Operation *Allied Force* which had the capacity to drop precision-guided munitions.
9. Upgrades will include the purchase of new operational flight program software from the U.S. Navy, the installation of new radio and radar systems, friend or foe identification systems, various displays and electronic warfare jamming equipment, a helmet-mounted sight and cueing system, and simulators.
10. The Canadian Military Satellite Communications System (SATCOM) will give the Canadian military a satellite communications capability in conjunction with the US military via a Canadian communications system onboard a US satellite.
11. Office of the Auditor General of Canada, 'Equipping and Modernizing the Canadian Forces', in *1998 Report of the Auditor-General of Canada*, April 1998.
12. William B. Scott, 'Bolder Budgets Restore Canada's Air Force', *Aviation Week and Space Technology*, June 26 2000, p.81.
13. See John E. Peters and Howard Deshong, *Out of Area or Out of Reach? European Military Support for Operations in Southwest Asia* , Santa Monica, Cal.: RAND Corporation 1995, pp.95–117; and Michael O'Hanlon, 'Transforming NATO: The Role of European Forces', *Survival*, Vol.39, No.3, Autumn 1997, pp.5–15.
14. See O'Hanlon, 'Transforming NATO', *Survival*, pp.5–15; and Michael O'Hanlon, *Technological Change and the Future of Warfare*, Washington, DC: Brookings, 2000, pp.153–60.

15. Lawrence Freedman, *The Revolution in Strategic Affairs*, Adelphi Paper No.318, Oxford University Press, 1998; and Michael O'Hanlon, *Technological Change and the Future of Warfare*, Washington, DC: Brookings, 2000.
16. As noted, the US Marine Corps does enjoy benefits from its sibling services that Canada would not have equal access to. However, the Marine Corps maintains three deployable combat divisions and combat wings; under our proposal, Canada would only need to develop the lift, logistics and technology for one-third as many forces.

Back to the Future:
UN Peacekeeping in Africa

ADEKEYE ADEBAJO and CHRIS LANDSBERG

Forty years after its difficult and controversial mission in the former Belgian Congo, the United Nations (UN) has deployed peacekeepers to the same unfortunate country to manage yet another struggle over the carcass of this huge country at the heart of Africa. This essay provides a historical overview of seven important UN peacekeeping missions undertaken in Africa between 1960 and 2000: Congo (1960s and 1999), Mozambique, Angola, Somalia, Rwanda and Sierra Leone.[1] All the conflicts examined are cases of civil war, reflecting the changing nature of post-Cold War peacekeeping (see Wermester and Malone in this volume). In this contribution the varied cases, most of which involve the large-scale deployment of troops, have been selected for the significant lessons that they provide for UN peacekeeping in Africa. The essay focuses neither on the UN's role in managing interstate conflicts nor on its dispatch of small military or electoral observer missions to Africa.

We will investigate several important questions related to the changing fortunes of UN peacekeeping missions in Africa: What are some of the factors that have determined the success, and contributed to the failure, of UN peacekeeping missions in Africa? Why was the UN Security Council reluctant to send peacekeepers to Africa after 1964? What factors account for the seeming resurgence of UN peacekeeping in Africa after 1990? Why did the Security Council become disillusioned with Africa again after 1993? Do the mandating of new UN peacekeeping missions to Africa in 1999 signify the failure of Africa's regional organizations and a revival of UN peacekeeping in Africa? How can a new division of labour be established between the UN and Africa's regional security organizations to manage conflicts on the continent?

Africa has been a giant laboratory for UN peacekeeping and has repeatedly tested the capacity and political resolve of an often dysfunctional 15-member UN Security Council. Since 1960, the world body has deployed 18 peacekeeping missions in Africa. Of the 34 UN operations established since the end of the Cold War, half of them have been in Africa. Under the loose heading of peacekeeping,[2] the UN has conducted a variety of tasks ranging from ending secession in mineral-rich Congo, to facilitating the feeding of starving populations in war-torn Somalia, to disarming and demobilizing soldiers in poverty-stricken Mozambique, to managing a transition to independence in apartheid-ruled Namibia, to registering voters for a self-determination referendum in the sands of Western Sahara.

Since the UN's peacekeeping successes and failures are often contingent on the domestic, regional and extra-regional dynamics of conflict situations, we examine these factors in detail in each case. We focus more heavily on the politics of peacekeeping than on its technical and logistical constraints. While these technical and logistical deficiencies are often important, we regard the existence of political consensus among domestic, regional and extra-regional (particularly the powerful members of the Security Council) actors as more significant in determining the success of UN peacekeeping missions in Africa. Technically-deficient peacekeeping missions can still succeed with strong political support, while the most technically brilliant peace operations are likely to be undermined by a lack of political commitment on the part of key actors. The essay has three important goals: to place UN peacekeeping missions in Africa in their larger geo-political contexts; to assess the internal, regional and external factors that affect the outcome of peacekeeping missions in Africa; and to draw general lessons from these cases in order to determine the factors that are most likely to contribute to future peacekeeping successes.

Based on a thorough assessment of our seven cases, we have identified six factors which, in our view, have most often contributed to success in UN peacekeeping missions in Africa: first, the existence of a political accord between the warring parties[3] and the willingness of internal parties to disarm and accept electoral results; second, the development of an effective strategy to deal with potential 'spoilers'; third, the absence of conflict-fuelling economic resources in war zones (see Alao and Olonisakin; and Keen in this volume); fourth, the cooperation of regional players in peace processes; fifth, the cessation of military and financial support to local clients by extra-regional actors and their provision of financial and diplomatic support to peace processes; and finally, the leadership of peacekeeping missions by capable envoys. It is worth noting that the presence or absence of these factors is not automatically determinant of the outcome of these peacekeeping missions. All the factors will clearly not be met in every case of success or failure.

This point was clearly illustrated by the UN mission in the Congo in the 1960s, which succeeded in its goals of reuniting a fractious country in spite of regional divisions and extra-regional meddling. The US-backed candidate, General Joseph Mobutu, eventually won power, and the Congolese parties agreed to cooperate in a political system led by an African *caudillo*, an outcome which was also accepted by regional states. The UN mission in Mozambique, however, met all our criteria for success:

the internal parties were willing to cooperate with the peace process and accept electoral results (an outcome doubtless helped by the end of the Cold War which facilitated the successful exertion of external pressure on the warring parties); regional and extra-regional players provided crucial diplomatic and financial support to the peace process and stopped arming Mozambique's warring factions; and the UN had an effective and energetic Special Representative in the person of Aldo Ajello. In stark contrast, Angola lacked most of the criteria for success: Jonas Savimbi proved to be a successful 'spoiler' who refused to disarm or abide by election results; he had the economic resources and military strength to frustrate the UN; continued US support for Savimbi was unhelpful to UN efforts to win the cooperation of the warlord; and the UN mission sent to Angola in 1991 was grossly under-funded and under-staffed.

Rwanda was tragically tarred with the Somali brush of failure. The UN missions in both countries were, in a sense, contrasts in failure. Somalia was a well-funded mission that had some of the best-equipped soldiers in the world. The UN, Ethiopia and extra-regional actors provided support for diplomatic efforts to end the conflict. But Somalia also lacked a peace accord among the parties before the UN intervention in 1992, and Mohammed Farah Aideed, the most powerful warlord and chief 'spoiler', was unprepared to share power with other factions. The aggressive military approach adopted by the UN Special Representative, Jonathan Howe, contributed to the confrontation with Aideed that led to the loss of political support for, and the eventual termination of, the mission. In contrast, Rwanda was, from the start, a mission based largely on ill-equipped armies from developing countries which lacked strong political and financial backing from the powerful members of the UN Security Council. This weakness encouraged Rwanda's extremist factions to force the withdrawal of the UN by killing its peacekeepers. France also continued to provide military support to the incumbent regime.

Internal parties in both Somalia and Rwanda were unwilling to implement peace agreements that would force them to share power. They adopted a zero-sum approach to the conflicts and signed accords that they had no intention of implementing. The regional spillover of both conflicts into neighbouring states was destabilizing to neighbours who sought unsuccessfully to mediate an end to the conflicts. These regional actors were too weak to impose peace on the belligerents and their role was sometimes compromised by past support for individual factions. The UN Special Representatives in Somalia and Rwanda were widely considered to be political liabilities, while the Security Council lacked the political will to continue with the two missions once Western peacekeepers had been killed by warlords in a bid to force their withdrawal.

The two current UN peacekeeping missions in Sierra Leone and the Democratic Republic of Congo (DRC) are still being increased to full strength but appear, so far, not to have met most of our criteria for success. In both cases, there appears to be a lack of commitment to implementing peace agreements reached by internal parties. The existence of mineral resources in both countries, which have been exploited by the warring factions, does not augur well for an early end to these conflicts. Regional actors in both Sierra Leone and Congo also appear to be deeply divided: in Sierra Leone, the leaders of Liberia and Burkina Faso backed rebels against a subregional military force spearheaded by Nigeria, and also involving Ghana, Guinea and Mali. While the former group have sought lucrative gains from Sierra Leone's illicit diamond and arms trade, the latter justified their intervention on the basis of the need to restore subregional stability.

In Congo, regional rivalries have also created difficulties for the UN. Zimbabwe, Angola and Namibia have sent soldiers to back the incumbent regime against a coalition of Rwandese and Ugandan soldiers who are supporting assorted Congolese rebels. The powerful members of the Security Council, distracted by more strategically important UN missions in Kosovo and East Timor and scarred by earlier experiences in Rwanda and Somalia, have provided only sporadic and often inadequate assistance to these two missions in Africa. In contrast to Kosovo and East Timor, Western countries have failed to provide significant troops for these peacekeeping missions which are largely staffed by poorly-equipped soldiers from developing countries.

The proposed increase of peacekeepers in the UN mission in Sierra Leone to 20,500 and recent tough economic measures announced against the rebels and their allies still seem to be half-hearted efforts to appear to be 'doing something' rather than a genuine attempt to provide the logistical and financial support that the mission so sorely lacks. The mission in Congo suffers from the opposite problem of a lack of peacekeepers. Just as the Rwanda mission was adversely affected by events in Somalia, so also has the UN mission in Congo been negatively affected by the UN's difficult experiences in Sierra Leone, involving the killing and holding hostage of its peacekeepers. In Congo, a clearly insufficient 5,500 peacekeepers have been mandated to police a huge territory with six foreign armies and a plethora of armed factions. The two missions clearly demonstrate that the UN Security Council and Secretariat have not learned many lessons from earlier failures in Angola, Somalia, and Rwanda, nor from success in Mozambique.

This essay identifies three distinct phases of UN peacekeeping in Africa. The first phase was epitomized by the Cold War-fuelled Congo crisis of the early 1960s which effectively ended large-scale UN peacekeeping in Africa for the next three decades. The second phase occurred after the end of the Cold War in the early 1990s when the early euphoria of successes in Namibia and Mozambique were dampened by disappointments in Angola and Western Sahara and destroyed by the twin *débâcles* in Somalia and Rwanda. The third phase entails efforts by several African regional organizations to fill the vacuum left by the disappearance of the UN, discussed here briefly before assessing the significance of the reappearance of the UN in Africa in 1999 with the establishment of two peacekeeping missions in Sierra Leone and the Democratic Republic of Congo.

Cold War Follies (1960–64)

'No more Congos!' The forlorn cry rang out unmistakably across the African continent in 1964 as the UN struggled with this first-generation peacekeeping challenge. The world body was expressing its deep frustration at a four-year intervention in the former Belgian Congo. It had lost its revered Secretary-General, Dag Hammarskjöld, in a mysterious plane crash, and got bogged down in a protracted civil war in the shadow of an ideological Cold War in an emerging Africa divided into several political blocs.

The 20,000-strong United Nations Operation in the Congo (ONUC) was dispatched to Central Africa in July 1960.[4] Although it soon became embroiled in civil war, the UN's original purpose was to preserve the sovereignty of the new state from foreign intervention, having been invited into Congo by its new leaders. Belgium had forgotten that the world had changed and that its peculiar brand of colonialism had become an anachronism in post-independence Africa. Having hastily and irresponsibly abandoned its former colony, it sent Belgian paratroopers to their former stomping ground within days. The Congolese army had mutinied, and amidst the chaos, Moise Tshombe, a mercurial renegade, declared the Congo's richest province, Katanga, independent, with Belgian connivance. A bitter power struggle erupted between the 'moderate' President Joseph Kasavubu and his 'radical' premier Patrice Lumumba. The United States and Soviet Union considered the Congo – a mineral-rich, strategically-located state the size of western Europe – a vital prize in the early Cold War stakes.[5] Moscow provided transport aircraft for pro-Lumumba troops, while Washington's Central Intelligence Agency (CIA) was reportedly involved in the assassination of Lumumba in 1961.[6] Following Lumumba's death, members of the 'Casablanca group' of 'radical' African states like Egypt, Guinea and Morocco withdrew their peacekeepers from the Congo.

The UN's reputation suffered tremendous damage as a result of this mission. Western powers accused the Indian UN Special Representative in

Congo, Rajeshwar Dayal, of Lumumbist leanings, while London accused the UN's Irish Representative in Katanga, Conor Cruise O'Brien, of leftist sympathies. Both were replaced by Hammarskjöld. The Soviets and many African states strongly criticized the UN's failure to protect Lumumba who had been killed under the nose of its peacekeepers. Hammarskjöld was sympathetic to the Western view that the Congo was threatened by Soviet expansionism and felt that Lumumba should be under-cut.[7] The fact that his closest UN advisers were American did not help.

Having achieved its strategic goals of eliminating Lumumba and elevating General Joseph Mobutu, the Congolese army chief of staff, to power, Washington eventually devised the military plan to end the secession in Katanga.[8] For the first time in its history, the UN embarked on peace enforcement, using force to incorporate Katanga back into the Congo by January 1963. The control of the central government in Leopoldville had become a game of musical chairs. Governmental authority was fully restored only after Mobutu staged a successful *coup d'état* and, by 1965, he was in full control of the country. He remained in power for the next three decades.

After the controversies of the Congo crisis, the UN Security Council refused to intervene in civil wars in Africa, citing the difficulties of keeping peace in the shadow of a Cold War in which two ideological superpowers waged proxy wars, the French *gendarme* intervened in its *chasse gardée* with reckless abandon, and obstinate Portuguese colonialists and reactionary white albinocracies in southern Africa clung desperately to power. For the next three decades, no major UN peacekeeping mission took place in Africa, even as conflicts proliferated, often fuelled by Cold War patrons.

The Rise and Fall of 'The New World Order' (1990–94)

The West was in triumphalist mood after the fall of the Berlin Wall and the disintegration of the Soviet Union by the early 1990s. Following the liberation of Kuwait by an American-led UN coalition in 1991, US President George Bush vaingloriously declared the advent of a 'New World Order' in which the UN would act as a noble Leviathan protecting the international society from 'rogue states' and truculent warlords. Bush ordered American troops to lead a humanitarian mission into Somalia to feed a starving population. Meanwhile, other UN missions had been launched in Angola, Mozambique, Rwanda and Western Sahara. But the killing of American peacekeepers in 1993 signalled the end of the second generation of UN peacekeeping in Africa. It also symbolized the death of the ephemeral New World Order and a serious retrenchment in UN peacekeeping in Africa. It is to these events that we now turn our attention.

A Tale of Two Conflicts: Mozambique and Angola

This section will examine the domestic, regional and extra-regional dimensions of the UN's efforts to bring peace to Mozambique and Angola. Both cases had 'spoilers', but the presence of economic resources in Angola and the greater cooperation of the warring parties in Mozambique were crucial in explaining the different outcomes in the two peace processes. The sustained interest and cooperation of the powerful members of the UN Security Council and their contribution of financial, diplomatic and logistical support to the UN mission was important to success in Mozambique and was mostly lacking in Angola. In Mozambique, the UN also had a dynamic Special Representative who was able to take advantage of more auspicious circumstances for peacekeeping.

In April 1974, a military coup in Lisbon had led Portugal to abandon its former African colonies. Democratic transitions collapsed in Mozambique and Angola, leading to civil wars in both countries in which Washington and Moscow backed ideologically compatible clients. The end of the Cold War made it possible for the installation of UN peacekeeping missions in both countries.[9] While the UN succeeded in ending Mozambique's war, the Angolan conflict continues unabated.

The international community's role was decisive in bringing an end to Mozambique's war. Between 1975 and 1990, the Front for the Liberation of Mozambique (FRELIMO) government and the Mozambique National Resistance (RENAMO) rebels were locked in a brutal civil war.[10] From 1988, intermediaries from the Community of Sant 'Egidio, a Catholic international lay association, began to facilitate informal negotiations between the warring parties.[11] By early 1989, Kenya, Zimbabwe, Botswana, Malawi and members of southern Africa's Frontline States (FLS) were also playing a role in peacemaking.[12] These efforts were supported by Italy, Portugal, Britain, the US and the UN.[13]

The first of a series of direct meetings between FRELIMO and RENAMO took place at the Covenant of Sant' Egidio in Rome in July 1990.[14] A genuine spirit of compromise developed, and the facilitators did not attempt to impose their solutions on the players. At further talks in November 1990, a Joint Verification Committee was established, with Botswana and Zimbabwe playing prominent mediation roles.[15] A month later, a ceasefire was agreed. The two warring parties then signed the *'Basic Principles' of the Mozambican Peace Agreement,* in October 1991, covering six key areas: the law on political parties, the electoral system, military issues, security guarantees, a ceasefire, and an international donors conference.[16] A year later, FRELIMO and RENAMO sealed a comprehensive peace accord that included, *inter alia,* agreement on the establishment of a new Mozambican army, the creation of a commission to supervise and monitor the peace process, and the recognition of all political parties in Mozambique.[17]

In December 1992, the Security Council approved a UN Operation in Mozambique (ONUMOZ), mandated to undertake five main tasks: monitor the ceasefire, carry out disarmament and demobilization, facilitate the return of two million refugees from neighbouring countries,[18] oversee the coordination of humanitarian assistance and verify national elections.[19] ONUMOZ experienced several difficulties: it took the UN almost six months to establish the mission; soon after the UN's arrival, RENAMO's mercurial leader, Afonso Dhlakama, acted as a 'spoiler', refusing to demobilize his troops unless more funds were provided for transforming his guerrilla movement into a political party. On the eve of elections, he threatened a boycott of the poll.

The mediation role played by the UN's Special Representative, Aldo Ajello, combined with external pressure, was crucial in convincing Dhlakama to implement the peace agreement. The Italian diplomat interpreted his mandate with flexible dexterity. He effectively used the Ceasefire Commission to resolve military issues, tirelessly lobbied donors to provide funds for implementing the agreement, and skilfully coordinated the political mission with the humanitarian activities.[20] ONUMOZ eventually succeeded in disarming and demobilizing 64,130 FRELIMO and 22,637 RENAMO fighters between January and August 1994.[21] The 1,200 UN electoral observers oversaw parliamentary and presidential elections in October 1994, which FRELIMO won. RENAMO had lost the support of its foreign patrons, and unlike the belligerents in Angola, had no access to domestic natural resources (oil and diamonds) with which to fund continued war. ONUMOZ deployed nearly 6,000 peacekeepers, 130 civilian police and cost $332 million a year.

Like FRELIMO and RENAMO in Angola, the Popular Movement for the Liberation of Angola (MPLA) and the National Union for the Total Independence of Angola (UNITA)[22] were engaged in a protracted civil war from 1975. The MPLA was able to secure the capital, Luanda, with the help of about 50,000 Cuban troops. UNITA and the National Front for the Liberation of Angola (FNLA) entered into an alliance with South Africa, the US, France and Zaire. A major rationale behind Pretoria's foreign policy was to make the region safe for Apartheid,[23] particularly after the withdrawal of its Portuguese ally from Africa.

The conflict in Angola, like that in Mozambique, was affected by the end of the Cold War which opened a window of opportunity for external mediation. Internationally-brokered talks had earlier led to commitments from Cuba and South Africa to withdraw their troops from Angola.[24] The first United Nations Angola Verification Mission (UMAVEM I) was created in December 1988 to monitor this withdrawal at an estimated cost of $19 million and was completed by June 1991. Because of the mission's size and straightforward mandate, planning was relatively uncomplicated.[25] These efforts led to the MPLA and UNITA signing the Portuguese-sponsored Bicesse peace accords in May 1991. The agreement called for the cessation of all foreign military support to both sides, for troops to be disarmed and demobilized, for a national army to be created, and for multi-party elections to be held. Bicesse also called for the establishment of a Joint Political-Military Commission, with the participation of the US, the Soviet Union and Portugal. The Commission was mandated to ensure that the ceasefire held and that the peace agreement was fully implemented.

In May 1991, the MPLA government requested the UN's participation in verifying the Peace Accords.[26] In the same month, the Security Council approved UNAVEM II[27] which had about 700 peacekeepers and a paltry budget of $118,000, and was charged with verifying that the Joint Monitoring Groups (JMGs) carried out their responsibilities. But the JMGs were soon wracked by infighting between the belligerents. UNAVEM II lacked the human and financial resources to execute its mandate effectively. Its peacekeepers proved to be too few for their demobilization tasks.[28] Even UN Special Representative, Margaret Anstee, complained bitterly about the weak mandate, insufficient resources, and lack of political will among the powerful members of the Security Council.[29] The UN's electoral role in Angola was to verify the polls. However, its observers were confronted with violence and intimidation and the government-controlled media was criticized for its bias. Voting took place in September 1992, with the UN deploying 400 electoral observers to cover all 18 Angolan provinces and 6000 polling stations. The presidential election was won narrowly by incumbent president, José Eduardo dos Santos and required a run-off.

But the UN's tasks were soon further complicated by the refusal of UNITA's Jonas Savimbi to conclude the electoral process and to disarm his fighters. Acting as a classic 'spoiler', Savimbi openly defied the peacekeepers and instead continued to rebuild his army. Angola's warlord was emboldened in his recalcitrance by continued foreign support. As late as June 1991, Washington provided UNITA with $30 million in covert aid.[30] The warlord returned to the bush to continue his guerrilla war funded by the sale of diamonds. After reneging on his promise to respect the electoral results, Savimbi's international backers started to abandon him. Washington offered diplomatic recognition to the MPLA government and the UN Security Council eventually imposed economic sanctions on UNITA in October 1997.[31]

The third UN mission in Angola (UNAVEM III) followed the signing of the Lusaka protocol of November 1994. It was a deliberate effort to correct the flaws of the earlier accord by providing 7,000 peacekeepers and by bringing UNITA representatives into a transitional government in Luanda. But neither side was serious about implementing the agreement, and by 1998, full-scale war had returned to Angola.[32] The UN withdrew its military observer mission (MONUA) from Angola in 1998 and only in August 2000 did it start to re-establish a political office in Luanda.

The UN failed to bring peace to Angola for several reasons. First, the two parties continued to see the war in zero-sum terms, mutual suspicions persisted, and the MPLA and UNITA continued to benefit from lucrative resources in their areas of control, a factor that was lacking in Mozambique. Second, collaboration between Washington and Moscow proved less successful in Angola than in Mozambique, while international donors failed to provide the necessary financial backing for the UN missions in Angola. Finally, the under-funded UNAVEM II lacked the leverage to pressure the parties to fulfill their commitments.[33]

Africa's Tragic Twins: Somalia and Rwanda

Both Somalia and Rwanda were orphans of the Cold War in the era of intervention by external powers in Africa. Somalia had been fought over by the superpowers, while Rwanda was entangled in French efforts to maintain a sphere of influence in Africa. Both conflicts were erroneously treated by the UN Security Council as humanitarian disasters and the political will for stronger military action was lacking after Western peacekeepers were killed in both countries. Political support for the UN missions in Somalia and Rwanda simply crumbled in the Security Council, and rather than bolster the UN presence, its peacekeepers were instead withdrawn.

Somalia's civil war erupted in full force in January 1991 after Siad Barre, a brutal autocrat who had been in power since 1969 and was backed by Washington between 1978 and 1988,[34] fled Mogadishu. The central government collapsed and Somalia joined the growing ranks of 'failed states'. Mohamed Farah Aideed and Ali Mahdi Mohamed, both members of the opposition United Somali Congress (USC), fought for control of the capital. In Kismayo, two rival warlords, General Siad 'Morgan' and Colonel Omar Jess, fought for control, while northwestern Somaliland declared itself an independent republic.

With growing starvation in Somalia, the Security Council established the UN Operation in Somalia (UNOSOM I) involving the deployment of 500 peacekeepers to protect food convoys. UN Secretary-General, Boutros Boutros-Ghali, sent experienced Algerian diplomat Mohamed Sahnoun to Somalia as his Special Representative in April 1992. Sahnoun sought to rebuild Somalia through a strategy of encouraging a legitimate political process based around Somalia's warlords, intellectuals, and elders. He eventually resigned in October 1992 following disagreements with Boutros-Ghali over UN tactics in Somalia.[35]

As Somalia's warlords continued to blockade food convoys and with UNOSOM I's unarmed military observers unable to stop them, 300,000 deaths resulted and one million refugees spilled into neighbouring Kenya and Ethiopia. Amidst the continued suffering, 38,301 peacekeepers, including 25,426 Americans and other contingents from Europe, Canada, Asia, and Africa, entered Somalia from December 1992 as part of the United Nations Task Force (UNITAF). 'Operation Restore Hope' was mandated to facilitate the delivery of humanitarian goods to Somalia. The mission started well enough with the presence of the peacekeepers ensuring the delivery of food, reducing looting and banditry, rebuilding roads and bridges, and facilitating the repatriation of Somali refugees from neighbouring countries. Between December 1992 and October 1993 a staggering $2 billion was spent on the international effort.[36]

But Washington had quixotically assumed that it could deploy its troops and feed Somalis while avoiding any confrontation with the country's warlords. It refused Boutros-Ghali's frequent requests to disarm Somalia's factions. However, Aideed, who had been consolidating his military position before the UN's arrival, felt that the entry of the peacekeepers would deprive him of the presidency. He also feared that the intervention might seek to endorse his rival Ali Mahdi's questionable election as President of Somalia at a conference in Djibouti in 1991.[37] The mere presence of the UN force changed the military balance on the ground. While Aideed reluctantly accepted the peacekeepers, his less powerful rival, Ali Mahdi, enthusiastically supported their presence.[38] Further complicating the UN's tasks, Aideed distrusted Boutros-Ghali, whom he had considered pro-Barre since the latter's tenure as Deputy Foreign Minister of Egypt. Aideed's suspicion of the UN was further heightened when a Russian plane with UN markings delivered military equipment to Ali Mahdi in northern Mogadishu.[39]

US Special Envoy, Robert Oakley, a former Ambassador to Somalia, arranged reconciliation meetings between Aideed and Mahdi as well as regular security meetings between their factions. Two UN-led peace conferences were also held in Addis Ababa with fourteen Somali factions in January and March 1993, with Ethiopia playing a strong mediation role. A rift developed between Aideed and his allies who favoured a decentralized, regional reconstruction of local administration which would give greater powers to clan-based militias, and Mahdi and his allies who championed a stronger national government to protect militarily weaker clans. An agreement was eventually signed, calling for a two-year Transitional National Council (TNC) with a parliament, rotating presidency, and regional and district councils.[40] But the agreement was never implemented and Aideed in particular did much to subvert the functioning of the councils, fearing that they were an effort to empower civil society against his own nominees.

In May 1993, UNITAF was transformed into UNOSOM II, which still had 4,000 American troops. The new UN mandate was ambitious in calling for the revival of national and regional institutions and the establishment of civil administration throughout Somalia.[41] Aideed's relations with the UN soon began to deteriorate, as he blamed the peacekeepers for his ally's loss of Kismayo in March 1993. Growing human rights abuses by UN peacekeepers, involving the killing of Somali civilians, also resulted in the civilian population turning against the UN.[42] Belgian troops in Kismayo beat and killed many unarmed Somalis sometimes without provocation.[43] A Canadian regiment had to be disbanded after some of its members were involved in sadistic acts of torture and murder. American and other contingents acted with unparalleled impunity in taking pot shots at often innocent civilians in a trigger-happy feast utterly unbeffitting of UN peacekeeping.

After the killing of 24 Pakistani UN peacekeepers by Aideed's fighters in June 1993, Washington successfully championed a Security Council resolution calling for the warlord's capture and trial.[44] It was within this context that the American UN Special Representative, Admiral Jonathan Howe, virtually declared war on Aideed, sending US helicopters to kill or capture his supporters, including respected elders, in Mogadishu[45] (see Berdal in this volume). Oakley's discreet style, based on prior knowledge of Somalia, contrasted sharply with Howe's aggressive and confrontational tactics. Admiral Howe adopted 'Wild West' tactics of putting a $25,000 bounty on Aideed's head. Sent out to carry out the sheriff's orders was a posse of American Rangers. The mission went disastrously wrong when the Rangers became caught in a firefight with Aideed's men, resulting in the death of eighteen American soldiers and about one thousand Somalis, mostly civilians. In order to deflect the strong domestic backlash at the sight of a dead American soldier being dragged through the streets of Mogadishu by enraged Somalis, the Clinton administration and much of the US media inaccurately blamed the botched mission, planned entirely under American command, on the United Nations. In early 1995, the UN withdrew all its peacekeepers from Somalia, leaving the country as anarchic as it had found it. Operation *Restore Hope* had become Operation *Return Home*.

Following Somalia, Washington, placed severe restrictions on the approval of future UN missions through the heavy-handed Presidential

Decision Directive 25.[46] Boutros-Ghali's requests for new UN peacekeeping missions in Burundi and Liberia met with an eloquent silence, even as the West continued to employ the UN for 'rich men's wars'[47] in more strategically important places like Bosnia and Haiti. Six months after the Somali *débâcle*, Washington led the opposition to a UN response to the genocide in Rwanda, in a situation that was tragically and erroneously viewed through a tainted Somali prism.

The Rwandese Patriotic Front (RPF) had invaded Rwanda from Uganda in October 1990. These refugee warriors were mostly the vengeful progenitors of Rwanda's Tutsi minority who had been forced out of their homeland and denied the right to return by the Hutu-dominated government of Juvenal Habyarimana. Uganda's Yoweri Museveni, whose successful guerrilla army had included Tutsi exiles, backed the RPF, while France, which sent a military contingent to Rwanda, and Zaire, supported Habyarimana. The Organization of African Unity (OAU) arranged peace talks in Arusha, which resulted in a comprehensive peace settlement by August 1993. Arusha called for a transitional government involving the country's political groups, a power-sharing arrangement, the establishment of a new army composed equally of Hutu and Tutsi, and the demobilization of the remaining fighters.[48]

The 2,500-strong and $120 million a year UN Assistance Mission in Rwanda (UNAMIR) was mandated to implement the agreement. The Security Council resolution establishing UNAMIR, however, made two crucial changes which weakened the peacekeeping force before its deployment. Arusha had called for the peacekeepers to guarantee the overall security of Rwanda and to confiscate illegal arms. The UN resolution mandated the force only to contribute to security in Kigali and its environs and did not sanction a seizure of arms. The UN peacekeepers arrived in Rwanda two months behind schedule and without the armoured unit and helicopters which had been authorized by the Security Council.

General Roméo Dallaire, the UN's Canadian Force Commander, had called for a contingent that was twice the size of the one deployed.[49] The force, consisting largely of soldiers from Belgium, Bangladesh, Ghana, and Tunisia, also lacked an intelligence unit, it had a small civilian police unit and no human rights cell, limiting its ability to monitor abuses.[50] To make matters worse, the situation in Kigali was scarcely conducive to peacekeeping: the transitional government was not installed, Rwanda's soldiers were not demobilized, and arms were flooding illegally into the capital. Jaques-Roger Booh-Booh, Cameroon's former Foreign Minister and the UN Special Representative in Rwanda, was seen by many to be out of his depth. He annoyed the RPF by calling for the inclusion of the extremist *Comité pour le Défense de la République* (CDR) in the future government,[51] and raised further suspicion by accepting an invitation to visit Habyarimana's village.[52] His criticisms of Habyarimana's delay in establishing the transitional government annoyed Hutu parties.

On 6 April 1994, Habyarimana's plane was shot down over Kigali, signalling the start of a devastating genocide against the Tutsi minority and moderate Hutus. The genocide had been planned by a group of extremists within the Habyarimana regime including members of the ruling party, officers of the Presidential Guard, the *interahamwe* and *impuzamugambi* militias, and members of the CDR. This group saw power-sharing as not only a betrayal but a threat to their own positions and privileges. They also feared that the RPF's presence in a new national army would facilitate the launching of a Tutsi military coup, fears heightened by the assassination of neighbouring Burundi's first Hutu President, Melchior Ndadaye, by Tutsi military extremists in October 1993.

Within 24 hours of the start of the genocide, 250,000 Rwandan refugees flooded into Burundi, Uganda, Tanzania and Zaire. Over the next three months, the *gnocidaires* eliminated 800,000 mostly Tutsi people.[53] The killing of ten Belgian UN peacekeepers led to the irresponsible withdrawal of its entire contingent, the backbone of the UN force, from Rwanda on 12 April 1994. Brussels then lobbied for the withdrawal of all UN peacekeepers from its former colony so as to avoid the historical stain on its peacekeeping record. The slaughter ended only with an RPF military victory on 17 July 1994. The genocidal militias and Rwandan army retreated into eastern Zaire with a hostage Hutu population of about one million people. This retreat was facilitated by the controversial UN-sanctioned French intervention, Operation *Turquoise,* which had ostensibly been launched to save lives. However, revelations that France had trained and continued to arm many of Rwanda's death squads raised troubling questions.[54]

Led by strong American and British demands,[55] the UN Security Council withdrew most of its peacekeepers from Rwanda, leaving a token force of 270. It pursued an utterly inappropriate diplomatic posture in search of an elusive ceasefire. Many observers, including General Dallaire and his Ghanain deputy, General Henry Anyidoho, have since convincingly argued that a strengthened UN force could have prevented many of the civilian deaths which were mostly carried out by gangs using machetes, clubs, knives and spears. A month later, the Security Council reversed its decision and authorized the dispatch of 5,500 peacekeepers (UNAMIR II) who arrived too late to save victims of genocide. The international community had fiddled while Rwanda burned.[56] The crisis had simply been dismissed as another bout of primordial bloodletting on 'the dark continent'. As Kofi Annan, the current UN Secretary-General, aptly commented at the time:

'Nobody should feel that he has a clear conscience in this business. If the pictures of tens of thousands of human bodies rotting and gnawed on by dogs…do not wake us up out of our apathy, I don't know what will.'[57]

Back to Africa? (1995–2000)

Subregional organizations in Africa attempted to step into the vacuum created by the departure of UN peacekeepers from Africa after the *débâcles* in Rwanda and Somalia. But the lack of logistical and financial support for intervention in Africa's civil wars was epitomized by the travails of a Nigerian-led West African peacekeeping force, the Economic Community of West African States Ceasefire Monitoring Group (ECOMOG), which attempted for over eight years to bring peace to Liberia and Sierra Leone.[58] A South African-led effort to restore order to Lesotho in 1998 was similarly embroiled in military and political difficulties. Regional actors in Africa often became entangled in parochial political and economic agendas, even as neighbours complained about the bullying instincts of regional hegemons like Nigeria and South Africa. These difficulties resulted in the return of UN peacekeepers to Africa with new missions in Sierra Leone and the Democratic Republic of the Congo in 1999.

Two More Congos? Sierra Leone and DRC

In both Sierra Leone and the Democratic Republic of Congo, decades of bad governance eventually resulted in state collapse and civil war. During peace negotiations, internal parties have failed to demonstrate genuine commitment to implementing peace agreements, and they have used their access to economic resources to fund their military campaigns. Despite the destabilizing regional consequences of these conflicts, key regional actors continued to provide military support to the warring parties. While energetic international diplomacy helped seal peace agreements, the permanent members of the UN Security Council have not shown the political commitment or provided adequate resources to support the UN's efforts in Sierra Leone and Congo.

Before the outbreak of its civil war in 1991, Sierra Leone had suffered from three decades of poor management of its economic resources and vast disparities in wealth between a corrupt elite in the capital, Freetown, and impoverished masses in the countryside.[59] An army of unemployed youths provided easy recruits for Sierra Leone's warlords who waged an often brutal, decade-long war against successive civilian and military regimes in Freetown which were supported by soldiers from Nigeria, Ghana and Guinea.

By the end of 1998, nearly 12,000 of ECOMOG's 13,000 troops, 90 per cent, came from Nigeria, while Ghana, Guinea and Mali also provided contingents.[60] Following the 6 January 1999 rebel invasion of Freetown, ECOMOG eventually forced the rebels to withdraw from the capital with the loss of over 100 Nigerian soldiers[61] and 3,000 civilians, amidst reports of human rights abuses by ECOMOG troops. This event marked a turning point for ECOMOG's ill-equipped peacekeepers as Nigeria, frustrated by the lack of international financial and logistical support, increasingly expressed its desire to rid itself of this thankless burden.[62]

But it was difficult for ECOWAS to turn its back on a conflict with such devastating effects on its own West African subregion. Sierra Leone's eight-year conflict had erupted in 1991 after Revolutionary United Front (RUF) rebels, backed by Charles Taylor's National Patriotic Front of Liberia (NPFL), invaded the country from Liberia.[63] During the war, Liberia and Burkina Faso have backed the RUF by providing it with arms and rear bases in return for a cut in the lucrative diamond trade from the rebels' control of diamond fields in eastern Sierra Leone.[64] The conflict rendered the entire Mano River basin unstable and has sporadically spilled over into Liberia and Guinea, resulting in hundreds of deaths, attacks on refugees, and creating tensions between the two countries. This situation has forced ECOWAS to plan a deployment of military observers along Guinea's borders with Sierra Leone and Liberia. A total of 500,000 Sierra Leonean refugees remain in Guinea and Liberia.

The Lomé peace agreement, spearheaded by the UN and the Economic Community of West African States (ECOWAS), was signed on 7 July 1999, raising hopes for an end to Sierra Leone's civil war. The accord called for the RUF to be transformed into a political party, provided it with cabinet posts in a Government of National Unity, and gave RUF leader, Foday Sankoh, the Vice-Presidency as well as the Chairmanship of a Commission for the Management of Strategic Resources. A controversial amnesty was offered for war crimes committed during the conflict, and the UN agreed to contribute personnel to help oversee disarmament and elections. A Joint Implementation Committee was to meet every three months to oversee the agreement's implementation.[65]

Shortly after being installed as Nigeria's president in May 1999, Olusegun Obasanjo announced the phased withdrawal of most of the Nigerian troops from Sierra Leone. With enormous domestic problems, the new civilian regime was not prepared to continue the sacrifices, involving costs of $1 million a day, which Nigeria's former military junta had incurred. In order to fill the void left by the departure of Nigerian peacekeepers, the 12,443-strong United Nations Mission in Sierra Leone (UNAMSIL) was established under an Indian Force Commander, General Vijay Jetley, at an annual cost of $476 million. Oluyemi Adeniji, a Nigerian diplomat who had served as the UN Special Representative in Central African Republic, was appointed Special Representative to Sierra Leone. The core contingents of UNAMSIL consisted of Nigerian, Indian, Jordanian, Kenyan, Bangladeshi, Guinean, Ghanaian and Zambian battalions.

But UNAMSIL faced tremendous problems, as Foday Sankoh employed similar 'spoiler' tactics as Somalia's Aideed to frustrate the peacekeepers. As in Somalia, the RUF accused the UN of compromising its neutrality by taking sides with the government troops of the elected President Ahmed Tejjan Kabbah. Using similar tactics as Dhlakama in Mozambique, Sankoh complained that RUF members were not being appointed to government positions as agreed at Lomé.[66] The RUF continued to fight the Armed Forces Revolutionary Council (AFRC) and Civil Defence Forces in the countryside, prevented the deployment of UN peacekeepers to the diamond-rich eastern provinces, and, from May 2000, attacked UN peacekeepers, holding them hostage and seizing their heavy weapons and vehicles.[67]

Aside from the RUF's obstructionist tactics, UNAMSIL also experienced its own problems. A UN assessment mission sent to Sierra Leone in June 2000 found serious managerial problems in UNAMSIL and a lack of common understanding of the mandate and rules of engagement. It also noted that some of UNAMSIL's military units lacked proper training and equipment.[68] There were constant reports of tension between the UN's political and military leadership[69] even before a confidential report written by General Jetley was published in the international press in September 2000. In the report, the Indian UN Force Commander accused senior Nigerian military and political officials of attempting to sabotage the UN mission in Sierra Leone by colluding with the RUF rebels to prolong the conflict in order to benefit from the country's illicit diamond trade. No evidence was provided for the allegations. Tremendous political damage was done to UNAMSIL by this incident: Nigeria refused to put its peacekeepers under Jetley's command and India subsequently announced the withdrawal of its entire 3,000-strong contingent from Sierra Leone in September 2000, followed shortly after by Jordan. Kenyan General Daniel Opande, took over as UNAMSIL'S force commander in November 2000.[70]

Aside from the political problems, UNAMSIL has also failed to fulfil important parts of its mandate. The disarmament process in Sierra Leone has been fraught with difficulties. Of the estimated 45,000 fighters, only 24,042 had entered demobilization camps by 15 May 2000, many without weapons,[71] and most have since been rearmed as part of the government effort to wage war on the RUF. The payment of the $150 remittance to demobilized fighters was slow, and there remained a $20 million shortfall in international contributions to Sierra Leone's disarmament programme in March 2000.[72]

There have recently been some encouraging signs of international resolve in Sierra Leone. UNAMSIL responded more forcefully against the

RUF in July 2000 by freeing some of its hostages in Kailahun, recapturing the strategic town of Masiaka from the rebels, and clearing illegal checkpoints from the Occra hills.[73] A brief British military intervention between May and June 2000 helped stabilize the situation in Freetown and its environs. Following the difficulties with the RUF, ECOWAS agreed to send a 3,000-strong rapid reaction force, consisting largely of Nigerians, to bolster UNAMSIL. The US helped to train and equip this force in the last months of 2000.[74] Though there has been much discussion about the need for strengthened peace enforcement powers for UNAMSIL and though Kofi Annan, urged on by strong British diplomatic pressure, has called for a gradual increase of UN peacekeepers to 20,500,[75] it is unlikely that these powers and numbers alone will make up for the lack of equipment and training of many of these contingents. The problems of UN peacekeepers in Rwanda and Angola are being replicated in Sierra Leone.

The International Contact Group, consisting of donors and ECOWAS states, continues to hold periodic meetings in a bid to mobilize funds for Sierra Leone. In recognition of the role of the illicit diamond trade in fuelling this conflict, in July 2000 the Security Council prohibited the global importation of rough diamonds from Sierra Leone. At a UN hearing in the same month, Washington and London strongly criticized Liberia and Burkina Faso for their role in diamond-smuggling and gun-running in support of RUF rebels in Sierra Leone. Richard Holbrooke, the American Ambassador to the UN, described Liberia's president, Charles Taylor, as 'Milošević in Africa with diamonds'.[76] A war crimes court is being established in Sierra Leone with UN support.[77]

But there remains an urgent need for Western donors to demonstrate a similar generosity in Sierra Leone as they have done in Bosnia, Kosovo and East Timor. For example, in early 2000, while $2 billion was pledged for the reconstruction of the Balkans, barely $150 million was pledged for Sierra Leone. As the UN Special Representative in Freetown, Oluyemi Adeniji, noted: 'The international community has to realize that there can be no double standard. Whatever the cause of the conflict in Africa, human suffering is universal, you can not respond to some countries and not to the emergencies in Africa.'[78]

The UN faces an even more difficult and complicated mission in the Congo than it does in Sierra Leone. Since 1965, when Mobutu seized power, there were countless attempts to topple him. His regime was saved from near collapse by his Western patrons – France, the US, and Belgium – in 1977 and 1978. The autocratic Mobutu embezzled an estimated $5 billion in foreign aid as his country sank into a deepening economic and political crisis.[79] By the mid-1990s, there was a sense of *fin de régime* as Mobutu was abandoned by his Western allies with the end of the Cold War. In early 1997,

Laurent Kabila's Alliance of Democratic Forces for the Liberation of Congo-Zaire (AFDL) launched a devastating rebellion against Mobutu, plunging the country into another civil war. Under Kabila's leadership, and with help from Uganda, Rwanda and Angola, the revolt succeeded in toppling Mobutu in May 1997.

But Kabila's political honeymoon proved to be short-lived. Until his death in January 2001, he had employed similar repressive tactics as his predecessor to remain in power, and insecurity continued to afflict the DRC.[80] Barely one year after helping to deliver him to power, Kabila's former allies, Uganda and Rwanda, invaded the Congo in support of anti-Kabila rebels.[81] Kigali was particularly angered by Kabila's ousting of Rwandan-supplied Tutsi officers from his army. In response to the invasion by Uganda and Rwanda, a pro-Kabila alliance of Zimbabwe, Namibia and Angola sent troops to the DRC to prop up Kabila's regime. Foreign armies in the Congo have sought financial rewards from the country's rich mines, with Uganda and Rwanda clashing militarily three times in mineral-rich Kisangani with the loss of hundreds of civilians.[82] Though most Western countries have strongly criticized Zimbabwe for its role in DRC, they have been muted in their criticism of the flagrant violation of Congolese sovereignty by Rwanda and Uganda. While he was alive, Laurant Kabila restricted internal political activity, while his relations with the UN turned sour over the world body's attempts to investigate allegations of human rights abuses by his army in 1997.

On 10 July 1999, the parties in the DRC signed the Lusaka Peace Accord. Lusaka is based on four central pillars:[83] first, it affirms the sovereignty and territorial integrity of the DRC and all its neighbouring states; second, it advocates a program of national reconciliation to resolve the internal Congolese crisis; third, it urges the signatories to put an immediate halt to any assistance, collaboration or giving of sanctuary to negative forces bent on destabilizing neighbouring countries; finally, the accord commits its signatories to address the security problems posed by the continuing activities of forces identified with the 1994 Rwandan genocide, and calls for the establishment of 'a mechanism for disarming militias and armed groups, including the genocidal forces'.

The UN and other regional organizations like the OAU and the Southern African Development Community (SADC) have been instrumental in supporting peace efforts in the DRC. But as Kofi Annan has noted, in order to be effective, any UN peacekeeping mission in the DRC, whatever its mandate, will have to be large and expensive.[84] Soon after the signing of the Lusaka agreement, African states began to canvass the UN for an international peacekeeping operation in the Congo. Powerful actors like the US Ambassador to the UN, Richard Holbrooke, persuaded their governments and legislatures to support the mission.[85]

On 24 February 2000, the UN Security Council approved a proposal to send 5,537 UN peacekeepers, later reduced to 3,000, to the Congo to implement the 1999 Lusaka accord. Nigeria, South Africa, Egypt, Pakistan, Jordan and Senegal have all pledged troops, mandated to protect military observers, as well as civilians living near UN bases. The Security Council insisted that it would deploy troops only after receiving security guarantees from the warring parties. The UN operation in the Congo is expected to cost $142 million per annum and is at least $250 million under-budgeted.

With its decision to return to the Congo four decades after its most controversial mission, the UN may be staring a major calamity in the face. Both the budget and the size of the mission are derisory for keeping peace among six neighbouring armies and a myriad of rebel groups in a large country with dilapidated infrastructure. Zimbabwe has an estimated 10,000 troops in the DRC, Angola 2,000, Namibia 2,000, Uganda 5,000, and Rwanda 10,000.[86] An unknown number of Hutu *génocidaires* from Rwanda are also in the Congo. Anti-Kabila forces control most of eastern Congo, while Kabila's 70,000-strong army retains power in the west. Before his death, Laurent Kabila obstructed the entry of more UN military observers, refused to engage in political dialogue with his opponents, and acted like a 'spoiler'. Following the assassination of Laurent Kabila on 16 January 2001 reportedly by one of his bodyguards, Kabila's allies, Angola, Zimbabwe and Namibia, as well as South Africa and UN Secretary-General Kofi Annan, have seen this incident as an opportunity for peace, stressing the importance of implementing the Lusaka Accord. Kabila's youthful son, Joseph, became the DRC's new head of state following his father's death, though it remains unclear whether he can establish his legitimacy and control over the country. During Joseph Kabila's visit to the UN in February 2001, he called on the UN to deploy more military observers to the Congo, and met with Rwanda's leader, Paul Kagame, in Washington D.C., a meeting facilitated by new US Secretary of State Colin Powell. At a meeting in Lusaka on the DRC peace process in February, Joseph Kabila met with Congo's other warring factions and invited former President Kethumile Masire, the facilitator of the yet to be held inter-Congolese dialogue.

Unless the UN takes advantage of this new window of opportunity, the UN mission in Congo runs the real risk of meeting with the same fate as its mission in Sierra Leone. If it comes under fire, how will it react? Will it surrender or will it fight? One thing seems certain: the UN Security Council is on the horns of a dilemma. On the one hand, it remains reluctant to beef up the Congo mission to a substantial and full-fledged Chapter VII operation. On the other hand, there are demands and expectations by African countries that it does exactly that, as was done with missions in

Kosovo and East Timor (see Griffin and Jones in this volume). The end result may well be more foot-dragging and procrastination, resulting in inaction and eventual failure.[87]

Learning Lessons

These seven cases of UN peacekeeping in Africa offer important lessons for the future. There is an urgent need to establish a proper division of labour between the UN and Africa's security organizations, which need to be vastly strengthened. The Arusha agreement of 1993 clearly revealed the military weakness of the OAU whose members lacked the resources to implement an agreement they had negotiated. In the case of Sierra Leone, the UN also had to take over peacekeeping duties from ECOMOG which was ill-equipped and poorly-funded. Rather than relying on mercenaries and private security firms (see Brooks in this volume) to maintain security, the UN must work more closely with the OAU, SADC, ECOWAS, the Intergovernmental Authority for Development (IGAD) and the Economic Community of Central African States (ECCAS) to strengthen their fledgling security mechanisms.[88] As argued below, UN peacekeeping could be built around African pillars. There is no shortage of African soldiers with UN peacekeeping experience, with over 20 OAU states having participated in UN peacekeeping missions around the world since 1960.

It is important to note that only in three cases – Angola, Sierra Leone and Western Sahara – did the UN take the lead in negotiating peace agreements, and in none of these cases have the accords so far been implemented.[89] This at least suggests the importance of regional and powerful external actors in negotiating an end to Africa's conflicts. External mediation and funding was important to the success of UN missions in Mozambique and Namibia. Lack of political support and consistent external funding eventually contributed to failures in Rwanda and Angola and could yet lead to failures in Sierra Leone and Congo.

The case of Somalia underlines the importance of impartiality to UN peacekeeping. Boutros Boutros-Ghali was distrusted by Aideed due to his past service as an Egyptian official and due to his Special Representative's military tactics. This reduced the UN's ability to influence events on the ground. The quality of diplomats serving as UN Special Representatives can be important to the success of a mission, as the example of Ajello in Mozambique showed. Less skilful Special Representatives can, on the other hand, make a difficult situation worse as appears to have been the case with Howe in Somalia and Booh-Booh in Rwanda. But it is important to note that adroit diplomacy alone is insufficient to achieve success. While personalities do matter in peacekeeping, it should be stressed that the will of the parties to implement agreements and the availability of resources with which to work appear to be the most important factors in determining success. It is highly unlikely, for example, that Ajello could have done much to prevent the genocide in Rwanda given the lack of political will demonstrated by the Security Council and the determination of domestic 'spoilers' to wreck the process.

There is a strong case to be made for developing strategies to deal with 'spoilers' like Aideed, Sankoh, Savimbi, and the *interahamwe*, who are determined to see the UN fail and attempt to ensure its withdrawal by attacking its peacekeepers.[90] In Angola, Rwanda and Somalia, peacekeepers were introduced into situations in which there was no peace to keep and in which certain parties were determined to force the withdrawal of the UN's peacekeepers. It is difficult to remain neutral under such circumstances, and the economic, political, and legal sanctions of the sort that are currently being applied on the RUF in Sierra Leone and UNITA in Angola would seem appropriate in such cases.

Political *élites* in the West have to show far more leadership in educating their publics about the utility and difficulties of UN peacekeeping. The commitment of important members of the Security Council to UN peacekeeping in Africa and the politics surrounding their interactions within the Council are often vital to the outcome of these missions. The recent US role in the Congo and Britain's role in Sierra Leone have been crucial to the establishment of UN missions in these countries. Washington's role was critical in leading the UN mission into Somalia in 1992 and in preventing UN action during the genocide in Rwanda in 1994. The decision to send a UN peacekeeping force to Rwanda in 1993 was pushed strongly in the Security Council by France which hoped to use the peacekeepers for its own parochial national interests of keeping Habyarimana in power and blunting the RPF's growing military strength.[91]

Despite some important recent thinking on UN peacekeeping reforms,[92] the success of future UN missions will continue to depend heavily on the willingness of the Security Council's powerful states to muster the political will and provide the military and financial resources to get the job done. The willingness of Western peacekeepers, who have both the equipment and resources, to continue to contribute to UN missions in Africa remains important. Even previously generous countries like Canada, the Netherlands and the Nordic countries are shying away from such missions.[93] As the recent, limited British intervention in Sierra Leone demonstrated, even if only to provide logistical support, the involvement of such armies is important in filling gaps created by the deficiencies of armies from developing countries. French logistical support was vital to the successful deployment of African peacekeepers to the UN mission in Central African

Republic in 1997. Despite the presumed domestic political risks of participating in such missions, it is important that a new aristocracy of death not be established where the lives of Western soldiers are worth more than those of non-Western peacekeepers and African civilians.

Building Regional Peacekeeping Pillars

Two events have contributed significantly to the recent turn away from regional peacekeeping and the apparent reassertion of the UN's role as the primary body responsible for international peacekeeping: the emergence of black majority rule in South Africa in 1994 and the death of Nigerian dictator, General Sani Abacha, in 1998. Abacha's death and the election of the civilian regime of Olusegun Obasanjo led to the emergence of a regime in Nigeria that could no longer ignore public opinion on the mounting costs and casualties of regional peacekeeping. Nigeria's recent ethnic clashes and continuing instability in its oil-producing region have focused attention on events closer to home.

In South Africa, Nelson Mandela's election raised great expectations in the West that Africa's richest country would lead the charge to keep the continental peace. Mandela chose instead to alleviate poverty at home and argued that South Africa's army needed restructuring, having acquired a notorious reputation for wreaking destruction on its neighbours. Mandela's successor, Thabo Mbeki, has promised to engage more in ending Africa's wars. With his army now largely restructured, there are no more excuses for not contributing soldiers to peacekeeping missions in Africa.[94] Both Mbeki and Obasanjo, internationally respected leaders, have promised to contribute peacekeepers to the Congo and Sierra Leone respectively, with the important proviso that they serve under a UN umbrella. But while both leaders have committed their countries to peacekeeping in Africa, questions remain about their capacity to undertake such missions. What is needed is to turn these countries into what John Stremlau recently called 'politically capable partners'.[95] Stremlau's idea is that the UN and US should assist in developing the capacities of African regional powers like South Africa and Nigeria to be able to keep peace in Africa.

The new missions in Congo and Sierra Leone could signify a new, innovative approach to UN peacekeeping in Africa based on regional pillars supported by local hegemons whose political dominance is diluted by multinational peacekeepers from outside their regions. By placing largely regional forces under the UN flag, the hope is that the peacekeepers will enjoy the legitimacy and impartiality that the UN's universal membership often provides, while some of the financial and logistical problems of regional peacekeepers can be alleviated through greater burden-sharing.

These new missions should also be more accountable, since the peacekeepers will have to report regularly to the UN Security Council. This might also force the Council to focus more attention on African conflicts.

Peace remains fragile in both Congo and Sierra Leone. The two missions, as Sierra Leone has already demonstrated, will be dangerous and fraught with difficulties. The mission in Sierra Leone will need better-equipped troops and more logistical support from Western armies. The number of troops for the Congo is clearly inadequate for the size of the country. 3,000 UN peacekeepers will be up against 100,000 African troops in a country the size of western Europe. If the UN is to avoid a repeat of the *débâcles* in Angola, Somalia and Rwanda, it will have to increase drastically its operation in Congo as a matter of urgency. The proposed UN peacekeeping force to monitor the Ethiopia/Eritrea border appears to be a more straightforward interposing force to separate two armies[96] but is also not completely risk-free.

The UN's credibility in Africa, already badly shaken by events in the Congo in the 1960s, suffered enormous damage after its peacekeepers abandoned Somalia and Rwanda to their fate in the early 1990s. It now has a golden opportunity to repair some of this damage by establishing a proper division of labour with Africa's regional organizations to keep the continental peace. But who would have thought that the UN would return to the Congo to deal with another sordid tale of mines, mercenaries, warlords and war-chests, four decades after the last such intervention? UN peacekeeping in Africa has come full circle.

ACKNOWLEDGEMENTS

The authors would like to thank Mats Berdal, Geoffrey Best, John Hirsch, David Malone, John Stremlau and Margaret Vogt for their invaluable comments on an earlier draft of this essay.

NOTES

1. See Christopher Clapham, 'The United Nations and Peacekeeping in Africa', in Mark Malan (ed.), *Whither Peacekeeping in Africa?*, Halfway House: Institute for Security Studies, 1999, pp.25–44; Oliver Furley and Roy May (eds.), *Peacekeeping in Africa*, Aldershot and Vermont: Ashgate, 1998; Marrack Goulding, 'The United Nations and Conflict in Africa since the Cold War', *African Affairs*, April 1999, Vol.98, No.391, pp.155–66; and Agostinho Zacarias, *The United Nations and International Peacekeeping*, London: I.B. Tauris, 1996.
2. On the distinction between peacekeeping, peacemaking and peace-enforcement, see Boutros Boutros-Ghali, *An Agenda For Peace*, New York: United Nations, 1992.
3. We would like to thank John Stremlau, Professor at Witwatersrand University, for drawing our attention to this point, as well as the point about the role of natural resources in fuelling conflicts.
4. See Georges Abi-Saab, *The United Nations Operation in the Congo 1960–1964*, Oxford: Oxford University Press, 1978; Catherine Hoskyns, *The Congo since Independence, January*

1960–December 1961, London: Oxford University Press, 1965; Conor Cruise O'Brien, *To Katanga and Back: A UN Case History*, London: Hutchinson, 1962; and Indar Jit Rikhye, *Military Adviser to the Secretary-General: UN Peacekeeping and the Congo Crisis*, London: Hurst; New York: St. Martin's, 1993.

5. See Brian Urquhart, *A Life in Peace and War*, New York and London: W.W. Norton, 1987, pp.145–70.

6. See Peter J. Schraeder, 'Removing the Schackles? US Foreign Policy Toward Africa After the End of the Cold War', in Edmond J. Keller and Donald Rothchild (eds.), *Africa in the New International Order*, Boulder and London: Lynne Rienner, 1996, pp.187–205; and John Stockwell, *In Search of Enemies: A CIA Story*, New York: W.W. Norton, 1978.

7. Alan James, 'The Congo Controversies', *International Peacekeeping*, Vol.1, No.1, Spring 1994, pp.44–58.

8. Ibid., p.53.

9. For a comparative analysis, see Assis Malaquias, 'The UN in Mozambique and Angola: Lessons Learned', *International Peacekeeping*, Vol.3, No.2, Summer 1996, pp.87–103.

10. See, for example, William Finnegan, *A Complicated War: The Harrowing of Mozambique*, Berkeley: University of California Press, 1992; and Alex Vines, *RENAMO: Terrorism in Mozambique*, Bloomington and Indianapolis: University of York and Indiana University Press, 1991.

11. Moises Venacio, 'Mediation by the Roman Catholic Church in Mozambique, 1988–91', in Stephen Chan and Vivienne Jabri (eds.), *Mediation in Southern Africa*, London and Basingstoke: Macmillan, 1993, p.147.

12. United Nations Department of Public Information, *The United Nations and Mozambique 1992–95*, New York: United Nations, Blue Book Series, Vol.5, 1995, p.14.

13. Ibid., p.15.

14. See Andrea Bartoli, 'Mediating Peace in Mozambique: The Role of the Community of Sant'Egidio', in Chester Crocker, Fen Osler Hampson and Pamela Aall (eds.), *Herding Cats: Multiparty Mediation in a Complex World*, Washington DC: United States Institute of Peace, 1999, pp.245–73.

15. Hasu P. Patel, 'Zimbabwe's mediation in Mozambique and Angola, 1989–91', in Chan and Jabri (eds.), *Mediation in Southern Africa*, p.119.

16. United Nations Department of Public Information, *The United Nations and Mozambique 1992–95*, p.4; and Chris Landsberg, 'Directing from the Stalls? The International Community and South Africa's Multi-party Negotiations Forum', in Steven Friedman and Doreen Atkinson (eds.), *The Small Miracle: South Africa's Negotiated Settlement*, Johannesburg: Raven Press, 1994, p.287.

17. Moises Venancio, 'Mediation by the Roman Catholic Church in Mozambique, 1988–91', p.166.

18. United Nations Department of Public Information, *The United Nations and Mozambique 1992–95*, p.4.

19. Philip Sibanda, 'Lessons from UN Peacekeeping in Africa: From UNAVEM to MONUA', in Jakkie Cilliers and Greg Mills (eds.), *From Peacekeeping to Complex Emergencies: Peace Support Missions in Africa*, Johannesburg and Pretoria: The South African Institute of International Affairs and the Institute for Security Studies, 1999, p.123.

20. See Aldo Ajello, 'Mozambique: Implementation of the 1992 Agreement', in Crocker, Hampson and Aal (eds.), *Herding Cats*, pp.619–42.

21. Chris Alden, 'Bullets, Ballots and Bread', Paper presented at the International Workshop on Southern Africa after Democratization, IDE, Tokyo, January 1996, p.34.

22. For an overview of the Angolan war, see Alex Vines, 'Angola: 40 years of War', *Track Two*, Vol.9, No.2, Occasional paper, Centre for Conflict Resolution, Cape Town, June 2000; and Margaret J. Anstee, 'Angola: The Forgotten Tragedy, A Test Case for UN Peacekeeping', in *International Relations*, Vol.11, No.6, December 1993.

23. For an analysis of South Africa's regional policy strategy, see Deon Geldenhuys, *The Diplomacy of Isolation: South African Foreign Policy Making*, Johannesburg: Macmillan, 1994; James Barber and John Barratt, *South Africa's Foreign Policy 1948–88: The Search for Status and Security*, Johannesburg and Cambridge: Southern Book Publishers and

Cambridge University Press, 1988; and Joseph Hanlon, *Apartheid's Second Front: South Africa's War against its neighbours*, London: Penguin Books, 1986.

24. Moises Venancio and Carla McMillan, 'Portuguese Mediation in the Angolan Conflict in 1990–91', in Chan and Jabri (eds.), *Mediation in Southern Africa*, p.105.
25. See Virginia Page Fortna, 'United Nations Angola Verification Mission I', in William Durch (ed.), *The Evolution of UN Peacekeeping*, New York: St. Martin's Press, 1993, pp.376–405.
26. United Nations Department of Public Information, *The UN and the Situation in Angola, May 1991–June 1994*, Reference paper, 1994, p.1.
27. Ibid., p.2.
28. Sibanda, 'Lessons from UN Peacekeeping in Africa', p.125.
29. 'The Blue Helmets Return', *Africa Confidential*, Vol.40, No.24, December 1999, p.2.
30. M.R. Bhagavan, 'Angola', *The Oxford Companion to Politics of the World*, Oxford: Oxford University Press, 1993, p.29.
31. Vines (n.22 above), p.8.
32. *Keesings Record of World Events*, London: Longman, June 1998.
33. See Margaret Anstee, *Orphan of the Cold War: The Inside Story of the Collapse of the Angolan Peace Process, 1992–3*, Macmillan: Basingstoke, 1996.
34. See Hussein Adam, 'Somalia: A Terrible Beauty Being Born?', in I. William Zartman (ed.), *Collapsed States: The Disintegration and Restoration of Legitimate Authority*, Boulder and London: Lynne Rienner, 1995, pp.69–78.
35. See Mohamed Sahnoun, *Somalia: The Missed Opportunities*, Washington DC: United States Institute of Peace, 1994, pp.25–41.
36. Alex de Waal, *Famine Crimes: Politics and the Disaster Relief Industry in Africa*, Oxford and Bloomington: James Currey and Indiana University Press, 1997, p.185.
37. Walter Clarke, 'Failed Visions and Uncertain Mandates in Somalia', in Walter Clarke and Jeffrey Herbst (eds.), *Learning From Somalia: The Lessons of Armed Humanitarian Intervention*, Boulder and Oxford: Westview Press, 1997, p.5.
38. John L. Hirsch and Robert B. Oakley, *Somalia and Operation Restore Hope: Reflections on Peacemaking and Peacekeeping*, Washington DC: United States Institute of Peace, 1995, p.54.
39. Sahnoun (n.35 above), p.39.
40. Terrence Lyons and Ahmed I. Samatar, *Somalia: State Collapse, Multilateral Intervention, and Strategies for Political Reconstruction*, Washington DC: The Brookings Institution, 1995, pp.49–51.
41. See Ameen Jan, 'Peacebuilding in Somalia', IPA Policy Briefing Series, July 1996.
42. See Alex de Waal (n.36 above), pp.183–8.
43. Ibid., p.186.
44. Boutros Boutros-Ghali, *Unvanquished: A US–UN Saga*, London: I.B. Tauris, 1999, p.95.
45. For his own interpretation of events, see Jonathan T. Howe, 'Relations between the United States and United Nations in Dealing with Somalia', in Clarke and Herbst (eds.), *Learning from Somalia*, pp.173–90.
46. See Mats Berdal, 'American, French and British Peacekeeping in Africa after the Cold War', in Furley and May (eds.) (n.1 above).
47. This expression was coined by Boutros Boutros-Ghali.
48. See Turid Laegreid, 'UN Peacekeeping in Rwanda', in Howard Adelman and Astri Suhrke (eds.), *The Path of a Genocide: The Rwanda Crisis from Uganda to Zaire*, New Brunswick and London: Transaction Publishers, 1999, pp.231–51; and Ami Mpunge, 'Crisis and Response in Rwanda', in Malan (ed.) (n.1 above), pp.14–24.
49. Laegreid (n.48 above), p.232.
50. Astri Suhrke, 'UN Peacekeeping in Rwanda', in Gunnar Sorbo and Peter Vale (eds.), *Out of Conflict: From War to Peace in Africa*, Uppsala: Nordiska Afrikainstitutet, 1997, pp.107–8.
51. Gérard Prunier, *The Rwandan Crisis: History of a Genocide*, New York: Columbia University Press, 1995, p.204.
52. Henry Kwami Anyidoho, *Guns over Kigali*, Accra: Woeli Publishing Services, 1999, p.11.
53. For an eye-witness account by UNAMIR's Deputy Force Commander, see ibid., pp.20–38.
54. Prunier (n.51 above), p.287.

55. Boutros-Ghali (n.44 above), p.138.
56. See Organization of African Unity, *The International Panel of Eminent Persons to Investigate the 1994 Genocide in Rwanda and the Surrounding Events*, July 2000; and *Report of the Independent Inquiry into the actions of the United Nations during the 1994 genocide in Rwanda*, 16 December 1999, S/1999/1257.
57. Quoted in Prunier (n.51 above), p.276.
58. Abiodun Alao, *The Burden of Collective Goodwill: The International Involvement in the Liberian Civil War*, Brookfield and Aldershot: Ashgate Publishing Company, 1998; Karl Magyar and Earl Conteh-Morgan (eds.), *Peacekeeping in Africa: ECOMOG in Liberia*, Hampshire, London and New York: Macmillan and St. Martin's Press, 1998; Robert Mortimer, 'From ECOMOG to ECOMOG II: Intervention in Sierra Leone', in John W. Harbeson and Donald Rothchild (eds.), *Africa in World Politics: The African State System in Flux*, Colorado and Oxford: Westview Press, Third Edition, 2000, pp.188–207; and Margaret Vogt (ed.), *The Liberian Crisis and ECOMOG: A Bold Attempt at Regional Peacekeeping*, Lagos: Gabumo Press, 1993.
59. See *African Development*, Vol.22, nos.2 and 3 (1997), special issue on 'Youth Culture and Political Violence: The Sierra Leone Civil War'; and Paul Richards, 'Rebellion in Liberia and Sierra Leone: A Crisis of Youth?, in Oliver Furley (ed.), *Conflict in Africa*, New York and London: Tauris Academic Studies, 1995.
60. Personal Interview with Lt. Colonel Chris Olukolade, ECOMOG's Chief Military Information Officer, Freetown, 3 July 1999.
61. Personal Interview with ECOMOG officers, Freetown, July 1999.
62. See, Adekeye Adebajo, 'Nigeria: Africa's New Gendarme?', *Security Dialogue*, Vol.31, No.2, pp.185–99.
63. For accounts of the Sierra Leone conflict, see Ibrahim Abdullah and Patrick Muana, 'The Revolutionary United Front of Sierra Leone: A Revolt of the Lumpenproletariat', in Christopher Clapham (ed.), *African Guerrillas*, Oxford, Kampala and Bloomington: James Currey, Fountain Publishers and Indiana University Press, 1998; pp.172–93; Adekeye Adebajo and David Keen, 'Banquet for Warlords', *The World Today*, Vol.56, No.7, July 2000, pp.8–10; William Reno, *Warlord Politics and African States*, Boulder and London: Lynne Rienner Publishers, 1998; and Paul Richards, *Fighting for the Rainforest: War, Youth and Resources in Sierra Leone*, Oxford and New Hampshire: James Currey and Heinemann, 1996.
64. See report of the panel of experts appointed pursuant to Security Council Resolution 1306 (2000), para. 19, in relation to Sierra Leone, S/2000/1195, 20 Dec. 2000.
65. See Seventh Report of the Secretary-General on the United Nations Observer Mission in Sierra Leone, 30 July 1999, S/1999/836, pp.1–3.
66. Fourth Report on the United Nations Mission in Sierra Leone, 19 May 2000, S/2000/455, p.4.
67. Third Report on the United Nations Mission in Sierra Leone, 7 March 2000, S/2000/186, pp.3–4; and Fifth Report on the United Nations Mission in Sierra Leone, 31 July 2000, S/2000/751, p.4.
68. Fifth Report on the United Nations Mission in Sierra Leone, 31 July 2000, S/2000/751, p.9.
69. See Lansana Fofana, 'A Nation Self-destructs', *NewsAfrica*, 31 July 2000, Vol.1, No.5, pp.25; and Chris McGreal, 'UN to Sack Its General in Sierra Leone', *Guardian Weekly*, 29 June–5 July 2000, p.2.
70. See eighth report of the Secretary-General on the United Nations mission in Sierra Leone, S/2000/1199, 15 Dec. 2000.
71. Fourth Report on the United Nations Mission in Sierra Leone, 19 May 2000, S/2000/455, p.5.
72. Third Report on the United Nations Mission in Sierra Leone, 7 March 2000, S/2000/186, p.14.
73. Fifth Report on the United Nations Mission in Sierra Leone, 31 July 2000, S/2000/751, pp.4–5.
74. See Jane Perlez, 'GIs to be Sent to Train Africans for Sierra Leone', *The New York Times*, 9 August 2000, pp.A1 and A10.
75. See Sixth Report of the Secretary-General on the United Nations Mission in Sierra Leone, 24 August 2000, S/2000/832, pp.4–6.

76. Blaine Harden, 'Two African Nations Said to Break UN Diamond Embargo', *The New York Times*, 1 August 2000, p.A3.
77. See report of the Secretary-General on the establishment of a special court for Sierra Leone, S/2000/915, 4 Oct. 2000.
78. 'We Don't Want Another Angola'. Interview with Olu Adeniji, *West Africa*, 13–19 March 2000, No.4217, p.14.
79. See Georges Nzongola-Ntalaja (ed.), *The Crisis in Zaire: Myths and Realities*, Trenton: Africa World Press, 1986; Herbert Weiss, 'Zaire: Collapsed Society, Surviving State, Future Polity', in Zartman (ed.) (n.34 above), pp.157–170; and Crawford Young and Thomas Turner, *The Rise and Decline of the Zairian State*, Madison: University of Wisconsin Press, 1985.
80. See Musifiky Mwanasali, 'Peacebuilding in the Democratic Republic of the Congo', IPA Policy Briefing Series, April 1998.
81. Claude Kabemba, *Whither the DRC? Causes of the Conflict in the Democratic Republic of Congo, and the Way Forward*, Centre for Policy Studies, Johannesburg, Policy, Issues and Actors, Vol.11, No.6, Johannesburg, March 1999, p.10.
82. Ibid., p.11.
83. International Crisis Group (ICG), *The Agreement on a Cease-fire in the Democratic Republic Congo: An analysis of the agreement and prospects for peace*, ICG Democratic Republic of Congo Report No.5, 20 August 1999.
84. Report of the Secretary-General on the United Nations Preliminary Deployment in the Democratic Republic of the Congo, 15 July 1999, S/1999/790.
85. We would like to thank David Malone, President of the International Peace Academy, for drawing our attention to this point.
86. International Crisis Group (ICG), *Africa's Seven-nation War*, ICG Democratic Republic of Congo Report No.4, 21 May 1999; and Ian Fisher, 'Congo's War Triumphs Over Peace Accord', *The New York Times*, 18 September 2000, p.A1 and A8.
87. See International Crisis Group (ICG), *The Agreement on a Cease-fire in the Democratic Republic of Congo*, p.5.
88. See Adekeye Adebajo and Chris Landsberg, 'Pax Africana in the Age of Extremes', *South African Journal of International Affairs*, Vol.7, No.1, Summer 2000, pp.11–26; Ibrahim Gambari, 'The United Nations as an External Actor in Sub-Regional Security', in *Militaries, Democracies, and Security in Sub-Saharan Africa*, Papers Presented at a Conference in Abuja, Nigeria 1–4 December 1997, pp.166–74; International Peace Academy/Council for the Development of Social Science Research in Africa, 'War, Peace, and Reconciliation in Africa', Consultation, Senegal, Nov.–Dec. 1999; and Margaret Vogt, 'Co-operation between the UN and the OAU in the Management of African Conflicts', in Malan (ed.) (n.1 above), pp.45–60.
89. Goulding, 'The United Nations and Conflict in Africa since the Cold War', p.161.
90. See Stephen Stedman, 'Spoiler Problems in Peace Processes', *International Security*, Vol.22, No.2, Fall 1997, pp.5–53.
91. Surkhe (n.50 above), p.105.
92. See Kofi Annan, 'Challenges of the New Peacekeeping', in Olara Otunnu and Michael Doyle (eds.), *Peacemaking and Peacekeeping for the New Century*, Maryland and Oxford: Rowman & Littlefield, 1998, pp.169–87; Mats Berdal, *Whither UN Peacekeeping?*, Adelphi Paper 281, October 1993; and *Report of the Panel on United Nations Peace Operations*, 21 August 2000, S/2000/809.
93. *The Economist*, 'The UN's Mission Impossible', 5–11 August 2000, p.24; and David Malone, 'The Battle for Peace', *Toronto Globe and Mail*, 23 August 2000.
94. See Chris Landsberg, 'Promoting Democracy: The Mandela–Mbeki Doctrine', *Journal of Democracy*, Vol.11, No.3, July 2000, pp.107–21.
95. John Stremlau, 'Ending Africa's wars', *Foreign Affairs*, July 2000, pp.117–32.
96. See Report of the Secretary-General on Ethiopia and Eritrea, 30 June 2000, S/2000/643.

In the Shadow of Kargil:
Keeping Peace in Nuclear South Asia

WAHEGURU PAL SINGH SIDHU

Since December 1971, when India and Pakistan fought their last full-fledged war, South Asia has been in a state of 'violent peace' – a state where though there have not been any wars, declared or undeclared, military confrontations, albeit of a limited nature, have erupted regularly. The Kargil confrontation in the summer of 1999 was only the most recent episode in the long history of crises that have plagued the region in the last three decades. These crises, particularly in the 1980s, which all stopped short of full-scale war, were clearly played out in the shadow of the emerging nuclear capabilities in the sub-continent.

There were three crises which nearly led to full-scale war in 1983–84, 1986–87 and 1990.[1] During the crisis of 1983–84, there were persistent reports that India would attack Pakistan's nuclear weapon production facilities and Islamabad threatened to retaliate with a similar attack on Indian facilities. The crisis in 1986–87 occurred when India conducted *Brasstacks*, its biggest military exercise ever, close to the Pakistani border. Pakistan, fearing that the exercise might be converted into an attack, launched its own defensive disposition Operation *Sledgehammer*. The Indians then responded with a mobilization to counter Pakistan's deployment – Operation *Trident*. Although the crisis was peacefully resolved, Pakistan indicated shortly after that it had acquired nuclear weapons capability.

The 1990 crisis erupted soon after Pakistan had conducted its biggest military exercise, *Zarb-i-Momin*, in late 1989. In the wake of this exercise, there was a sudden spurt in the insurgency movement in the disputed Kashmir region. The insurgents were reportedly operating out of camps in Pakistan. India accused Pakistan of training and supporting the militants and rushed reinforcements to the valley. New Delhi threatened to carry out 'hot pursuits' across the border into Pakistan to strike at the reported training camps. Pakistan considered this a hostile act and as tension mounted, Islamabad reportedly threatened to weaponize its nuclear capability to counter any Indian attack. Although none of these crises was conducted with the possession of nuclear weapons, they were all certainly about nuclear weapons – the threat to build them, the threat to prevent their construction, and the threat of their future use. While the nuclear dimension may not have been explicitly conveyed to the other side, it was always present in the background and would certainly have had a bearing on the decisions taken by policy-makers on both sides of the border.[2] These incidents were nuclear-related crises even though there was no overt deployment of weapons.

Although the Kargil confrontation in 1999 was a continuation of this trend, it was also different from earlier crises in three important respects. To begin with, this was the first major crisis after both India and Pakistan had tested several nuclear devices and openly declared themselves to be nuclear powers in May 1998. Unlike the past where there may have been some doubt about the nuclear weapons capability of each side, in this instance, both sides were well aware of the presence of nuclear weapons in each other's arsenal. In fact, according to one account, India is reported to have prepared at least half a dozen nuclear weapons for delivery during the course of the conflict.[3] Second, in the South Asian context, this was the first time since 1971 that one side had occupied a disputed territory. Thus the Pakistani action of crossing the Line of Control (LoC) signalled a major breakout and challenged the relative stability that had been established under the non-weaponized deterrence relationship between the two antagonists since the early 1980s. Finally, Kargil was different from earlier crises because it was the longest, and perhaps bloodiest, military confrontation between the two countries, which unlike other crises did not end with a bilaterally negotiated peace treaty. To a large extent the crisis was resolved at the behest of a third party – the United States.

At least two myths were challenged by the Kargil episode. The first myth is the belief that going overtly nuclear automatically ensures the cessation of all conflict and the creation of stability between two adversaries. Kargil in fact demonstrated that a dyad nuclear relationship is not inherently stable but can lead, in some cases, to situations where it may actually provoke one side (or both sides) to take steps to undermine the status quo. As a corollary, the belief that India's alleged conventional superiority would prevent military action by Pakistan was also brought into question by the incident. Kargil proved that while India may appear to be the more powerful country, at least in sheer size and numbers, this is not necessarily a qualitative edge nor is it likely to deter a nuclear-armed Pakistan. The second myth which Kargil challenged is that the Line of Control between India and Pakistan in the state of Jammu and Kashmir is not sacrosanct – indeed, it is now considered inviolable and is being accepted as the international border whether India and Pakistan like it or not. India's statements and actions have clearly demonstrated that New Delhi considers the LoC unalterable by force, although it is still unwilling to convert the LoC into an international border.

This essay begins with a brief description of the Kargil confrontation. It then explores the origins of the myths of strategic stability and the inviolability of the LoC. It assesses how these myths were challenged by Kargil and what impact this episode is likely to have on the future of Indo-Pakistan relations. Will both sides attempt to revive these myths? Or will they try to establish a new and more realistic relationship in the wake of the Kargil confrontation in order to keep peace in nuclear South Asia? The essay will argue that these myths are unlikely to be resurrected and that both New Delhi and Islamabad will have to fashion a new post-Kargil relationship which could turn out to be either antagonistic or cooperative. The nature of the emergent relationship will depend on several factors: strategic considerations, domestic political compulsions, economic and technological capabilities, and the role of the international community. In concluding, the essay will explain why it is in the interests of both India and Pakistan to adopt a cooperative approach to keeping peace in South Asia.

The Kargil Crisis

The genesis of the Kargil operation remains a contentious issue. One report suggests that the operation was planned as far back as 1987 under Pakistan's military ruler, General Zia-ul-Huq.[4] Pakistani military analysts, however, assert that the operation became feasible only after 1995 when a *pucca* road was completed on the Pakistani side of the LoC. This made it possible to set up forward logistic support for any military operation in the area.[5] The actual plan and timing of the operation was decided by Pakistan's Chief of Army Staff, General Pervez Musharraf, and shared with only three or four other senior officers. Pakistan's Prime Minister at the time, Nawaz Sharif, may have approved of the operation in principle, but he was not provided with (and may not have asked for) the specifics of the operation. Consequently, in the spring of 1999 (the exact date remains a matter of some debate) around 800–1000 officers and men of Pakistan's Northern Light Infantry and the Special Service Group, supported by *mujahideen* groups, crossed the LoC into India in the Kargil sector and occupied strategic heights all along the ridgeline. This deployment not only posed an immediate danger to the Srinagar-Leh National Highway 1A – the lifeline between the Kashmir valley and Ladakh – but also threatened India's hold over the Siachen glacier area.[6]

The Indian army spotted these intrusions in early May 1999 and launched Operation *Vijay* to evict the invaders. The seriousness of the invasion became clear when two Indian Army reconnaissance patrols went missing and Pakistani artillery scored direct hits on the ammunition dump and district headquarters at Kargil. On 26 May, the Indian Air Force (IAF) launched Operation *Safed Sagar* and began air strikes to dislodge the well-entrenched intruders on the Indian sides of the LoC. India lost two aircraft, probably to shoulder-fired surface-to-air-missiles, during the first few days of the incursion. Interestingly, although Pakistani fighter aircraft were spotted in the area, they did not engage the Indians either in the air or on the ground and the IAF continued to enjoy air superiority throughout the conflict.[7] The Indian Navy established an offensive posture (Operation *Talwar*) along the Makran coast of Pakistan. On 31 May, a year after he declared India a nuclear weapon state, Indian Prime Minister, Atal Behari Vajpayee, described the situation as 'war-like'[8] and both the Indian and Pakistan armed forces went on full alert along the International Border. At this juncture India is reported to have deployed nuclear-capable missiles in Rajasthan and Punjab.[9] The Indian Navy in particular established an offensive posture along the Makran coast of Pakistan.[10]

As reinforcements were rushed into the Mushko Valley, Dras, Kaksar and Batalik in Kargil and the air and ground campaign continued (without crossing the LoC) it became clear that the Indian military simply did not have the wherewithal to eject the intruders from all the locations simultaneously. Thus, India prioritized the assaults: Tiger Hill and Tololing complex in Dras sub-sector, which dominate the Srinagar-Leh highway, were accorded the highest priority. The Batalik-Turtok sub-sector came next as it provided access to the Siachen region through the Shyok river valley.[11] The Indian military suffered heavy losses, particularly as it attempted to regain the strategic heights in the Tiger Hill-Tololing complex and contemplated crossing the LoC. Several officials and strategists called for escalation but a minority urged restraint.[12]

Interestingly, all through this period, both the Indian and Pakistani prime ministers remained in regular telephone contact. For instance, Vajpayee called Sharif on 24 May (two days before the air strikes were launched) and warned him that 'all possible steps' would be taken to clear the intruders from Kargil. Similarly, Sharif called Vajpayee four days later and offered to send his foreign minister for talks. Sharif called Vajpayee again on 13 June, a day after the talks between the foreign ministers were deadlocked, to urge the resumption of dialogue.[13]

In addition to talking directly, the two prime ministers had also established a back channel of communication through former Pakistani Foreign Secretary, Niaz A. Naik, and R.K. Mishra, an Indian publisher close to Vajpayee. This back channel had reportedly been established between the two Prime Ministers' offices soon after the Lahore Declaration in February 1999 to discuss a number of bilateral issues, including Kashmir.[14] While there is some indication that the Indian Ministry of External Affairs was involved to some extent in this back channel, there is no evidence to suggest that the same was true in Pakistan. In fact, information suggests that the Pakistan army, which had opposed the Lahore process, was deliberately kept out of this channel. This back channel was particularly useful in ensuring communication between the two prime ministers during the early days of Kargil, although it was not designed for this purpose. It was apparently shut down around 29 June after Islamabad publicly distanced itself from Naik's peace mission to India.

However, the back channel notwithstanding, on a visit to the front line on 21 June Sharif warned, 'there will be more Kargil-like situations' in future.[15] A few days later, the Pakistani Prime Minister threatened to use the 'ultimate weapon' and warned of 'irreparable losses' if India crossed the LoC, issuing the clearest nuclear threat to date.[16] Significantly, none of India's leaders issued a counter threat. India's Defence Minister, George Fernandes, merely cautioned that Sharif's threat should 'not be taken casually' and hoped that international pressure would deter Pakistan from using its nuclear weapons in the heat of battle.[17] India's Home Minister, Lal Krishna Advani, who, in May 1998, had warned Pakistan by talking of 'hot pursuits' and issuing a tacit nuclear threat, reiterated the government's stand not to cross the LoC as this approach 'has given the country decided advantages'.[18]

But it would appear that India's decision not to escalate the crisis had more to do with the success of international pressure on Pakistan than with Sharif's nuclear threat. The international pressure, led primarily by the United States, was evident in American President Bill Clinton's telephonic admonitions to Sharif, a Group of Eight (G-8) communiqué, and the visit of General Anthony Zinni, Commander-in-Chief of the US Central Command, to Islamabad for a one-to-one meeting with General Musharraf. This external pressure forced an increasingly diplomatically isolated Pakistan to look for a way out of the crisis.[19] Sharif went to Washington DC to meet with Clinton in early July 1999. In the joint statement issued at the end of the meeting, it was agreed that Pakistan would take steps 'for the restoration of the LoC in accordance with the Simla Agreement'.[20] Following Sharif's visit to Washington and his decision to withdraw his troops unilaterally, a meeting was held between the Indian Director General of Military Operations (DGMO) and Pakistan's Director of Military Operations (DMO) at the Attari (Wagah) border outpost near Amritsar on 11 July, to work out a time frame for the Pakistani troop withdrawal. Pakistan's DMO agreed that the withdrawal, which had already begun, would be completed by 16 July 1999.[21] Pakistani intruders, however, remained entrenched in small numbers in pockets of Dras, Mushko Valley and Batalik. They eventually retreated from these areas by 25 July. The next day, the Indian DGMO declared that all Pakistani soldiers had been evicted from Kargil district, bringing the longest Indo-Pakistan military confrontation to an end.[22]

As a post-script to the Kargil episode three events are noteworthy. First, India set up a committee to review the Kargil imbroglio and the army raised a new corps headquarters (XIV corps) with the objective of having a permanent force east of the Zoji La pass to man the 140-km LoC in the Kargil sector as well as the disputed Siachen glacier.[23] The second incident was the downing of a Pakistan Navy Bergeut Atlantique aircraft by the IAF on 10 August 1999, killing all the personnel on board.[24] While Pakistan claimed that the 'unarmed' aircraft was on a 'training' mission, India accused its neighbour of 'spying' over Indian airspace.[25] The third event was the failed attempt by Sharif to oust his army chief, General Musharraf and the dramatic counter-coup by the Pakistan army on 12 October 1999, which led to the ouster of Sharif instead.[26] Although there were several reasons behind the falling out of the prime minister and his army chief, one of the significant factors was the serious differences between the two over the handling of the Kargil issue.

The 'Stability' Myth

Although nuclear weapons are widely believed to provide stability between pairs of nuclear-armed states, every dyad has experienced a crisis or a series of crises before nuclear stability was achieved. The US and the former Soviet Union had several tense stand-offs starting with the Berlin Crisis and culminating in the eyeball-to-eyeball confrontation during the 1962 Cuban missile crisis. Only after these crises was a level of stability achieved through a series of formal measures between the two. Similarly, the China–Soviet dyad experienced a serious crisis that led to a shooting match over the Ussuri river boundary in 1969 before nuclear stability was achieved. And yet until very recently both Indian and Pakistani officials maintained that the mere presence of nuclear weapons in their dyad relationship would inherently provide stability. Indeed officials proudly proclaimed that South Asia presents a 'brighter picture' and that the Lahore Declaration of February 1999 showed the 'commitment of both governments to manage their nuclear responsibility'.[27] In reality, however, India and Pakistan too have been through at least three nuclear-related crises since 1984. This led Kanti Bajpai, an academic, to point out that while nuclear capabilities may be 'deterrence stable' they are not 'crisis stable'. In fact, 'nuclear capability on both sides of the border has made the region positively safe for insurgencies aided and abetted by outsiders'.[28] This has certainly been borne out by the events in Kargil, the only difference being that insurgents did not lead this particular operation.

Like the previous three crises, the Kargil crisis too had its genesis in the nuclear equation and Pakistan's interest in testing the limits of this relationship. While the Pakistani army's plan to cross the LoC into Kargil is at least several years old, its implementation at this juncture revealed that the military leadership may have been emboldened by Pakistan's newly demonstrated nuclear capability and the perception that this provided an umbrella to carry out Kargil-type military operations. Simply put, Islamabad was convinced that New Delhi would be deterred and would not put up much of a fight or would only engage in a limited operation for fear of escalation. Another factor that might have bolstered the conviction among Islamabad's military top brass was India's unilateral nuclear no-first-use declaration.

During the conflict, however, when India resorted to the use of air power and also brought its navy into play, Pakistan did not escalate in response, indicating that the engagement was being limited to ground troops in Kargil.[29] The Pakistan Air Force (PAF), for instance, refrained from crossing the LoC and did not engage the IAF aircraft, even from a distance, while they were attacking Pakistani troops. Had the PAF done so, the IAF may have responded with strikes beyond the LoC, thereby escalating the conflict beyond the Kargil region and bringing it closer to the nuclear threshold: a scenario that Islamabad appeared unwilling to entertain. However, when India contemplated crossing the LoC, Sharif warned of 'irreparable losses', thereby threatening to go nuclear if the engagement was not confined to the Kargil region.

From the Indian perspective, the Kargil experience reinforced New Delhi's existing posture of dealing with threats by using its conventional forces first, a position that has been reaffirmed in the draft Indian nuclear doctrine of 17 August 1999.[30] Even the no-first-use posture, which could be regarded as one of the factors that prompted the Pakistani action in Kargil, has been retained in the draft doctrine. Indeed, only a passing reference was made to the Kargil crisis during the release of the draft doctrine. India's National Security Adviser, Brijesh Mishra, stated, 'the recent operations in Kargil have demonstrated, our ... great responsibility and restraint,' revealing that Kargil has had little or no impact on the nuclear debate.[31] It also indicated that India continues to believe in the myth that the 'responsibility and restraint' of one power in a nuclear dyad is enough to ensure stability.

On the other hand, the Kargil episode may also have proved to both Pakistan and India, that it is possible to have a limited conventional engagement (although the risk of escalation exists) that will remain below the nuclear threshold, only if both sides tacitly agree to limit the conflict either in terms of area, time, and/or weapons. The certainty that this message was delivered and understood by both sides may be based on the direct communication between the two prime ministers and the indirect parlays through their back channel. This could explain why Sharif declared at the height of the confrontation that 'there will be more Kargil-like situations' in future. It may also explain why in the wake of Kargil, Indian defence officials made pointed references to the Ussuri incident of 1969 and started propagating the concept of 'limited war' including the need to maintain a conventional edge so as to 'ensure that conventional war... is kept below the nuclear threshold'.[32] There is no indication so far, however, that Pakistan has accepted this 'limited war' concept.[33] On the contrary, senior Pakistani officials cite Moscow's actions in Hungary (in 1956) and Prague (1968) at the height of the Cold War as a rationale for Islamabad's post-Cold War aggression in Kargil. Thus, it is unclear whether India and Pakistan have realized that unless their dyad nuclear relationship is formalized and its lines clearly delineated, there is a real danger of escalation if either side misinterprets the tacit signals, misreads intentions and crosses the nuclear threshold.

The 'LoC' Myth

The Line of Control (LoC), which runs for 740 kilometres from Sangam (near Jammu) to point NJ 9842 (short of the Siachen Glacier), was demarcated using a six-point grid reference under the 1972 Simla Agreement reached between India and Pakistan.[34] Although the LoC marks the positions where Indian and Pakistani troops were physically located at the end of the 1971 war, and can still be altered by troops from both sides moving positions, it has become the *de facto* border, as the international outcry against Pakistan's action in Kargil revealed. In one of the more telling incidents during the conflict, when Pakistan's Ambassador in Washington, Riaz Khokhar, was making his case about the violability of the LoC before a US State department official, the American official presented him with the documents and maps outlining the LoC and asserted that the Line was not disputed.[35] The sanctity of the LoC was also reiterated in the joint Clinton–Sharif statement which categorically stated that the 'Line of Control in Kashmir be respected by both parties, in accordance with their 1972 Simla Accord'.[36] This was also endorsed in a separate statement made by China, one of Pakistan's key allies.[37] Thus, in post-Cold War South Asia the LoC has gained the sanctity that the Iron Curtain had in Cold War Europe.

International opprobrium apart, neither India nor Pakistan can alter the LoC by force for two reasons. First, given the overt nuclear posture of both sides, any large-scale attack across the LoC would eventually bring both countries to the brink of nuclear Armageddon. For instance, were India unable to block and evict the intruders in Kargil (or if international pressure had failed to bring about a unilateral Pakistani withdrawal), New Delhi would almost certainly have escalated the conventional conflict either by crossing the LoC or by opening up another front. Such a move would have posed an unacceptable level of threat to the state of Pakistan in general and the cities of Karachi, Lahore and Islamabad in particular. In such a scenario, Pakistan would almost certainly have been compelled to unsheathe its nuclear sword. Similarly, were India to try and alter the LoC, initiate a Kargil-like conflict, cross the LoC and occupy Pakistani territory, the nuclear threshold would be reached even sooner. This is because Islamabad continues to adhere to a first-use posture and reserves the right to bring its nuclear weapons into play whenever it deems it necessary. Although the common Indian perception is that Pakistan considers its nuclear arsenal to be weapons of last resort and would use them only when the very existence of the state was threatened, the thinking in Islamabad is rather different. According to Zafar Cheema, a leading Pakistani strategist, nuclear weapons are not necessarily weapons of last resort but could be employed if India was to cross the LoC even in hot pursuit.[38] Hence, theoretically Pakistan could play the nuclear card as soon as the first Indian intrusion across the LoC was detected. This was clearly the message that Sharif's 'ultimate weapon' statement during Kargil sought to convey.

Even without the presence of nuclear weapons, a military option to alter the LoC is unlikely to be effective beyond a certain point. This is primarily because neither India nor Pakistan possesses the necessary manpower, equipment or resources to carry out a decisive offensive military operation that will enable them to alter and hold new military positions. Such an operation would require not just an infiltration across the LoC but the ability to interdict and hold vital supply bases and routes well beyond the *de facto* border. This would mean not just controlling the heights but also major highways and valleys on either side of the LoC. Although Pakistan may have attempted this in the recent operation, it was clearly unable to sustain its hold or advance further. The Pakistani army, in particular, appears to have designed its equipment and tactics for more Kargil-type of operations, rather than the traditional full-scale wars of the past. Hence, with just one thousand lightly armed men backed by limited artillery, the Pakistani army was able to engage a significant proportion of the Indian army and air force for well over two months. Islamabad's incursion not only threatened India's hold over the Siachen area but also weakened its military presence in the Kashmir valley.[39] However, it is doubtful whether Pakistan could have sustained this hold indefinitely.

Similarly, although the Indian army is nearly twice as large as the Pakistan army and has two and a half times the artillery guns of the latter, New Delhi is unprepared for Kargil-like operations, and in the early days of Kargil it was out-manned, out-gunned and ill-equipped. According to one assessment, it took three weeks to build up sufficient force levels and an additional twelve days for the acclimatization of these troops.[40] Even when reinforcements did arrive, they did not have adequate equipment to provide them with real-time data of the immediate battlefield. Consequently, the Indian army suffered inhuman losses fighting a twentieth century war with turn of the century equipment.[41] Even India's Chief of Army Staff, V. P. Malik, admitted that 'we would have reduced our casualties had we the right equipment'.[42] Similarly, the IAF, though numerically and technologically superior to the PAF, was equally inappropriately equipped to operate in Kargil. By its own admission, the IAF had neither the right equipment nor the right tactics for the Kargil operation.[43]

Another way to alter the LoC would be to negotiate a new and mutually agreed upon boundary as part of the composite dialogue between India and Pakistan. Alternatively, both sides could decide to accept formally the present LoC as the international border, thus converting the *de facto* border into a *de jure* one. However, both these prospects appear unlikely, given the bitterness generated by the Kargil crisis and the derailment of the Lahore process. For instance, after Kargil, the then Pakistani Foreign Minister, Sartaj Aziz, categorically stated that Islamabad would not entertain any proposal to convert the existing LoC into an international border.[44] Similarly, India's Foreign Minister, Jaswant Singh, while 'reaffirming the inviolability and sanctity' of the LoC ruled out converting the LoC into an international border.[45] However, even in the absence of a formal understanding (and despite attempts by either side to alter the Line), the *de facto* LoC, like the Iron Curtain in Europe before it, is almost certain to be preserved unaltered as is manifest by the Kargil experience; only the cost in men and material in similar episodes will be inevitable.

Keeping Peace in South Asia

Kargil is not an isolated incident but sets the pattern for the future of Indo-Pakistan relations. There are two principal ways to manage this new relationship. One is the non-cooperative, antagonistic approach where each side unilaterally fortifies the LoC and deploys a string of sensors and other early warning devices so as not to get caught off guard. The other, discussed in greater detail below, is the cooperative, non-antagonistic bilateral approach in which both sides reaffirm the inviolability of the LoC. In the first scenario, each side would build up its defences to respond rapidly and with overwhelming force to any intrusion. This appears to be the preferred option of both India and Pakistan. India, which raised a new corps, has now deployed units all along the LoC, particularly on the high-points in the Kargil, Dras and Batalik sectors so as to ensure that the line is manned all year round. The same is true on the Pakistan side of the LoC where troops have been stationed on a permanent basis. In addition, the Kargil Review

Committee, set up by New Delhi to suggest means to try to ensure that such an episode does not recur, has recommended the indigenous development of a 'world-class satellite capability' and has advocated the acquisition and use of unmanned aerial vehicles (UAVs) for reconnaissance at the high altitudes of the Kargil sector.[46] Similarly, Islamabad announced a new National Command Authority to develop and employ 'strategic forces'.[47] The approach of both countries, however, presents at least three problems.

First, this military-build up is likely to be untenable in the long run both in terms of men and money.[48] According to one Indian estimate, maintaining a year-round deployment in the Kargil sector would cost the Indian exchequer at least $900 million a year.[49] This does not include the cost of high-technology surveillance equipment, like satellites or UAVs, but covers just troop deployment. The cost for Pakistan may be marginally less, given that the approach from its side of the border to the LoC is easier to access. From Islamabad's perspective, by having the Indian army deployed along these areas, the Pakistan military would have achieved its purpose of tying down a sizeable section of the Indian army without even crossing the LoC. It would achieve this goal while freeing the Pakistani army to be re-deployed in more critical areas.

Second, even if both India and Pakistan were in a position to spend the money to acquire state-of-the-art surveillance and reconnaissance equipment, such as UAVs, they do not have the technological means to build these items indigenously. While India can certainly build spy satellites, these are not very useful in monitoring the movement of a few troops in the rocky and snowy terrain of Kargil. In this terrain, only UAV's, which can provide ten-centimetre resolution pictures, are effective. However, while both India and Pakistan possess some aerial reconnaissance capability, they do not have UAVs which can effectively operate in the harsh Kargil environment.[50] The US is the only country which currently possesses all-weather UAVs that could operate at those heights and in those conditions. Such UAVs are, however, unlikely to be sold to either India or Pakistan as such technology transfer would require a higher degree of interaction between New Delhi, Islamabad and Washington than presently exists.

Third, the unilateral non-cooperative approach could lead to inadvertent escalation and accidents, as the shooting down of the Pakistan aircraft in August 1999 illustrated. For instance, were a UAV or a group of soldiers to cross the LoC, be detected and shot down, one side could justifiably accuse the other of spying and of violating the LoC. The presence of nuclear weapons manifoldly increases this danger of escalation. Thus, while both India and Pakistan have opted for the confrontational approach to keeping peace in South Asia, this is clearly not the best approach for either one of them, in the long term, on account of the factors mentioned above.

The second way to ensure that peace is kept in South Asia is the cooperative, non-antagonistic, bilateral approach whereby both sides mutually agree not only to reaffirm the sanctity and inviolability of the LoC but also to ensure that neither side crosses it with impunity. While re-establishing the LoC (based on the details contained in the 1972 Simla Agreement) would be relatively easy, it is important to stress the verification component (the 'trust but verify' approach) in ensuring the effective implementation of this agreement between Islamabad and New Delhi. In the past, such agreements were backed by declaratory Confidence Building Measures (CBMs) where both parties declared their intention to adhere to the spirit and letter of the agreement. However, Kargil has exposed the limitations of such declaratory CBMs and proved the need for mutually verifiable agreements. Such an agreement would not necessarily obviate the need for sensors and other early warning devices, or even manpower, but would make it possible for both sides to agree on troop levels and the type and number of sensors to be used. This approach would preserve the sanctity of the LoC, while reducing the danger of inadvertent nuclear escalation.

Although such an approach would be ideal, there are several hurdles to negotiating and implementing such a verification agreement. Perhaps the biggest (apart from political will) would be that both India and Pakistan lack the experience in the art and science of cooperative monitoring. Although India has some experience in negotiating such arrangements, based on the verification provisions of the 1993 and 1996 Sino-Indian agreements with respect to the 'Line of Actual Control' between the two countries, New Delhi has little practical verification experience as these provisions have yet to be implemented. In contrast, none of the Indo-Pakistan agreements have a verification arrangement.[51] This is primarily because neither side has been comfortable with the prospects of having the enemy over-fly, let alone visit, its territory to verify troop and equipment numbers. In this context, going back to the Lahore process (which started with the Vajpayee visit to Lahore and the signing of the Lahore Declaration and a Memorandum of Understanding [MOU] in February 1999) would seem to present the best way to move forward. As part of efforts at reviving the Lahore process, both sides should now try to work out a verification arrangement, particularly with respect to Kargil, the LoC and their nuclear arsenal. According to General V.R. Raghavan, a retired Indian army officer, the MOU could be called the 'Memorandum of Military Understanding because eighty percent of... it was related to military actors'.[52]

Ironically, while the Kargil crisis has highlighted the need for both sides to establish a verifiable agreement, it has also created the most formidable hurdle to the efforts made by the Lahore process to move in this direction. Clearly, the Kargil episode, followed shortly afterwards by the coup in Pakistan, have interrupted this process. First, Kargil not only vitiated the cordial atmosphere that had been established between India and Pakistan but also revealed that the Lahore process was not endorsed by a key constituency of the Pakistani establishment – the military. Moreover, the manner in which the conflict was resolved – at the behest of a third party and without a formal agreement to disengage – meant that the opportunity to use the cessation of hostilities to revive the normalization process was also lost. In the past, the process of resolving a crisis has often led to the beginning of new measures to ensure peace and stability. For instance, following the 1983–84 crisis, which revolved around the possibility of India and Pakistan attacking each other's nuclear facilities, General Zia-ul-Huq of Pakistan and Rajiv Gandhi of India verbally agreed in 1985 to refrain from carrying out such attacks. This agreement was formalized and signed in 1988 by Prime Ministers Benazir Bhutto of Pakistan and Rajiv Gandhi of India in the wake of the resolution of the 1986–87 *Brasstacks* crisis. Both sides have strictly adhered to this agreement which requires that the two sides exchange lists of their nuclear facilities.

In addition, the coup in Pakistan made both democracy and the Lahore process a hapless victim of Kargil. According to Pakistani scholar, Zafar Cheema, the differences between the Army Chief, General Musharraf, and Prime Minister Nawaz Sharif over the handling of Kargil was one of the primary reasons behind the coup that led to the ousting of Sharif on 12 October 1999.[53] This event, apart from retarding democracy in Pakistan, adversely affected the return to the Lahore process in several ways. First, it removed one of the key players in the process from the scene and replaced him with a General who was regarded in India as the 'hawk' who not only masterminded the Kargil intrusions but also opposed the Lahore process itself. This realization (more than the subversion of democracy or the reluctance to deal with a military dictator) will make it difficult for India to return to the Lahore process. Not surprisingly, Pakistan's offer to resume talks has been turned down by India.[54]

Hence the return to the Lahore process will occur only when both sides are ready to deal with each other. However, in the interim, there are several unilateral steps which both India and Pakistan can take to keep peace in the region. First, both could unilaterally reaffirm their commitment to the principles and CBMs enunciated in the Lahore Declaration and MOU, particularly the commitments to a moratorium on nuclear testing and the non-deployment of nuclear forces. In this context the practice of prior notification of missile tests, also agreed to in the Lahore MOU, and adhered to by both Islamabad and New Delhi since April 1999, is a step in the right direction. In addition, there are a host of other unilateral steps that both India and Pakistan could undertake to ensure that, while they retain their nuclear weapons, the danger of accidental or inadvertent use, particularly in a conventional crisis, is reduced.[55] Both Pakistan and India should be encouraged to provide unilateral declarations to maintain peace and tranquillity along the LoC. Here General Musharraf's declaration (soon after his seizure of power) to withdraw troops from the international border, however tokenistic in practice, should be welcomed. Second, both sides should encourage track-two diplomacy which would not only keep the process active but would also prepare the ground for the official track as and when it begins. Moreover, track-two diplomacy would also provide both sides an opportunity to understand each other better and may remove some of the misperceptions that exist at present.[56] Finally, at a later stage, key official actors from either side should make a dramatic gesture (like Vajpayee's bus trip to Lahore in 1999 or General Zia's visit to watch a cricket match between Pakistan and India in Jaipur in 1987) to resume the stalled process of negotiations.

In addition to unilateral steps, the international community could also play a role in keeping peace in South Asia by putting the India–Pakistan normalization process back on track. A credible third party mediating between India and Pakistan could do this. While Washington has offered its services and Islamabad has expressed its willingness, India is unlikely to agree to a formal US role. This became evident both before and during American President Bill Clinton's visit to India in March 2000.[57] Although India had agreed to let Washington play a limited role as a conduit to convey messages to Pakistan and vice versa (during the 1990 crisis) and in resolving an on-going crisis (during the 1999 Kargil confrontation), New Delhi remains reluctant to allow any third party to mediate between itself and Islamabad on core issues, such as nuclear risk-reduction measures and maintaining peace and tranquillity along the LoC. This may explain why three of the four 'Rs' to reduce tension suggested by President Clinton during his visit to India are primarily unilateral steps. The four 'Rs' are – respect the line of control; exercise restraint; reject violence or a military solution; and restore dialogue.[58] Of these only the last requires bilateral or multilateral or third-party efforts.

Given this attitude, a third party could alternatively conduct separate bilateral interactions with both Islamabad and New Delhi to convince them to take unilateral steps to ensure peace and stability in the region. This is clearly the approach that Washington has pursued: senior American officials have been negotiating separately with their Indian and Pakistani counterparts since the two countries conducted nuclear tests in May 1998. Although the bulk of these negotiations have dealt with bilateral relations between Washington and Islamabad and between Washington and New Delhi, as well as concerns regarding further nuclear proliferation, a part of them have also addressed the issue of keeping peace between India and Pakistan, particularly in Kashmir. Thus, even the Kargil Review Committee

Report, submitted to the Indian parliament on 24 February 2000, grudgingly acknowledged that the 'US-sponsored withdrawal of the intruders from the Indian side of the LoC probably came as a welcome face-saving device for the Pakistani establishment.'[59] Clearly, despite its protestations to the contrary, New Delhi has not been averse to letting Washington play the role of conveying the Indian perspective to Islamabad.

This approach was much in evidence during the course of Clinton's visit to South Asia in March 2000. When it was initially announced that the US President would visit India and Bangladesh from 19 to 25 March and briefly touch down in Islamabad for a few hours after the end of his visit to India, the government in New Delhi tried its best to dissuade him from visiting Pakistan. However, once Clinton was in New Delhi, the Indian government was not disinclined to let the American President raise certain issues on India's behalf with Pakistan's military leadership during his brief stopover in Islamabad. In a particularly telling incident, Vajpayee publicly asked Clinton to discuss the issue of cross-border incursions into Kashmir when the latter was in Islamabad, a subject that Clinton promised to (and subsequently did) raise.[60] Although this exchange was prompted by the brutal massacre of 36 Sikhs in Kashmir at the start of Clinton's official visit to India, there is little doubt that, following this historic visit, New Delhi has now endorsed Washington's potential role in ensuring the absence of violence and respect for the LoC, particularly in Kashmir. Following these events, India will now find it difficult not to acknowledge, no matter how tacitly, some sort of facilitating role for the US in prompting the two estranged neighbours to negotiate a more durable peace in South Asia.

Not surprisingly, on 29 March, just days after Clinton's visit to Islamabad, Pakistan's Foreign Secretary, Imam-ul-Huq, made a formal offer to the Indian High Commissioner in Islamabad, G. Parthsarathy, to hold bilateral talks on security issues of mutual concern. Clearly, a third-party role, however effective and benign, can only be an interim measure. Ultimately both India and Pakistan will have to sit down face- to-face to negotiate and implement more enduring measures to keep peace in South Asia. This is a long and difficult path for both New Delhi and Islamabad, but it is by no means impossible. The US and Russia, Israel and some of its Arab neighbours, Brazil and Argentina, and even India and China have successfully gone down this road before. The time has come for India and Pakistan to embark on this arduous but inevitable journey.

NOTES

1. Only recently have scholars studied these crises in some detail. For the 1984 crisis see Ravi Rikhye, *The Fourth Round*, New Delhi: ABC Publishing House, 1984 and Waheguru Pal

Singh Sidhu, 'The Development of an Indian Nuclear Doctrine Since 1980', PhD dissertation, University of Cambridge, February 1997, pp.119–43. For discussion of the *Brasstacks* crisis, see Kanti Bajpai, P.R. Chari, Pervaiz Iqbal Cheema, Stephen P. Cohen and Šumit Ganguly, *Brasstacks and Beyond: Perception and Management of Crisis in South Asia*, New Delhi: Manohar, 1995; Inderjit Badhwar and Dilip Bobb, 'Game of Brinkmanship', *India Today*, 15 February 1987; and 'The War That Was Not – Happily', *Sainik Samachar*, 19 April 1987. On the 1990 crisis, see B.G. Deshmukh, 'Spring 1990 Crisis', *World Affairs* Vol.3, No.2, December 1994, pp.36–7; General V.N. Sharma's interview, 'It's All Bluff and Bluster', *Economic Times*, 18 May 1990; Dilip Bobb and Raj Chengappa, 'War Games', *India Today*, 28 February 1990; C. Uday Bhaskar, 'The May 1990 Nuclear Crisis: An Indian Perspective', *Studies in Conflict and Terrorism* Vol.20, 1997, pp.317–32; Devin Hagerty, 'Nuclear Deterrence in South Asia: The 1990 Indo–Pakistani Crisis', *International Security*, Vol.20, No.3, Winter 1995–96, pp.79–114; William E. Burrows and Robert Windrem, *Critical Mass*, New York: Simon & Schuster, 1994, pp.349–77; Seymour Hersh, 'On the Nuclear Edge', *The New Yorker*, 29 March 1993, pp.56–73 and Michael Krepon and Mishi Faruqee (eds.), *Conflict Prevention and Confidence Building Measures in South Asia: The 1990 Crisis*, Occasional Paper No.17, Washington, DC: The Henry L. Stimson Center, April 1994.

2. Scholars have variously called this condition 'recessed deterrence', 'non-weaponized deterrence' or 'existential deterrence'. See Devin Hagerty, 'Nuclear Deterrence in South Asia: The 1990 Indo-Pakistani Crisis', *International Security*, Vol.20, No.3, Winter 1995/96, p.87; George Perkovich, 'A Nuclear Third Way in South Asia, *Foreign Policy*, No.91, Summer 1993, p.86; and Air Commodore Jasjit Singh, 'Prospects for Nuclear Proliferation', in Serge Sur (ed.), *Nuclear Deterrence: Problems and Perspectives in the 1990s*, New York: United Nations Institute for Disarmament Research, 1993, p.66.

3. Raj Chengappa, *Weapons of Peace*, New Delhi: Harper Collins, 2000, p.437. This, however, has been denied by Indian officials.

4. 'Kargil intrusion was scripted in 1987', *United News of India*, 13 September 1999.

5. Personal conversation with senior Pakistani military experts.

6. 'Pakistan Army's Misadventure in Kargil', Army Liaison Cell, Army Headquarters, New Delhi, p.8.

7. See 'Understanding Air Operations in Kargil', Indian Air Force briefing on Operation *Safed Sagar* at http://armedforces.nic.in/kargil/kargil-web.htm.

8. 'Soldier's Hour', *India Today*, 26 July 1999, p.23.

9. Chengappa, *Weapons of Peace*, p.437.

10. Dinesh Kumar, 'Naval Build-up by Pakistan: India Ready to Meet Sea-borne Attack', *The Times of India*, 17 June 1999; 'Navy Played a Major Role in Kargil: Kumar', *Deccan Herald*, 31 July 1999. See also C. Uday Bhaskar, 'The Maritime Dimension', *The Economic Times*, 21 July 1999.

11. See Gurmeet Kanwal, 'Pakistan's Military Defeat in Kargil', in Jasjit Singh (ed.), *Kargil 1999: Pakistan's Fourth War for Kashmir*, New Delhi: Knowledge World, 1999.

12. Lt. Gen. (Retd) V.R. Raghavan, 'Crossing LoC Not an End in Itself', *Hindustan Times*, 29 June 1999.

13. See 'Dial-A-PM', *India Today*, 28 June 1999 and 'Kargil Calander', *India Today*, 26 July 1999.

14. Vajpayee and Sharif signed the Lahore Declaration on 21 February 1999 following a high-profile bus trip made by Vajpayee from Delhi to Lahore. The Declaration called for the 'resolution of all outstanding issues, including Jammu and Kashmir'. This was the first time that India had agreed to put Kashmir on the agenda. Along with the Declaration a Memorandum of Understanding was also signed by the Indian and Pakistani foreign secretaries. This too called for a resolution of Jammu and Kashmir in addition to measures to reduce the risk of accidental or unauthorized use of nuclear weapons and the need to implement 'existing Confidence Building Measures' and upgrade communication links between the two directors-general of military operation. See http://www.meadev.gov.in/lahore.htm.

15. 'Sharif Warns of More Kargil-like Situations, Urges Dialogue', *Deccan Herald*, 21 June 1999.

16. 'Nuclear Blackmail?', *Hindustan Times*, 26 June 1999.
17. 'Pak Nuke Threat Not to be Taken Casually: Fernandes', *Hindustan Times*, 30 June 1999.
18. 'Intruders Will Be Evicted by Winter: Advani', *Hindustan Times*, 30 June 1999.
19. W.P.S. Sidhu, 'The U.S. and Kargil', *The Hindu*, 15 July1999.
20. Text of joint Clinton–Sharif statement at http://www.economictimes.com/kargil/update 72.htm.
21. Indian Army Headquarters Press Release, 11 July 1999. Also see, 'Lull After Storm as Pak Troops Start Withdrawing', *The Economic Times,* 13 July 1999.
22. 'Last Three Pockets of Intrusion Vacated', *The Hindustan Times,* 27 July 1999.
23. Rahul Bedi, 'New Indian Corps for Kashmir Duty', *Jane's Defence Weekly*, 8 September 1999.
24. 'IAF Shoots Down Pak. Intruder Plane', *Indian Express*, 11 August 1999.
25. See Amit Baruah, 'Pakistan Warns of Appropriate Response', *The Hindu*, 11 August 1999; Air Commodore Jasjit Singh, 'Atlantique Mission Had to Be Cleared at the Highest Level', *Indian Express*, 12 August 1999 and 'Atlantique Intruded Thrice, Turned Hostile', *Indian Express*, 14 August 1999.
26. 'Coup in Pakistan, Sharif Under House Arrest', *Indian Express*, 13 October 1999.
27. Dilip Lahiri, 'Formalising Restraint: The Case of South Asia', paper presented at the Ninth International Arms Control Conference, Entering the New Millennium: Dilemmas in Arms Control, organized by Sandia National Laboratories at Albuquerque, New Mexico, 16–18 April 1999. Pakistani officials have also made similar statements at other international conferences. See for instance remarks made by Director General (South Asia), Zamir Akram, a senior Pakistani diplomat at a conference on Trust- and Confidence-Building Measures in South Asia, organized by the United Nations Institute for Disarmament Research at Palais des Nations, Geneva, 23–24 November 1998.
28. Kanti Bajpai, 'Thinking the Unthinkable', *Security, Technology and Arms Control News,* Vol.2, No.3 (February 1996), p.2.
29. This is not the first time that India and Pakistan have reached such an unwritten tacit understanding to limit the engagement. The battle for the Siachen Glacier being fought since 1984 has also been confined to the ground troops and artillery with the air forces providing only logistic support. According to some Pakistani strategists, the Kargil operation could be seen as an extension of the Siachen conflict.
30. See 'Draft Report of the National Security Advisory Board on Indian Nuclear Doctrine', para. 2.7 at http://www.meadev.gov.in/govt/indnucld.htm, which asserts that 'effective conventional military capabilities shall be maintained to raise the threshold of outbreak both of conventional military conflict as well as that of threat or use of nuclear weapons'.
31. Opening remarks by National Security Adviser Brijesh Mishra, at the release of the Draft Indian Nuclear Doctrine, 17 August 1999. http://www.meadev.gov.in/govt/opstm-indnucld.htm.
32. Inaugural address by Raksha Mantri [George Fernandes], at National Seminar on The Challenges of Limited War: Parameters and Options, organized by the Institute for Defence Studies and Analyses (IDSA) in New Delhi, 5–6 January 2000. Senior Indian strategists, however, have challenged the limited war concept. See, for instance, V.R. Raghavan, 'Limited War & Strategic Liability', *The Hindu*, 2 February 2000.
33. Indeed, all indications are that Pakistan has summarily rejected this 'limited war' concept. For instance, a senior Pakistani diplomat warned that 'the thesis promoted by India's Defence Minister and Army Chief that it is possible to pursue a "limited" conventional war against Pakistan amounts to dangerous brinkmanship.' See Ambassador Maleeha Lodhi, 'New Security Architecture for South Asia', paper distributed at International Institute for Strategic Studies Conference on Minimum Deterrence, Concepts and Practices, Mauritius, 22–23 June 2000.
34. For details and a brief history of the demarcation see Lt. Gen. (Dr) M.L. Chibber, 'Line of Control in Jammu & Kashmir – A part of Simla Agreement' at http://www.vijayinkargil.org/perspectives/LoC.html.
35. Personal communication with senior US State Department Official, Washington DC, June 1999.

36. Text of joint Clinton–Sharif statement (n.20 above).

37. C. Raja Mohan, 'Respect LoC, Says China', *The Hindu*, 2 July 1999.

38. Remarks made by Professor Zafar I. Cheema at the conference on Peace and Security in South Asia: After India–Pakistan Nuclear Tests, organized by Quaid-I-Azam University, Islamabad and Hanns Seidel Stiftung Foundation, Munich at Islamabad, 3–5 December 1998.

39. According to one report during Operation *Vijay*, all 58 battalions involved in counter-insurgency operations in Kashmir were diverted to Kargil. See Harinder Baweja and Ramesh Vinayak, 'Reaction Plans', *India Today*, 31 January 2000.

40. Kanwal (n.11 above).

41. According to official Indian figures, 474 Indian soldiers were killed and another 1109 wounded. See *Kargil Review Committee Report* presented to the Parliament of India on 24 February 2000.

42. 'There Are Tough Days Ahead', interview with General V.P. Malik, *India Today*, 19 July 1999.

43. 'Understanding Air Operations in Kargil' (n.7 above).

44. 'Pakistan Will Never Accept Kashmir LoC as International Border: FM', *Indian Express*, 8 August 1999.

45. See Jaswant Singh 'Kargil and Beyond', talk at the India International Centre, 20 July 1999 at http://www.meadev.gov.in/opn/kargil/jaswad-2007.htm and 'Jaswant rules out change in country's stand on LoC', *The Hindu*, 2 September 1999.

46. 'Overhaul national security apparatus', *The Times of India*, 24 February 2000.

47. 'Pakistan tests a new missile and revises command structure', *Jane's Defence Weekly*, 15 February 2000.

48. See Murali Krishnan, 'The New Cold War', *Outlook*, 29 November 1999 and Ramesh Vinayak, 'Winter Warriors', *India Today*, 21 February 2000.

49. 'Kargil to Hit Economy Hard: Assocham', *The Asian Age*, 5 July 1999.

50. See Lawrence C. Trost, 'Unmanned Air Vehicles (UAVs) for Cooperative Monitoring', *Sandia Report*, SAND 2000–0185 (Sandia National Laboratories: Albuquerque, January 2000).

51. W.P.S. Sidhu, 'Kargil: the role of technology', *The Hindu*, 13 August 1999.

52. Lt. General V.R. Raghavan (Retd.), presentation on 'Confidence Building Measures after Kargil: Possibilities' at the Henry L. Stimson Center Asian Security Luncheon Series, 14 September 1999 at http://www.stimson.org/cbm/asls/raghavan.htm.

53. Professor Zafar I. Cheema at the International Institute for Strategic Studies Research Associates' Seminar in London on 9 November 1999.

54. 'Pakistan Calls for Talks with India', *Associated Press*, 22 February 2000 and 'Pak. Must Revert to Path of Peace: Jaswant', *The Hindu*, 27 April 2000. In fact the first time Musharraf and Vajpayee spoke was after the tragedy of the Gujarat earthquake in India.

55. For a sample of such measures see Nazir Kamal, 'Pakistani Perceptions and Prospects of Reducing the Nuclear Danger in South Asia', Cooperative Monitoring Centre Occasional Paper 6, January 1999 and Agha Shahi, Zulfikar Ali Khan and Abdul Sattar, 'Securing Nuclear Peace', *The News*, 5 October 1999. See also W.P.S. Sidhu, 'India's Security and Nuclear Risk-Reduction Measures', in *Nuclear Risk-Reduction Measures in Southern Asia*, Stimson Center Report 26, November 1998.

56. See for instance, Salman Haider, 'The Army Is King', *Indian Express*, 29 November 1999 which presents a more benign view of General Musharraf. The article written by a former foreign secretary of India was based on his personal impressions after a visit to Pakistan as part of a track-two process run by the Balusa group.

57. 'US Willing for Mediation on Kashmir If Asked: Clinton', *The News*, 17 February 2000. In fact, after President Clinton's visit to the region, particularly Islamabad, in late March 2000, even the US appears to have retreated from its offer to mediate. See Amit Baruah, 'US Will Not Mediate on Kashmir, Says Clinton', *The Hindu*, 26 March 2000. Interestingly, even Pakistan appears to have given up on direct mediation by the US. See 'Kashmir Ruining Economy: Pakistan May Forego Mediation Option, Says CE' *Dawn*, 31 March 2000.

58. See White House press release, 'Remarks by the President and Prime Minister of India in Joint Press Statement', Hyderabad House, New Delhi, 21 March 2000.

59. *Kargil Review Committee Report* (n.41 above), p.82.

60. See 'Remarks by the President and Prime Minister Vajpayee of India' (n.58 above).

Abstracts

War and Peace: What's the Difference? *by David Keen*
War and peace are normally considered opposites, but it is revealing to ask what they have in common, particularly when studying transitions from war to peace and from peace to war. Many of the actors helping to shape violence during a conflict have aims other than simply 'winning', and these aims often foster a limited but enduring violence. Peace can also be quite violent, and this violence embodied in peace may help to account for mass violence or civil war.

Economic Fragility and Political Fluidity: Explaining Natural Resources and Conflicts *by Abiodun Alao and Funmi Olonisakin*

This contribution questions some of the arguments in the recent literature on natural resources and conflicts, which attribute the emergence of armed conflict and civil wars largely to a ploy by protagonists to exploit the natural resources in a particular area. The real explanation involves elements of state collapse as well as economic greed. Transparent, accountable structures of governance and the promotion of a buoyant and educated civil society will best enhance the management of resource-based conflicts.

Boom and Bust? The Changing Nature of UN Peacekeeping *by David M. Malone and Karin Wermester*

With the end of the Cold War, the notion and practice of peacekeeping has undergone something of a revolution. Spearheaded by the UN Security Council, two significant shifts have occurred in peacekeeping in the past decade. First, the goals pursued by peacekeeping operations have changed from assisting in the maintenance of ceasefires to implementing the foundations of self-enforcing peace through, in particular, the increasingly detailed electoral, humanitarian, human rights, and civilian police components in peacekeeping mandates. Second, the level of enforcement brought to bear by peacekeeping operations has increased dramatically. New trends in UN peacekeeping include the increasing use of Chapter VII mandates to authorize the use of force under 'coalitions of the willing', the implementation of mandatory sanctions regimes, and the humanitarian intervention missions of the 1990s.

Lessons Not Learned: The Use of Force in 'Peace Operations' in the 1990s *by Mats Berdal*

The armed forces of several western countries have embraced the view that 'peace enforcement' constitutes a type of military activity that, while coercive in nature, remains distinct from 'war'. This view rests on two basic assumptions: that military force can be used impartially to enforce compliance with a given mandate without designating an enemy, and that using force in this manner will not prejudice the political outcome of the conflict in question. The experience of military operations in support of humanitarian objectives in the 1990s in places like Somalia and Bosnia, however, suggests that these assumptions are empirically unsustainable and optimistic in the extreme. Instead, decision-makers need to think in terms of a broad yet still basic distinction between consent-based operations and enforcement which must yet allow for the logic of war and war-fighting.

Building Peace through Transitional Authority: New Directions, Major Challenges by Michèle Griffin and Bruce Jones

The two new, surprisingly far-reaching peace operations in East Timor and Kosovo, authorized by the UN Security Council in 1999, are more challenging than previous similar peacebuilding missions in Namibia, Cambodia, and Eastern Slavonia, in that they involve the UN assuming vastly greater executive and legislative authority. The UN is assuming such powers in unstable environments which lack functioning institutions, and in the context of increasingly severe financial, political and logistical constraints on the UN's capacity to manage conflicts.

Truth Commissions and the Quest for Justice: Stability and Accountability after Internal Strife by Chandra Lekha Sriram

A key dilemma related to truth commissions is whether and to what degree accountability ought to be pursued after the end of civil conflicts or military dictatorships. A study of nearly 30 cases reveals that three factors frequently make accountability more or less possible: the international political and historical context, the history of past abuses, and the nature of civil–military relations and/or the balance between the government and opposition. There may be instances in which limiting, though not jettisoning, accountability may enable transitional regimes (and by extension external donors) to pursue greater levels of reform of security forces. This can be done, in particular, by transitional regimes cutting military budgets and personnel, and instituting wide-ranging reforms in doctrine and education – actions which may help to ensure long-term stability.

Protégés, Clients, Cannon Fodder: Civilians in the Calculus of Militias by Marie-Joëlle Zahar

The incentives of belligerents to respect or to violate the rights of civilians are little understood and have been even less systematically studied. This contribution develops a typology of civil–militia relations, ranking warring groups from most to least challenging in terms of their expected compliance with the letter and spirit of the provisions of the Hague conventions on the protection of non-combatants, the Geneva conventions, and other humanitarian laws. Two broad classes of factors that influence civil–militia relations are identified: the impact of militia objectives and militia structure, and the nature of the ties between combatants and the population.

Messiahs or Mercenaries? The Future of International Private Military Services by Doug Brooks

Private military companies (PMCs) or private security companies (PSCs) are different from the 'freelance mercenaries' of the past, both in terms of motivation and adherence to legal norms. The bias against these companies stems from two major concerns: that they threaten the traditional authority of the state, and that they are a key factor in the growth of multinational corporations. What makes private military services viable, however, is their ability to offer military services in a more efficient, timely and inexpensive manner than state militaries or non-military companies. This contribution predicts a rapid growth in the activities and functions of these companies, including their increased use in peace operations, particularly due to the weakness of some recent UN operations.

NATO's Underachieving Middle Powers: From Burdenshedding to Burdensharing *by Brian Finlay and Michael O'Hanlon*

The degree of US military supremacy in the post-Cold War era is unprecedented and ultimately harmful to the future of the NATO alliance. While the world decries *Pax Americana*, the international community is often helpless to conduct many of the military operations necessary to deter conflicts and maintain and re-establish peace without US military support. NATO's underachieving middle powers should restructure their armies to shoulder a heavier military burden in post-Cold War missions. Using Canada as a case study, this contribution demonstrates how NATO allies can potentially reconfigure their militaries to become more self-sufficient and more rapidly reactive. America's NATO allies must develop their military high-technology and strategic transport and logistics capabilities, reducing their dependence on the US while simultaneously increasing their ability to operate in conjunction with American forces.

Back to the Future: UN Peacekeeping in Africa *by Adekeye Adebajo and Chris Landsberg*

This essay focuses on seven important cases of UN peacekeeping in Africa, including the current missions in Sierra Leone and the Democratic Republic of the Congo (DRC). Factors identified as having often contributed to success in UN peacekeeping missions in Africa include: the existence of a political accord between the warring parties and the willingness of internal parties to disarm and accept electoral results; the development of an effective strategy to deal with potential 'spoilers'; the absence of conflict-fuelling economic resources in war zones; the cooperation of regional players in peace processes; the cessation of military and financial support to local clients by extra-regional actors and their provision of financial and diplomatic support to peace processes; and finally, the leadership of peacekeeping missions by capable envoys. In order to manage African conflicts there is an urgent need to strengthen regional organizations in Africa and to establish a new division of labour between the UN and these organizations.

In the Shadow of Kargil: Keeping Peace in Nuclear South Asia *by Waheguru Pal Singh Sidhu*

The 1999 Kargil conflict, the latest in a series of 'nuclear crises' between India and Pakistan, challenged two myths: that stability is inherent between a pair of nuclear-armed states, and that states, particularly nuclear-armed states in a post-Cold War dyad setting, can alter a boundary – even a disputed boundary – by force. The Kargil episode proved that while stability cannot be taken for granted, boundaries – even disputed ones – can. Any attempt to change such boundaries by force is not only likely to fail but may lead to dangerous escalation. Although, in the wake of Kargil, both India and Pakistan have sought unilateral and antagonistic approaches to ensure their security, this approach is fraught with danger and could lead to inadvertent escalation. It is in the interest of both countries to adopt a more co-operative and verifiable approach to keeping peace in South Asia. This contribution suggests several ways for India and Pakistan to move in this direction with the facilitation of influential external actors like the United States.

Notes on Contributors

Adekeye Adebajo is Director of the Africa Program at the International Peace Academy, New York. He has held research fellowships at the Brookings Institution and Stanford University, and was a Rhodes scholar at Oxford University. He has served on UN missions in South Africa, Western Sahara and Iraq. He is currently completing a book on the civil war in Liberia.

Chandra Lekha Sriram is an Associate at the International Peace Academy, New York, where she directs the project on strengthening UN capacities for the prevention of violent conflict. She also holds a law degree from the University of California-Berkeley, Boalt Hall School of Law, with an emphasis in international law, and she received her PhD in Politics from Princeton University in January 2000, with a thesis on transitional justice and the political trade-offs of transition.

David Keen is a Lecturer in Development Studies at the London School of Economics and Political Science. He is the author of *The Benefits of Famine* (Princeton) *and The Economic Functions of Violence in Civil Wars* (Adelphi Paper, Oxford). He is currently finishing a book on the political economy of war in Sierra Leone.

Abiodun Alao is with the Centre for Defence Studies, King's College, London, where he co-directs the African security issues project. His current research interest is resource conflicts in sub-Saharan Africa, and he is just completing a book titled "The Tragedy of Endowment: Natural Resources and Conflict in Sub-Saharan Africa".

'Funmi Olonisakin is a Research Associate at the African Security Unit, Centre for Defence Studies, King's College London. She has been a MacArthur Foundation Research Associate at the Department of War Studies, also at King's College London, and held a research position at the Institute for Strategic Studies at the University of Pretoria, South Africa. Her main areas of interest are African regional security and the reform of civil military relations in collapsed states, on which she has conducted extensive research. She is the author *of Reinventing Peacekeeping in Africa: Conceptual and Legal Issues in ECOMOG* (Kluwer Law International, 2000) and co-author of *Peacekeepers, Politicians and Warlords: The Liberian Peace Process* (United Nations University Press, 1999).

David M. Malone is President of the International Peace Academy, New York, where he has published extensively on peace and security issues, particularly on the activities of the UN Security Council. A career Canadian Foreign Service Officer and occasional scholar, he was successively, over the period 1994–98, Director General of the Policy, International Organizations and Global Issues Bureaus of the Canadian Foreign and Trade Ministry. During this period he also acquired a DPhil from Oxford University with a thesis on decision-making in the Security Council.

Karin Wermester is a program officer at the International Peace Academy, New York. She has an MA in Political Science from Columbia University and a BSc (Econ) in International Relations from the London School of Economics and Political Science. Her current focus is on the concept and practice of conflict prevention.

Mats Berdal is Director of Studies at the International Institute for Strategic Studies

(IISS) in London. Publications include *Whither UN Peacekeeping* (Adelphi Paper 281) and *Disarmanent and Demobilisation after Civil Wars* (Adelphi Paper 303). He is the co-editor with David Malone *of Greed and Grievance: Economic Agendas in Civil Wars* (Lynne Rienner, 2000).

Michèle Griffin is a Policy Advisor with the UN Development Programme, with particular responsibility for UNDP–UN partnerships at the political level, and an adjunct Lecturer in International and Public Affairs with Columbia University School of International Affairs. She has worked with the UN Secretariat, the International Peace Academy, the Irish Mission to the UN and the US Institute of Peace. She has degrees from the London School of Economics and Trinity College, Dublin.

Bruce Jones is currently Special Assistant to the UN's Special Coordinator for the Middle East Peace Process. He has worked for the UN in New York, was part of the UN Advance Mission in Kosovo, and worked on the design of the East Timor mission. Before joining the UN he worked with NGOs in the Great Lakes Region of Africa. He recently completed a PhD from the London School of Economics.

Marie-Joëlle Zahar is a Social Science and Humanities Research Council of Canada Post-Doctoral Fellow at the Munk Centre for International Studies, University of Toronto. She received her PhD in 2000 from McGill University with a thesis on militia institutions and their impact on the prospects for conflict resolution. She was a pre- and post-doctoral fellow at the Center for International Security and Cooperation, Stanford University.

Doug Brooks is a PhD student at the Graduate School of Public and International Affairs, University of Pittsburgh. He just finished a year as a Bradlow Fellow at the South African Institute of International Affairs in Johannesburg. He has written extensively on private military companies and the potential for private peace operations, and recently co-founded the International Peace Operations Association (IPOA) in Washington, D.C.).

Brian Finlay is the Foreign Policy Program Officer at the New York City-based Century Foundation (formerly the Twentieth Century Fund), and was formerly a Senior Researcher in the Foreign Policy Studies Program at the Brookings Institution in Washington, DC. He holds a Graduate Diploma from the Johns Hopkins School of Advanced International Studies. He specializes in global security policy, arms control and the non-proliferation of weapons of mass destruction.

Michael O'Hanlon is a senior fellow in the Brookings Institution Foreign Policy Studies program. He is the author, with Ivo H. Daalder, of *Winning Ugly: NATO's War to Save Kosovo* (Brookings, 2000).

Chris Landsberg lectures in the Department of International Relations, Witwatersrand University, South Africa, and was recently a Hamburg Fellow at Stanford University's Centre for International Security and Cooperation.

Waheguru Pal Singh Sidhu is an Associate at the International Peace Academy. He has written extensively on South Asian security issues in general and on confidence building measures in particular, and he is presently editing a book on the impact of South Asia's nuclear tests on other regions of concern.

Index

Titles of Related Interest

Beyond the Emergency
Development Within UN Peace Missions

Jeremy Ginifer, *Norwegian Institute of International Affairs* (Ed)

> '*The book makes a noteworthy addition to writings on UN conflict resolution, peacekeeping and peace building by exploring the often-neglected nature of development and when and how this feature – as a continuing long-term objective and end in itself – should fit into these processes.*'
>
> **Journal of Peace Research**

152 pages 1997
0 7146 4760 8 cloth
0 7146 4321 1 paper

The UN, Peace and Force

Michael Pugh, *University of Plymouth* (Ed)

This book examines the options for the UN in the use of force to secure peace, and the extent to which peacekeeping can be effectively extended to coerce warring factions.

224 pages 1997
0 7146 4759 4 cloth
0 7146 4320 3 paper

FRANK CASS PUBLISHERS
Crown House, 47 Chase Side, Southgate, London N14 5BP
Tel: +44 (0)20 8920 2100 Fax: +44 (0)20 8447 8548 E-mail: info@frankcass.com
NORTH AMERICA
5824 NE Hassalo Street, Portland, OR 97213 3644, USA
Tel: 800 944 6190 Fax: 503 280 8832 E-mail: cass@isbs.com
Website: www.frankcass.com

Mediating in Cyprus

The Cypriot Communities and the United Nations

Oliver P Richmond

> *'A significant step forward in our understanding.'*
> **Boundary and Security Bulletin**

This study sets out to investigate the Cypriot parties' views of the process of peacemaking in order to shed light on the Cyprus problem, and on the theoretical debates on mediation, from a new angle.

320 pages 1998
0 7146 4877 9 cloth
0 7146 4431 5 paper

Peacekeeping and the UN Agencies

Jim Whitman, *Cambridge University* (Ed)

This book is a long-overdue assessment of the role of UN agencies in peacekeeping operations. While based on the full range of recent history, the contributions to this volume are forward-looking and policy-oriented, bringing a hard-edged practicality to complex and hitherto under-examined issues.

152 pages 1999
0 7146 4897 3 cloth
0 7146 4451 X paper

FRANK CASS PUBLISHERS
Crown House, 47 Chase Side, Southgate, London N14 5BP
Tel: +44 (0)20 8920 2100 Fax: +44 (0)20 8447 8548 E-mail: info@frankcass.com
NORTH AMERICA
5824 NE Hassalo Street, Portland, OR 97213 3644, USA
Tel: 800 944 6190 Fax: 503 280 8832 E-mail: cass@isbs.com
Website: www.frankcass.com

Peacekeeping and Public Information

Caught in the Crossfire

Ingrid A Lehmann, *Director, United Nations Information Centre, Athens*

> '*Peacekeeping and Public Information ... proves how important an understanding of peace operations mounted by the UN is*'
> **Linda Melvern,** *Glasgow Herald*
> *(Books of the Year)*

The book provides a timely and challenging prescription for just how the goals of placing communication functions at the heart of the strategic management of the UN might be achieved – and a dramatic warning of the consequences of failing to do so.

192 pages maps 1999
0 7146 4930 9 cloth
0 7146 4490 0 paper

The Evolution of US Peacekeeping Policy under Clinton

A Fairweather Friend?

Michael MacKinnon, *Graduate Institute of International Studies, Geneva*

This fascinating study examines the dynamic process through which the Clinton administration developed a policy towards UN peace support operations, why policy-makers in the administration eventually adopted such a different posture towards UN operations from the one they set out to achieve.

224 pages 1999
0 7146 4937 6 cloth
0 7146 4497 8 paper

FRANK CASS PUBLISHERS
Crown House, 47 Chase Side, Southgate, London N14 5BP
Tel: +44 (0)20 8920 2100 Fax: +44 (0)20 8447 8548 E-mail: info@frankcass.com
NORTH AMERICA
5824 NE Hassalo Street, Portland, OR 97213 3644, USA
Tel: 800 944 6190 Fax: 503 280 8832 E-mail: cass@isbs.com
Website: www.frankcass.com

Peacebuilding and Police Reform

Tor Tanke Holm, *Police Advisor for the UN Programme at the NUPI* and **Espen Barth Eide,** *Director of the UN Programme, NUPI* (Eds)

The editors have brought together experts in the fields of peacekeeping, civilian police activities and police reform, both academics and practitioners, to discuss the issue of internationally assisted police reform in transitions from war to peace.

240 pages 2000
0 7146 4987 2 cloth
0 7146 8040 0 paper

Peacekeeping and Conflict Resolution

Tom Woodhouse and **Oliver Ramsbotham,** *Co-Directors at the Centre for Conflict Resolution, University of Bradford* (Eds)

This book is about the ways in which conflict resolution theory has become relevant to the various challenges faced by the United Nations peacekeeping forces as efforts are made to learn from the traumatic and devastating impact of the many civil wars that have erupted in the 1990s.

280 pages 2000
0 7146 4976 7 cloth
0 7146 8039 7 paper

FRANK CASS PUBLISHERS
Crown House, 47 Chase Side, Southgate, London N14 5BP
Tel: +44 (0)20 8920 2100 Fax: +44 (0)20 8447 8548 E-mail: info@frankcass.com
NORTH AMERICA
5824 NE Hassalo Street, Portland, OR 97213 3644, USA
Tel: 800 944 6190 Fax: 503 280 8832 E-mail: cass@isbs.com
Website: www.frankcass.com